THE IRON DUKE

Bobby Windsor –
The Life and Times of a
Working-Class Rugby Hero

BOBBY WINDSOR
WITH **PETER JACKSON**

To Gwen
don't forget your
protection
Love Bobby Windsor

MAINSTREAM
PUBLISHING

EDINBURGH AND LONDON

First published in Great Britain in 2010 by
MAINSTREAM PUBLISHING COMPANY
(EDINBURGH) LTD
7 Albany Street
Edinburgh EH1 3UG

ISBN 9781845966508

A catalogue record for this book is available
from the British Library

Typeset in Adobe Caslon and DIN

Printed in Great Britain by
Clays Ltd, St Ives plc

1 3 5 7 9 10 8 6 4 2

ACKNOWLEDGEMENTS

This book would never have been completed without those who gave freely of their time to help make it possible, like Fran Cotton. A tower of strength alongside the Iron Duke in every battle throughout the invincible Lions tour of South Africa in 1974, the former England captain readily agreed to write the foreword in glowing admiration of the Welshman with whom he ventured into the jungle all those years ago.

My thanks, too, to Ray Prosser, the legendary Pontypool coach and biggest single influence on the Duke's career, for taking the trouble to give his unique insight into what set Windsor apart from the rest. Eddie Butler, once part of the same fearsome pack, now BBC television's leading commentator, offered an expert, first-hand appreciation of what it took to be the middle member of the 'Viet-Gwent'. I am indebted to Stephen Jones of the *Sunday Times* for finding the time in his hectic schedule to provide his pre-publication verdict. Phil Bennett, Mike Burton, Mervyn Davies and Fergus Slattery, all 1974 Lions, also deserve special mention.

The story would never have been possible without the inspiration of schoolteachers like Dick Shotton and Hedley Rowland. In singling out both for special mention, the Duke also acknowledges the help given by lifelong friends like John Whitfield, kit-man, trainer, coach and first-aid expert at Whitehead's Steelworks RFC, where the teenaged Windsor began the climb which would take him to the summit of the world game; John 'Paddy' Burke, who did British and Irish rugby the colossal favour of shoving Windsor from prop to hooker, is another, along with George Thomas, in his capacity as captain of Newport Saracens RFC. The Old Lion will forever be grateful to those at Cross Keys for giving him his big break in the first-class game and those selectors, both Welsh and Lions, who acknowledged his rare talent. 'I'd like to thank you, gentlemen, one and all,' he says. 'Thank you very much.'

Most of all, he is indebted to the Windsor family, especially to his first wife, the late Judi, and to his six children for their enduring love and unfailing support – Joanne, Ricky, Mandy, Mark, Luke and Sean. I thank them, too, for all their help and am grateful to Ricky's partner, Ceri Edwards, for the endless cups of tea which kept us going through long interviews during the Welsh winter until the Iron Duke could take the cold no more and retreated to the warmth of Majorca.

I owe a million thanks to a whole host of people for their generosity, not least with photographic material – to Robin Davey and Jackie Davies of the *South Wales Argus*, Alan Walter of the *Daily Mail* and Rob Cole of the Westgate Agency in Cardiff. Others gave their time selflessly to check a multitude of facts – Alan Evans (the Barbarian Football Club), Horace Jefferies (Cross Keys RFC), Ray Ruddick (Pontypool RFC), Ivor Thom (Newport Saracens RFC), Mal Beynon (Monmouthshire RFC), Geoff Pritchard (Crawshay's Welsh RFC) and David Power (Welsh Charitables RFC).

The book would never have seen the light of day without the technological expertise of Ceri Jackson and Neil Hore, the encouragement of Bill Campbell, Graeme Blaikie and all at Mainstream Publishing. Lastly, my gratitude to the man himself, without whom there would have been no story to write. His *nom de guerre*, as you will discover, comes from a speech made by a senior French official in admiration of Windsor's courage after one particular match in Toulouse.

The French, after all, know an Iron Duke when they see one, the original, the Duke of Wellington, having seen Napoleon off at the Battle of Waterloo almost 200 years ago.

Peter Jackson, Cardiff, July 2010

CONTENTS

FOREWORD

Fran Cotton spent the most glorious summer of his international career cheek by jowl with Bobby Windsor all over South Africa in 1974 without losing a single match. No wonder the Welshman claims he would have fought Al Capone on the proviso that the 'great English oak' of a prop had been alongside him.

A native of Wigan, Cotton is the only Lion to have played in a winning Test series against the Springboks and then repeated the feat almost a quarter of a century later as manager of what has been acclaimed as the best tour since the '70s. Since retiring after ten years at the sharp end of Test rugby for England and the Lions, the Lancastrian has translated his success into the business world, as well as becoming one of the most respected figures during his time as a member of the Rugby Football Union. He is a director of his former club, Sale Sharks.

As you are about to find out, Bobby Windsor was a lot more than just one of Wales' and the Lions' greatest players. He was also one of the most colourful characters in the history of the sport.

Our paths first crossed shortly after we had been selected for the 1974 Lions tour to South Africa. For reasons fully explained in this book, Bobby had to be whisked straight from the plane on arrival to the nearest hospital. The gastric problem which meant he was missing for most of the first week may have had something to do with his being in the same drinking company as 'Swerve' [Mervyn Davies] and J.P.R. [Williams].

An interesting thing happened shortly after he rejoined the party at our first training camp in Serfontein. 'The Duke' returned just in time for our first choir practice led by Billy Steele of Scotland, who introduced us to some beautiful Scottish ballads, including the one which we adopted as a battle hymn, 'Flower of Scotland'.

9

THE IRON DUKE

During a break in rehearsals, Bobby took his do-it-yourself tobacco kit out and began rolling a cigarette before turning round to address all and sundry.

'Never mind all this singing,' he said. 'I want to know when the booting starts.'

All the forwards nodded their approval and while the three-quarters didn't understand what he was talking about, J.P.R. most certainly did. He was positively salivating at the prospect of joining in the forwards' fun, which he did, with typical enthusiasm, during the weeks and months which followed.

Bobby was true to his word every time he played. Never once did he take a backward step during some of the most brutal scenes in Test match history. In so many ways, Windsor set the tone for the no-nonsense, rugged approach which underpinned the unprecedented success of the only invincible tour ever made by the Lions, one which will never be matched, if only because modern tours barely involve half the number of games.

Off the field, Bobby could best be described as a likeable rogue. You needed to have your wits about you in his presence. Very often, if anybody left their Lions sweater or tracksuit lying around unattended for any length of time, it would be too late. By the time its loss had been discovered, the item of clothing would be all parcelled up and on its way to Windsor's mates in the steelworks at Newport where he worked.

The same with the cigarettes. A well-known manufacturer would leave large numbers of the company's product in the team room of every hotel on our itinerary, which only goes to show how attitudes to fitness have changed. Anyway, most of the cigarettes disappeared within hours of check-in. We all had our suspicions, but we could never prove anything.

Bobby was far too streetwise to be caught, but, for all that, we loved him to bits. We loved his mischief, we loved his sense of humour, but, above all, we loved his brutal honesty. I had the privilege in my time of playing with many great hookers and the Duke was unquestionably the greatest of them all.

To wrap your arms round this bull of a man from Pontypool just before locking horns with Springboks or All Blacks was a great feeling. It gave you an unshakeable sense of security and supremacy, that whatever trouble was coming our way, we could take it and give it back with a lot of interest. Nobody frightened Windsor, not even the great French pack of the second half of the '70s and they were the most frightening sight of all.

Bobby has certainly had his share of personal tragedy and trauma over the years, which makes this book all the more revealing. I have waited a long time for a book to be written about his life and times, because nobody can have quite as many hair-raising stories to tell.

This book will not be for the faint-hearted, but if you want to know all about what the violence of Test rugby used to be like, it is not to be missed.

Not for nothing is it entitled *The Iron Duke*. His ever-readiness to cut out the candyfloss and give it to you straight from the shoulder is bound to make this a sure-fire winner.

Fran Cotton, July 2010

1

. . . .

'BASH' STREET KID

Thursday, 31 January 1946. A world exhausted by six years of bloodshed recoils in horror at evidence from the International War Crimes Tribunal of more unspeakable Nazi atrocities. Day 47 of the trial of Hitler's high command at Nuremberg uncovers the full scale of the slaughter of 642 French men, women and children at Oradour-sur-Glane, the scorched village near Limoges which has been preserved exactly as the 2nd SS Panzer Division left it in June 1944, a permanent memorial of man's inhumanity to man.

On the other side of the Atlantic, car workers in Detroit begin the 71st day of their four-month strike. Elsewhere in America, Alfred Arnold Cocozza and Arnold Raymond Cream, better known as Mario Lanza, the American opera singer-cum-film star, and Jersey Joe Walcott, the aspiring world heavyweight boxing champion, are celebrating birthdays, their 25th and 32nd respectively.

Winston Churchill is preparing to make his landmark speech about 'an Iron Curtain descending across Europe' and Alistair Cooke comes up with the idea to broadcast a weekly *Letter from America*, the first of 2,869 – the longest-running weekly programme of its kind in radio history.

In New York, Ethel Merman, the Barbra Streisand of her time, is clearing her throat for the Broadway premiere of *Annie Get Your Gun*, Estée Lauder puts the finishing touches to the launch of her cosmetics empire and *Billboard* magazine declares that 'ol' leather tonsils', Vaughn Monroe, has knocked Bing Crosby off the top of the US chart with 'Let it Snow, Let it Snow, Let it Snow'.

Nearer home, one half of Merseyside is in gloom over Liverpool's 5–0 trouncing by Bolton Wanderers in the fourth round of the FA Cup. Newport Harriers are celebrating their first post-war title as cross-country champions of Wales. The Ministry of Transport revives a ten-year national plan, suspended at the outbreak of war, which includes a bridge across the Severn near Chepstow and a 'high speed' dual carriageway from the bridge to Newport.

A new phenomenon is bursting out all over the United States – the sound of the 'baby boomers'. Amongst them is a 12-day-old girl from Locust Ridge, Tennessee, whose lung power will make her famous the world over: Dolly Parton.

And several thousand miles west, shortly before midday on that last Thursday of January, the baby boom embraces a bruiser who will shake, rattle 'n' roll with the best.

Robert William Windsor enters the world at 25 Harrow Road, Newport, Monmouthshire, the only son of Victor Windsor, ex-Royal Navy, and his wife, Connie. It is just as well that the boy should be blissfully oblivious to developments in the world around him. Two days later, on the first Saturday of his life, at the St Helen's ground in Swansea, Wales are routed 25–6 by Scotland in a 'victory' rugby international which turns out to be anything but.

Harrow Road and its neat terraced houses are within sight and sound of Rodney Parade, home of Newport RFC, where, on the second Saturday of his life, the famous Black-and-Ambers defeat Leicester 15–5 before seeing Cardiff off the following week.

One of the Newport team had fought at Arnhem and been awarded the *Croix de guerre* by the French government for his bravery as an assistant major in the 1st Airborne Division of the Parachute Regiment. Back in civvy street as a schoolmaster, Hedley Rowland, alias 'The Poacher' in recognition of his 93 tries in 136 matches for Newport, would do more than anyone to keep the young Windsor out of the clutches of the police and put him on the road to fame with Wales and the Lions.

In that grim first winter of his life, the embryonic Duke is not to know that within a matter of months, a pair of barristers, one English, the other Australian, will create Mensa, the high IQ society; for a multitude of reasons, the new arrival never quite gets round to joining.

Instead, he ploughs his own fighting furrow through the rugby world, commanding more column inches and making more headlines than he could ever have dreamed about. A working-class boy born with fire in his belly, he keeps it alight by hook or by crook, or both, in defiance of the hardships of growing up in the severe austerity of post-war Britain.

'We lived with my mother's sister, Sarah, in a one-down, one-up house,' Windsor says. 'I'll always remember the tin bath in front of the fire. My dad had come back home from the war to what was supposed to be a land fit for heroes. Mind, you had to be heroic to find your way through the pitch-black night down to the toilet at the bottom of the back garden. And in winter it was freezing cold. But back then you had to be resourceful and make the most of what you had, because you didn't have much. Certainly nothing as fancy as a toilet roll. So the *South Wales Argus* was cut up into neat squares and used in the proper way.

'My dad had been in the Merchant Navy until war broke out, then he switched to the Royal Navy and worked his way up through the ranks to chief petty officer. Serving King and Country was all very well, but it didn't seem to count for much when it came to starting afresh in civvy street. The vast majority of the men who had been away fighting for the victory were asking themselves the same question – what do we do now? Dad got a job in Newport driving taxis, which kept a roof over our heads and allowed him a bit of time to devote to his real passion, for engines and engineering. He was always into that. For a while, he went to America to lecture at colleges on diesel engines, then came home and became a fitter and turner for the rest of his working days.

'He worked hard all his life. He'd work seven days a week whenever he could, for the overtime. We needed the money. People think times are hard now, but it's paradise compared to back then. Even bread was rationed. And they called it a land fit for heroes?

'My mother had seven sisters and three brothers, not that she ever told us much about her family. All we knew was that two of her brothers were killed at Dunkirk; the surviving boy, Uncle Tommy, died of cancer.

'We lived less than a hundred yards from one of the main entrances to Rodney Parade. When Newport were playing, I could hear the roar of the crowd before I opened the front door. In those early post-war years, the Black-and-Ambers were one of the biggest clubs in the country. I'd walk out of the house, turn right, cross the main road and sneak in with my sister, Sally, not to watch the match but to get in under the wooden stand to see if anyone had dropped any pennies or ha'pennies. We'd find one or two and go straight to the sweet shop. You could buy a bar of chocolate with a couple of those old pennies.

'Bonfire night was the big money-making night for us kids. You'd take the guy down to the front entrance and make a few bob from the fans going in and out to the match. The great Ken Jones would be playing on the wing for Newport and all I'd be interested in was going ferreting about under the stand to see what had been dropped by the spectators sitting above!

'The thing I remember more than anything else about my childhood was being hungry. It was that hunger which put the gravel in my gut – without it I'd never have been able to fight my way to the top as a rugby player.

'Although my parents did their very best, more often than not I'd be starving when I got to school. Maindee Junior was a concrete jungle with no room for a piece of grass, never mind a playing field. I had to cross a few roads to get there. One day, as a six year old coming home with my sister, I ran out into the Chepstow Road and got hit by a motorbike with a sidecar. I've never been so frightened in all my life. I got up and ran home, crying. The bloke on the motorbike followed me all the way home because he was concerned that I might have been seriously hurt. I was lucky not to have been killed and if I had been it would have been entirely my fault.

'On my way to school, I'd walk past the main Newport police station, which I did visit a few times later in my life, as will be revealed. As a kid, I only had one goal, and that was to be a professional footballer. Soccer wasn't so much my first love, it was my only love. I was absolutely football mad.

'During that time, my mum and dad got a council house up at St Julians, a brand-new estate with a brand-new junior school. Best of all, the school had a football pitch. For a working-class kid like me, I felt like I was going to Eton. Mr Shotton, the history master who was also in charge of games, had been a Navy man and he'd tell us the story of the sinking of the *Bismarck*.

'As kids of eight and nine, he'd have us mesmerised. Then the bell would go and he'd say, "We'll continue the story next week." And we'd say, "No, sir, more please." One or two teachers gave me a punch around the earhole – which I probably asked for – but Mr Shotton was brilliant. Years later, I went back to the school when they put up a plaque in honour of the fifty-six goals I scored in one season – which is still a record.

'I'd come home from school, change and play football until it got too dark. Our council house was at the end of the terrace. Next to it was a lawn and we'd play with a bald old tennis ball or whatever kind of ball we could find. If there were only two of us, one would keep goal until the other scored three goals and then we'd switch round.

'The old leather balls of the day were like a lead weight, especially when it was wet – and when wasn't it wet? Heading that was like being assaulted, but I was soccer daft. Being a centre-forward, I'd head it any time because you could barge the goalie then, so I'd often have the ball and the keeper in the back of the net.

'The first plastic ball I had was one my sister bought me for Christmas when I was nine. We headed straight out to play and we'd been going about 30 seconds when a boy booted it straight into a thorn bush.

'All you could hear was the sound of the air coming out. Flat as a pancake. It broke my heart. That was the only Christmas present I ever got, because my mother was a Jehovah's Witness. All my friends were getting presents and I wasn't. Try and explain that to a kid.

'Clothes were another thing. Being a Navy man, my father got me a pair of trousers with bell-bottoms. He'd say, "Oh, that's smart, son. Real smart." In 20 years' time, they'd be the height of fashion. Back then, all they did was make me a figure of fun. The bastard bell-bottoms were bigger than my bastard shoes, and they were another sight.

'I had to wear those big Tuf boots. "Good strong shoes, son," said my dad. So while everyone else was wearing winkle-pickers or whatever the fashion was at the time, I was in these big clodhoppers like I was going to work on a building site.

'Then I had a military mac with flaps. I was the new kid on the block and, boy, did they give me some stick. They'd nick my cap and boot it around the school yard. They gave me a bit of bumping, my mac was ripped and our mum went to the school to ask the headmaster, "What's gone on with my boy? Blah, blah blah."

'One of the prefects, a right bully-boy, had it in for me. I was out in the yard one day when he came up and put a snowball down the back of my neck. I turned round and beat the stuffing out of him, even though he was in the fourth form and I was in the second. Next thing, I'm up before the head, Mr Wilkinson, and I'm thinking I'm in shit street.

'He asked me why I'd done it and I told him. He thought for a moment, then he said, "Now you know how to look after yourself, Windsor." He called the prefect in and apparently tore a strip off him, said he was made of milk and water and that he wasn't a prefect any longer. From that day on, I never let anyone mess me about. I learned a valuable lesson, that if you let people get away with doing things to you, they'll keep on f*****g doing them until you do something about it.

'It was round about then that I first felt the long arm of the law. There was still building work being done on the estate after we moved in. One day I saw a heap of concrete blocks with a wheelbarrow beside them. So I loaded up the wheelbarrow and thought, I'll take these home for our dad. Be a nice surprise.

'The estate copper, a Mr Waters, who was a right bastard, stopped me on the way.

'He said, "Hello, hello. Where are you going with them?"

'I said, "I'm taking them home to my father." I had no idea I was stealing them. The way they were chucked on the ground made me think they were there to be picked up. He made me take them all the way back and stack them in a neat pile, and then he took me down to the house to see my father.

'I had to go to the police station. Our dad came with me. I loved my father, I could not have wished for a better one. He used to call me "Bash". When we got to the station, he said, "Sit there, Bash." My father was sticking up for me and I was just sitting there scared stiff in case they were going to lock me up.

'Anyway, after a while they let us go and the first thing Dad did was to stop at the nearest shop. He went in and came out with two bars of chocolate and a bottle of ice-cream soda for me and my sister while he nipped into the boozer for a pint.

'It wouldn't be the last I'd see of the inside of that police station, but I could go back to playing football without a care in the world.

'When I got a bit older, 11 or 12, I'd go with a few mates to Somerton Park and watch Newport County in the old Third Division (South). We'd be "up the County" every other Saturday, watching players like the goalie Len Weare, who a few years later made a name for himself as the first player from the Fourth Division to play in an international. For us kids, playing football for the County and getting paid to do it was the perfect job. Brilliant days.

'My life slowly began to change after I did the 11-plus and went to Brynglas Secondary Modern which was like a mansion with its own grounds. That meant a bus into town, a bus to Brynglas and two buses back. That was tuppence a day in old money and my mother gave me my lunch money on a Monday for the week, about half-a-crown [twelve and a half pence post-decimalisation], except that I'd have it all spent by Monday morning on sweets and chocolate eclairs.

'That meant I'd be starving all week. For the mid-morning break, some boys would bring cold toast. Now when you're hungry, cold toast smells like a sirloin steak. Beautiful. So you'd be following these boys round hoping they'd give you a crust or, if they were eating an apple, that they'd let you have the core.

'More often than not, I'd spend the bus fare on sweets as well as the lunch money. So I'd have to walk all the way from Brynglas. Must have been five miles. When I got older, I'd wonder why my mother didn't ask why I was so late getting home. Maybe she knew why and never let on.

'I'd always run home, in case my mates started the soccer match without me. Once, when I'd got into another scrape and had to report to the police station at one o'clock Saturday lunchtime, I ran a good mile from Brynglas to Maindee and said I was very sorry for what I did. Then I ran all the way back, sweating and praying I'd get to the match for kick-off.

'When you had a new estate, like the one I lived on at St Julians, you had people being rehoused from all over the place and there'd be a few territorial issues, which meant you'd always be scrapping. For some reason that I never understood, I got a bad name on the estate. I never broke into anyone's house or anything like that, but I always seemed to be in trouble. Coppers appeared to follow me round.

'At Brynglas I met the man who changed my life, Hedley Rowland. We had two teachers there who took sport, a fellow called Don Thomas who was soccer mad and Hedley who was rugby mad. So I'd play soccer for the school on a Tuesday and rugby on a Thursday. I only played rugby because Hedley Rowland said I wanted to play and I was trying to say, "But, sir, I play football." And he'd say, "You're playing rugby on Thursday."

'He played me at outside-half and full-back. At school I was small for my age, but I was quick, as I was when I was older. There wasn't a faster forward playing for Pontypool than me. Gradually, I was leaning more towards rugby. I was getting the feel of it, enjoying the contact and running with the ball. On the football field, I felt too small for my position as a centre-forward, jumping against centre-halfs who were at least a foot taller.

'Another thing struck me about rugby. I could see from the very early days that I had a brain for the game, not just to spot a gap but an instinctive feeling for what was going to happen next. Hedley was that much into sport, especially swimming, that I got my life-saving medallion. I'd swim for the school and play baseball in the summer.

'Monday afternoon was swimming, Tuesday rugby, Wednesday swimming, Thursday rugby. When it came to studying, we only really went to school on Friday! Brilliant, it was. The amount of time teachers gave up in those days outside school to organise sport was outstanding because they never got paid for it. I'm not sure whether that still happens now, but it did then, thank God.

'When you played at home, your teacher refereed and vice versa. There was always a lot of fighting. Brynglas would have been considered by some to have been a bit rough and ready, like the teams from Pill, the docks area of Newport. Anyway, on one particular day, we were playing Llantarnam, which was an upmarket place by comparison.

'We were fighting like bantam cocks. Their referee sent me off. He came up to me afterwards: "Windsor, come here. Do you realise you have no need to be doing what you're doing? You're messing yourself up. Stick to what you're good at, cut out the nonsense and you might go a long way in this game."

'It was nice of him to say so and it made me think – use your head instead of getting caught all the time. I was 14 and shortly after that, I'll never forget it, Hedley was a forward short and he said, "Windsor, you're playing hooker today." We were playing one of the local schools and everyone knew it was going to be a fight because they were full of the dull bastards who'd failed the 11-plus.

'I'd never been in a scrum in my life. This boy Stephen Hall was hooking for the other side. We became friends for life, but not then, because the front rows went down and bang, there was a fight straight away. The ref sent us both off. The next day, Hedley Rowland says, "Windsor, after watching that yesterday, I'm going to leave you in the forwards."

'He said something about me getting a couple of strikes against the head or some technical jargon like that. I thought he was having a dig at me hitting somebody and I felt like protesting that if I did strike anyone on the head it was in self-defence. Because I didn't know what the hell was happening in the front row, I didn't have a clue that he was complimenting me for winning the ball on the opposition put-in. The decision turned out to be a masterstroke by Hedley even though I was still on the small side.

'He had such a good influence on me that he even improved me academically, which, I admit, took some doing. Hedley taught history and I'd always be in the top four at history. Hopeless at every other subject, but I made a point of studying history because I wanted to please him so he'd say, "Well done, Windsor." He'd given me so much that I wanted to give him something back.

'Hedley Rowland used to drink at the Royal Albert in Newport, a real pukka pub where they would have chickens on the spit in the window. Just before the end of this one term, he came to a few of us and said, "Do you boys want to earn a few bob over Christmas working in the Royal Albert? All you do is go down into the cellar, they send the empty bottles down, you stack them in crates and send the full ones back up on a pulley."

'We said, "Right, sir." We'd get ten bob a night [50p] and have a bit of fun. That was the plan and it all went well until Christmas Eve. We'd had a few drinks in the cellar, then we were up in the bar clearing up the empties till the time came for us to take them back down. The boy I was with said that instead of taking the long way down he'd go down on the pulley and that I had to hold the rope. I was letting him down slowly when the rope came off the wheel and all I could hear was, "Aaaargh". He'd hit the ground, fallen out and smashed a few bottles.

'When I went down to grab him in the dark, I stretched out my right hand and caught it on a jagged piece of glass. Blood was spurting all over the place. They carried me out and straight down to the Royal Gwent. Nineteen stitches in my hand, then I went back to the pub to collect my money. They gave me half a quid and a roasted chicken, and took me home by car.

'I walked into the house and held the chicken up in my good hand for my parents to see – "Look what I've got!" In those days, you couldn't afford anything as fancy as a chicken. I'd just come from a pub plastered with decorations and full of all kinds of Christmas spirit, not all of it alcoholic. At home we didn't even have as much as a Christmas tree, never mind any fairy lights.

'I understood that was because of my mother's religion and while I respected that, I always resented it. I was jealous of all those other kids who were jumping about opening their presents and there was me with virtually nothing. One of my pals, a lad called Alan Jones, lived on the same block of houses and that Christmas my sister had given me a bar of toffee.

'I put it in a tin and wrapped it up as neatly as I could and knocked on Alan's back door, Christmas Day. I wasn't doing it entirely out of the kindness of my heart. I was hoping that I would get a present in return. Alan said, "Thanks very much," and closed the door. Nothing. But worse than that, I'd lost my bastard toffee. If someone had told me there and then that it is better to give than to receive, I would have told him to get stuffed.

'Christmas should have been the best time of the year. Instead it was probably the worst. In the early days when we lived at Harrow Road, we did celebrate Christmas in a small way and I'd hang up my stocking. I'd only get an apple, an orange, maybe a few nuts, but it was something. Then, once we'd moved and my mother got into her religion, all that stopped.

'At that time, I was doing a milk round, which meant my father got me up at half past four every morning. I'd walk from my house across the estate for about a mile to the milkman's. At five we'd load up the milk and I'd work with him until eight, then I'd go to school. I'd be on the go for eight hours without anything to eat. It was unbelievable how hungry I was. I worked with the milkman five weekdays and then until lunchtime on Saturdays.

'Weekends, I had a paper round. F*** me, was that hard work. Every house had a long drive, so I'd walk miles delivering 30 copies of the *Argus*. Sunday papers like *The Observer* and the *Sunday Times* were so heavy that you needed a crane to get them around. My father made a special bag for me, but it still felt like a ton weight. You'd always be hoping that someone at those houses would come out, say "Well done, son," and give you a tanner [sixpence in old money].

'I'd try to save a bit, but it was a losing battle. The Saturday before Mother's Day, I had no money to buy Mum something. I was working for the milkman down by St Julians and on a doorstep there was some money for him, four or five shillings, so I picked it up, went to the chemist down the road and bought her some lily of the valley perfume.

'The bloke who left the milk money out began to suspect something was up when the milkman asked him to settle the bill. The next thing I knew the coppers were on the case. The bloke who left the milk money out was a schoolteacher so my dad took me down to the house. My dad paid the money and, pointing at me, said, "He'll work it off, 'cos I'll make sure he does."

'I had lost my job with the milkman. I knew it was a very stupid thing I'd done. My dad said to me, "Right, Bash, any time you want any money, come to me. Don't steal it."

'I told him I was sorry and he took me home on his motorbike, a BSA 350.

'If I was ill, he would go and do the paper round for me. That's the kind of dad he was. Nothing was ever too much trouble. Because he was always ready to work all the hours he could to support us, Dad very rarely had time to come and watch me play. He did get along once, to Rodney Parade for the final of the Dewar Shield, a competition involving all the schools of Newport and Cardiff. I was in the Newport squad, one of two full-backs. There had been some doubt about the game because of the weather, but I'd told him before leaving the house that morning, "Dad, the game's on." They picked the team and left me out. Sod's law. So I stood beside our dad leaning on a crush barrier and watching a boy at full-back who wasn't fit to lace my boots. He missed two tackles that cost us the match.

'The fire in my belly was burning like hell that day.'

2

....

PIECE OF CAKE

January 1962. Adolf Eichmann, despised as the so-called architect of the Holocaust, awaits his execution in Israel after being found guilty of crimes against humanity. Another notorious case, albeit one on an infinitely smaller scale, opens at Bedfordshire Assizes: the A6 murder trial, which would end with James Hanratty becoming one of the last people to be hanged in Britain before the abolition of the death penalty.

In Rome, Pope John XXIII excommunicates the Cuban communist revolutionary Fidel Castro. New Zealand grants independence to Western Samoa, presumably on the understanding that they could take their pick of the island's best rugby players and convert them into All Blacks for decades to come.

A rising band of musicians have their first audition, then sign Brian Epstein as their manager and cut their first disc. The Beatles are on their way, but for the moment 'The Twist', as sung by an American called Chubby Checker, is all the rage and the newspapers run photographs of the new dance being performed by Norma Sykes, a voluptuous English model better known as Sabrina.

The Americans launch John Glenn into space from Cape Canaveral and bring the 40-year-old Marine back safe and sound. As the space race hots up, NASA (the National Aeronautics and Space Administration) launches its first space probe to the Moon, only for the rocket to miss by 22,000 miles.

At Twickenham, Wales, under the captaincy of Lloyd Williams, fire so many misguided missiles that they have to settle for a scoreless start to the Five Nations championship. In a classic case of much ado about nothing–nothing, they miss five shots at the English goal in a tricky breeze, the grim stalemate putting the wind up a crowd of more than

70,000. Mercifully, the championship has not witnessed a 0–0 draw since.

Rod Laver and Margaret Court win the singles titles at the first Grand Slam event of the tennis year, the Australian Open. On the American golf tour, Arnold Palmer is warming up for the second of his three US Masters titles and Benny 'Kid' Paret is in training for what would prove to be a fatal defence of his world welterweight title, the twenty-five-year-old Cuban dying from head injuries twelve days after losing to Emile Griffith.

Cliff Richard spends the first six weeks of the year on top of the charts with 'The Young Ones' and he's still there when Wales follow their pointless visit to HQ by contriving to lose at home to Scotland. Just as well, then, that before Cliff can be knocked off his perch by B. Bumble and the Stingers with 'Nut Rocker', a youngster who would rock a few nuts in the Swinging Sixties gets his first job.

'I was no great academic,' says Bobby Windsor. 'Hedley Rowland didn't need to be Einstein to work that out, but he did me the favour of getting me an interview at Whitehead's steelworks at the top of the docks in Newport. There was a vacancy in the accounts department as a junior wages clerk, a really pukka job. My father was chuffed to bits. His son was going to be on the staff. If you were on the staff and you kept your nose clean, you had a job for life.

'At the interview, they asked me about my family and whether my dad had been in the forces and that's what swung it. They thought I was from good stock, so I got the job, which was to get all the time sheets from the mill for the wage slips. You had to be 16 to work in the mill and I was 15.

'I was on £2 2s 6d and I didn't like the fact that there were boys of 16 getting up to £5 2s 6d, more than twice as much. I talked with Dad about getting a trade and he found out that there was a job going as an apprentice in the bakery where he was working. I got the job. After the boredom of the wages department, it was like going to work in Aladdin's cave. I'd have to say I was more of a taster than a baker. Working in a cake factory – I couldn't believe my luck. Put it this way: I never went hungry. I scoffed all the cakes I wanted. In the bakery there were slabs of chocolate, four-foot square and about a foot high, which I had to smash up with a mallet and put into a melting drum. What I didn't eat, I poured down onto the cakes below, stopping every so often to fill my face with it.

'Boy, did I make up for lost time on that caper. Those cakes were the main reason why I went from being a sort of skinny full-back or outside-half to a front-row forward. But the job was too good to last. I was an apprentice there for six months until one day my father came up to me and said, "Come on, Bash, we're finished here." He'd had a barney with one of the engineers and told them to stick their job – which meant sticking mine as well.

'There was a job going down in the hot mills at the steelworks, but you had to be 16. I went there on the 12th of January to see the trade union rep. He asked how old I was. I knew I couldn't start until the following Monday at the earliest, so I said, "I'm 16 on the 21st."

'They kitted me out with steel boot-protectors and clothing for working with red-hot steel. I reported for duty and they kept asking me for my P45. Eventually, I took it in. The personnel people played holy hell when they saw I was still 15 and I had to explain that I stretched a point about my age because I was afraid I wouldn't get the job.

'The union bloke stepped in, saying, "Come on, he's 16 now. It ain't a problem any more."

'That was when I began to turn the chubbiness I'd got from eating all those cakes into muscle – it was hot, heavy work slogging away at the blast furnace. One of the first things I did was to put my name down for the rugby trials on the Saturday for the works team. That was how I met another man who had a big influence on my life, Johnny Whitfield. He must have been the first trainer-coach in Welsh rugby. He did it all, Johnny, from first aid to sorting out the kit and marking the pitch. He was an absolute diamond.

'Johnny started off by asking us to name our position. I'd filled out so much that when I heard lads of similar size saying "front row", I said the same. For my first match, against Cardiff High School Old Boys at Tredegar Park, I was picked for the second team at prop. They didn't bother with any technicalities like loosehead and tighthead.

'Going to the match on the Saturday, I met a boy who was a bit older than me, John "Paddy" Burke. He asked if I'd ever played prop before and I said, "Never." So he said, "I've propped before, so I'll go there and you play hooker. OK?"

'And that, believe it or not, is how I became a hooker. At that time, props used to strike for the ball as much as the hooker. I'll never forget coming off at the end and bumping into Len Bingham, who was a committee man.

"Great game, Bob," he says. "Three against the head. Bloody marvellous." I thanked him, but I was thinking, what the hell is he talking about?

'Anyway, they put me straight into the first team. Away from the set scrums, I could play. I could knock opponents off, keep the ball alive and make it available because I was quick, strong and, thanks to the job, getting stronger all the time.

'In the hot mills, you'd have white-hot lengths of molten steel, forty foot long, six inches square, which would be pushed out into a set of rollers which would compress them into whatever size was required. You'd be stood there with the smoke billowing up and your feet feeling like they were on fire. You used tongs to pick up the steel and I worked night shifts until a job came up working days. By then I was 18 and married to the love of my life, Judi McCarthy of Frederick Street in Pill. She was from a big family of Irish ancestry. Her father was a coal-trimmer down the docks and Judi was the youngest of seven.

'I met her when I was 14 and I don't mind admitting that it was a shotgun wedding. But I wanted to marry her – I loved her. On the day of the wedding, the 5th of September 1964, our dad came along in his A35 van and said, "Hey, Bash, you haven't got to do this if you don't want to. Are you sure you're doing the right thing? Because if not, there's the keys for the van."

'He didn't like the thought of me being pushed into something I didn't want to do. I said, "No, Dad. I'm doing it because I want to."

'Judi's people were Catholics, which meant I had to go and see the parish priest six times and tell lies about how I would become a Catholic as well. It was a load of old bullshit, but I went along with it.

'We couldn't afford much of a reception. We had it in the back room of the Picton public house, a salad on a plate with a few pints. Our honeymoon was a week in a caravan in Porthcawl. We came back and moved to Wingate Street, into a room at the house where one of Judi's brothers, Bernard, lived with his wife, Rose, a Maltese lady.

'We had a front room and a bedroom. The problem was that to get to the kitchen we had to go through their room. Before long, Judi had a barney with Rose and the upshot of that was that we went over the road to Brunel Street to live with her sister Sheila, who was a wonderful woman, and her husband, Charlie McDaid. Their three kids were soon to be four. And there was me, Judi and the baby – Joanne – who had been born a few weeks earlier, in March 1965.

'Then we got a council house on a new estate in the suburb of Bettws. The problem was that we were flat broke, absolutely skint. We went to the furniture shop, got a three-piece suite, a dining-room suite and a bedroom suite on the never-never. We paid three quid a week. The furniture was nice, but we had no central heating and no gas fire and marley tiles on the floor. It was f*****g freezing.

'I couldn't afford to buy coal, but I couldn't sit there seeing the family shiver and do nothing. So I would cycle from Bettws to Newport docks down by the Ebbw Bridge. Coal got washed down all along the banks of the river. I'd feel through the mud and get what they call "patch coal". I'd then balance a sackful on the handlebars and pedal like hell all the way back to Bettws, from one end of Newport to the other.

'With the patch coal you'd get clay and when that went on the fire, bits would shoot out like bullets and make a mess of your front room unless you had a fireguard. Other times, I'd go to the canal or down to Tredegar Park, where I could cut logs from the fallen trees for the fire. Moneywise, we were really up against it.

'You'd have good weeks and bad weeks in the steelworks. In the bad weeks, you'd work three days and they'd give you one day's dole and that was it. Where you made your money was in overtime. I'd eat beans and chips all week because that was all I could afford. But I always made sure the kids had proper food.

'Then I got a lucky break. The M4 was being built and I got a job on the concrete gangs with an Irish firm. You started at seven in the morning and you shovelled ready-mixed concrete for twelve, sometimes fourteen hours. Shovelling, shovelling, non-stop except for a 15-minute break for tea in the morning and half an hour for lunch.

'That's where I got myself really physically fit. You'd work a stretch of at least 15 miles, all the way from the Cardiff side of Newport to the Severn Bridge, which was then under construction. I did that for two years and the experience taught me how the Irish always stuck together. The gangers were always Irish. If they wanted a brain surgeon and a brain surgeon from London applied for the job and there was a gravedigger from Cork called O'Reilly who needed some work, O'Reilly got the job.

'That's how much they stuck together and I only got a job there because I knew this Irishman who said they were looking for men and he put a word in for me. I'd earn £50 a week, big money back then, but you worked all the hours God sent. It got even better when the ganger gave me a bigger job as a screwsman, which meant that, as the machine went along on wheels, it was my responsibility to make sure the concrete stayed at the same level.

'That was more money. It was a fairly tough routine. I'd get home at nine o'clock every night, Judi would have my dinner ready and then I'd be off again at seven the next morning. But it made a big difference to our lives. We paid off our debt and, instead of having another hand-me-down television, I went into the shop and paid £75 cash for a brand-new one.

'I never stopped to think that it was too good to last, that maybe, like the cake job, it would suddenly disappear. And then I ran into a fella called Tony Lambrianides who was working on the same motorway job. He was a boxer who'd fought a pair of British welterweight champions, Wally Swift and Mick Leahy, so this Lambrianides could handle himself. I knew that because I'd talked to him about his boxing – he'd had to give it up because of an accident which damaged the sight in one eye – but he wasn't going to scare me.

'He'd been throwing himself around a bit, trying to put the frighteners on people. When people got their head off, they'd use the shovel. We were doing the levels when we had a bit of a barney and I told him, "It's got f*** all to do with you. The levels are wrong and we're going to stay here until we get them right."

'He threatened me, so I let him have it, not with the shovel but with my fist. What he didn't know was that I had a tape measure in my hand. I was as fit as a fiddle then. But I learnt soon enough that you can't do that and hope to keep your job. I got booted out straight away, after two years. They said, "Sorry, Bob, but you're causing too much trouble."

'It was the second unscheduled fight I had had with a boxer. I used to train in the Newport Sporting Club, run by a great man, "Buller" Walters. He'd take all the kids off the streets and get them working away on the punchbag and the speed ball. That's why you hardly had any trouble in those days, because everyone was letting off steam in the gym.

'The only proper fight I had there was against a local boy from Pill, Billy May, a middleweight who had 12 fights as a professional after winning the Welsh ABA title and boxing for Wales at the Commonwealth Games. I was in a pub one night and Billy was giving a lad by the name of Tony Pearce a hard time. I went up and told Billy to leave Tony alone and he threw a punch at me straight away. Then the coppers came and broke it up, but not for long.

'We went up to the next roundabout on the Ringland estate. We started scrapping again and the coppers broke that up too. There was no way I was going to let him off so we went to another place under the motorway. He was a bully-boy. We had a real ding-dong and in the end I laid him out. My face was a mess. I could take a punch, but he kept jabbing me and I had to take a lot of punches to get one in.

'Judi cleaned me up. Then the word got out that Billy was going to get me. When my boys were growing up, I taught them how to react to anyone threatening them. I told them that if they heard that Fred Jones was looking for them, they were to go look for Fred Jones. Billy was working then at Whitehead's, so I went down to the steelworks gate, saw the boys coming out and told them to go and tell Billy May I was out there. The word came back that he was busy working.

'Anyway, I went back to the sporting club and asked Buller Walters to put me in the ring with Billy. When you sparred, they'd give you gloves like balloons. I said to Buller, "Give me the little gloves." Billy and I had a bit of a ding-dong, then Buller rang the bell and said, "That's enough. Now shake hands."

'And we did. After that, me and Billy became the best of butties. Sadly, Billy's gone now. He died of a brain haemorrhage at the age of forty-three while on holiday on one of those islands in the West Indies. They brought the body home and gave him a real old-fashioned Pill funeral – big glass hearse, four black horses, top hats and a jazz band. While Billy concentrated on his boxing, I was taking a step up in my rugby, although sometimes you'd be hard pushed to notice the difference.

'Joining Newport Saracens took me from junior level with the steelworks team to second-class. There was no fanfare or roll of the drums when I turned up for my first match, in April 1967. If a fortune-teller had been there that day to let the Sarries in on the secret that they'd just signed a British Lion in the making, they'd have looked at him as if he had two heads. I started at the bottom, in the Sarries' 3rd XV, but I was as happy as a pig in the proverbial just to be playing at a higher level, even if it was still a million miles away from the international scene.

'I worked my way up into the first team and gave it everything I had every Saturday to make sure the selectors thought I was worth my place for the next match. I never had any fancy ambitions and I never saw myself playing for any of the first-class clubs. I'd finish work on a Saturday at midday and play for the Sarries, who had fixtures against most of the second teams of the bigger clubs – Pontypool, Ebbw Vale, Newbridge and others. We'd also run into top second-class clubs like Pontypool United (who were completely separate from Pontypool).

'You'd go into their clubhouses after the match for a few beers and some grub and you'd see all these wonderful display cabinets and the old jerseys hanging inside. I used to marvel at all that stuff. If it was an international weekend, I'd watch Wales play on the telly. I never thought that maybe one day I would play for Wales. As far as I was concerned, they were at their level and I was happy at mine, a second-class player always ready to bust a gut for the team.'

More than a few bust theirs trying to stop him. Tries rapidly became a Windsor speciality, hat-tricks included, like the one against Hereford, as reported by the *South Wales Argus*. 'Bob Windsor is heavily built yet extremely mobile,' they said. 'He was at his rampaging best. Hereford had no answer to his bullocking runs from the back of the line. He scored what appeared to be a perfectly legitimate fourth try, but the referee thought otherwise. It was an outstanding performance and the club records do not show another hooker having performed a similar feat.'

'In that first season with Newport Sarries at Sandy Lane, under a really good captain in George Thomas, we lost one game all season – one game,' Windsor says. 'I had Charlie Faulkner propping on one side of the scrum and my brother-in-law Bryn Allen, who also went with us to Cross Keys, on the other. We won everything there was to win, the Ben Francis Cup and the Monmouthshire League. You're bound to get noticed when you're winning all the time and we were halfway through that season when Cross Keys got in touch with the Sarries. They needed a couple of forwards for the Boxing Day game against Taunton.

'So it was agreed that Charlie and I could go on permit, which was a temporary transfer. Bloody hell, we were over the moon. Cross Keys were in the big league as far as we were concerned, a first-class club, and now we were going to be playing first-class football. You can't go any higher than that. We'd be rubbing shoulders with the likes of Cardiff, Newport, Swansea, Llanelli.

'The first-class bit extended to your appearance. You never dreamt of turning up in a pair of jeans, looking like a scruff, with a pair of earphones, the way they do now. You wore a shirt with the tie buttoned up and you wore a blazer. The Boxing Day game against Taunton was so much faster than anything I'd encountered before, but I was fit for it and able to enjoy the experience.

'I had a shower, put the shirt, tie and blazer back on. As I was going through the clubhouse for a bite to eat, one of the committee men came up and tucked something into my top pocket. "Thank you very much, Bob," he said. And I said, "Thank you."

'I couldn't wait to get into the toilet to see what he'd given me. Five pounds! One whole fiver. You could do a lot with that kind of money in 1970. You accepted the laws of rugby union, which made it a strictly amateur game, and therefore you never asked for anything. As long as I had a rugby ball in my hand, I was happy. Now, all of a sudden, I was playing first-class rugby, getting all the free beer I wanted and £5 in the back pocket – or, in my case, the front pocket.

'If they'd had a lottery back then, I'd have felt like I'd won it every week. What they did was strictly against the rules. If I'd been caught, they'd have kicked me out of the game, but I was never going to be mug enough to spill the beans. We were still struggling to make ends meet as a family, so the extra little bit came in very handy.

'In the clubhouse a little later, after I'd tucked the fiver safely away, the same fella came up to me and Charlie and said, "How would you two like to join us?" It must have taken us about a tenth of a second to accept and we stayed for the rest of that season. We weren't exactly what you'd call overnight sensations. I was coming up 24 and Charlie was nearer 30, although he always kept his age a secret; or, to be more accurate, he tried to keep it a secret.

'The great thing about playing first-class rugby was that some of the clubs had really posh programmes with the teams displayed in the middle. The first time I looked down the list I saw two stars against some of the names and there'd be one star against a few others. I'd never seen anything like that before and didn't know until someone pointed it out that two stars meant you were a Welsh international and one star meant you had been picked for a Welsh trial.

'Again, I thought those were things for other players, not me. After a few months at Cross Keys, someone asked me whether I'd fancy joining Cardiff. Cardiff! "Crikey," I said, "you're talking about big stuff now. Cardiff?"

'Anyway, I went down for the pre-season trials that summer. The first one I played in, I met a bloke called Peter Thomas, "Peter the Pies" and now the multimillionaire chairman of the club. He was also a hooker but far too good looking for the part. I got stuck into him and they must have thought Peter was too pretty because I got picked for one of the Cardiff 1st XV's first matches of the season, against, would you believe it, Pontypool, at the Arms Park. We beat them 26–3.

'Ray Prosser, then well into his marathon run as Pooler coach, went into the committee room after the match. He wanted to know the answer to two questions, so he gave them straight from the hip as usual, "Who's that ape you have in the middle of the front row? Where the hell did you get him from?" I hope they told him they'd got this particular ape from the local zoo.

'Hookers then were lighter than they are now. They were called "rubber men" or "swingers" because they swung on the prop because he was heavier and stronger. At 16 stone, I was built more like a prop. The driving scrum which came into fashion during the '70s was made for me. It was right up my street.

'Playing for Cardiff made me imagine how it must be to play for Manchester United. You walked into the dressing-room and your jersey was hanging on your peg, your towel was on the bench and you were treated like royalty. After training, you had egg and chips, and fairy cakes so good they almost made me think I was back in the bakery!

'I played nine matches for Cardiff and got a couple of tries and met some real characters, like Carl Smith, a back-row forward who could leap and run like a gazelle. I always thought Carl was good enough to play for Wales. Then there was John Hickey, the captain. He was a mad so-and-so. He'd tell you, "If you don't boot the opposition, I'll boot you." You always knew where you stood with John.'

As if sensing that he might not be there for long, the new boy wasted no time making an impact in a Cardiff team featuring Barry John at outside-half. Against Aberavon at the Talbot Athletic Ground, Windsor began by taking a strike against the head and by half-time he had used his deceptive pace to catch the Wizards by surprise. When Alex Finlayson made a 40-yard break and turned inside for support, who should be there to take the pass and hurtle over but Windsor.

'My problem was getting down to Cardiff and back. Every time it involved a journey of four buses – a bus to the centre of Cardiff, a second bus out to the training ground at Sophia Gardens, a third bus back to the city centre and a fourth one home. They didn't pay any expenses, so, over the course of a week, it was costing me a fair bit in bus fares as well as a lot of time. I came to the conclusion that I couldn't afford to carry on.

'Being skint, I also felt that I didn't really fit in. They were full of big-city boys who were mostly single fellas having a good time, while I was married with a wife and by then a second daughter, Mandy.

'Cross Keys let it be known that I had a standing invitation to go back there. I told them I would rejoin them on one condition: that I came back as a prop, not a hooker. It might not have sounded the smartest move in view of my subsequent success, but, as luck would have it, the club's regular hooker, Alan Talbot, broke his leg the week before I returned.

'And then, the following season, 1972–73, you'll never guess what happened. They made me captain. And if you'd told me then that I'd finish that season as first reserve for Wales and that I'd finish the season after that going to South Africa with the Lions, I'd have had you certified.'

Windsor would probably have been capped even sooner had he not punched himself out of immediate contention on the day Wales coach Clive Rowlands veered off the beaten track and pitched up to see the all-action man for himself – Cross Keys versus Swansea, Saturday, 4 September 1972 at Pandy Park, once famously referred to by the imaginative rugby journalist Dave Phillips as 'Pandemonium Park'. Unfortunately, the referee stopped Windsor 73 minutes inside the distance for creating his own pandemonium. Early baths, then, did not come much earlier.

That first sending-off also turned out to be his last, which, considering what he would give and receive in the years ahead, just goes to show that fact really can be stranger than fiction . . .

3

GANG OF THUGS

The mega-fights of 1971 demanded some serious demolition work in the Amazonian rainforests for the newsprint to satisfy public curiosity on a global scale. The pulp faction business went into overdrive before, during and after an event unique in the annals of the world heavyweight title, unique in that it featured not one unbeaten champion but two.

The hype merchants proclaimed it the Fight of the Century and, for once, nobody could accuse them of exaggeration. Joe Frazier and Muhammad Ali stepped into the ring at Madison Square Garden for the biggest pay day since the Marquis of Queensberry devised his rules. Each got $2.5 million for his work on a night when it seemed as though the rest of the world stopped to look, listen and read all about it.

After winning both comeback fights, Ali pronounced himself ready to reclaim the crown he had been forced to abandon without being allowed to throw a solitary punch, while the ferocious Frazier threatened to turn the prize into his own personal possession. Stripped of his title in 1967 for refusing to fight in Vietnam and banned from the sport for three years, Ali's reappearance had almost brought the United States of America to a standstill.

The great and the good occupied the best ringside seats and Frank Sinatra came armed with his own camera to take shots of a fight during which Frazier fired more than Ali to claim a unanimous points verdict in what would be the first of three epics between them. Elsewhere during the pugilistic year, other fights commanded tremendous interest.

There was Henry Cooper's last, against Joe Bugner at Earl's Court for the British, European and Commonwealth titles, the young challenger stealing all three by a quarter of a point and sending the revered old champion into retirement. A similar fate befell Nino Benvenuti, the stylish Italian taking the hint after his attempt to regain the world middleweight title from Carlos Monzon ended inside three rounds.

Ken Buchanan, the Welsh-based Scot managed in Merthyr Tydfil by the inestimable Eddie Thomas, finished off the durable Panamanian Ismael Laguna. But no catalogue of the fights of the year would be complete without an unscheduled catchweight contest which took place on the first Saturday of the 1972–73 rugby season, 4 September.

Within seven minutes of Cross Keys kicking off at home to Swansea, Pandy Park resembled Madison Square Garden without the fat cigars and Yankee accents. An open-and-shut case of Referee Stopped Fight resulted in Bobby Windsor being sent off and his opponent, Swansea's gangling second-row forward Mike James, carted off on a stretcher.

According to one Sunday newspaper, James had suffered a suspected broken elbow. Another claimed he had a suspected broken shoulder. 'After Cross Keys had taken the lead through Bill James (no relation),' the report read, 'the play deteriorated and a free-for-all ended with two Swansea players on the ground.'

The scrap put a temporary halt to the word around Pandy Park that it would be only a matter of time before Cross Keys doubled their number of post-war internationals. The first, Rex Richards, played against France in 1956 only to embark on an improbable change of career when the selectors failed to ask him back.

A one-cap wonder, 'Tarzan' Richards headed for America hoping to make it big in Tinsel Town on the strength of his nickname, given to him after he had finished runner-up in a nationwide contest to find the new Tarzan. Richards appeared in one film, *Wild Women of Wongo*, about apemen and Amazons, which was considered so bad that it has officially been listed among the ten worst Hollywood movies of all time.

At the moment Bridgend referee Stuart Morgan gave Windsor his marching orders, the Cross Keys captain might have had marginally more chance of landing the title role in *Raging Bull* for his Jake La Motta impersonation than of winning his Wales cap. Even if the suspension meant six weeks in purdah, Windsor never had any regrets about abiding by the first law of the rugby jungle as spelt out in the Old Testament: an eye for an eye, a tooth for a tooth.

Not then and not now . . .

'Cross Keys were always regarded as a chopping block for the pukka sides like Swansea, so when they came to Pandy Park they probably thought we'd be a bit of a pushover,' Windsor says. 'The first scrum goes down and Mike James, in the second row for Swansea, smacks me straight in the chops. It was impossible not to make a mental note. I decided to bide my time.

'We went to a lineout. They threw the ball in, he won it and passed it to the scrum-half. Then I slammed him and knocked him out. He went off on a stretcher and I got my marching orders, even though the referee never saw a thing. Swansea people in the crowd were shouting, "It was that number 2 who did it, the dirty bastard."

'I went straight into the Swansea changing-room, where James was lying on the stretcher. Who was there but Clive Rowlands, the Welsh coach. He said he'd come to look at me with a view to the Wales Under-25 team, who were playing Canada in a few weeks' time, and also to tell me I'd been picked for the Crawshay's invitational team, which was a big thing in those days.

'Rowlands said to me, "You stupid bugger."

'I told him that it wasn't me who started the trouble but him, and I pointed to the figure on the stretcher. And Mike James, fair play to him, said, "My fault, my fault." That wasn't much use to me, not when I spent the next six weeks banned from playing. As it was, we beat them with 14 men, but it meant I had to miss the Crawshay's tour to Cornwall. It taught me to be a bit smarter in future.

'I never apologised because I'd done nothing to apologise for. From time to time, some of my own teammates, like John Taylor the flanker, would say I'd been a bit naughty, that I shouldn't have done this or that. That comes from people who believed the game to be played by gentlemen and that everyone loves everyone else.

'Get one thing straight – rugby football at the sharp end, in other words the front five, is a game based on intimidation, physical and mental. Your job is to overcome your opposite number, that's why you are there – and you can't do it by pussyfooting around. You don't care who your opposite number is, you attack him.

'I did whatever it took. London Welsh thought they were the bee's knees then until they went on an Easter tour to Pontypool and they never came back again. How ridiculous that they would think they could come down to South Wales for a good time when all the Welsh clubs couldn't wait to get stuck into them.

'Anyway, one or two of their players would say, "Bob, I don't think that's really in the game." I said, "Let me tell you something now. Our job is to get the backs good ball so they can do their job. The glory boys out in the backs are waving to the girls in the crowd and I'm in the scrum. If the forwards didn't give them the chance to score tries and blow kisses to the crowd, they'd come to people like me and say, "We didn't get a chance today because you and the rest of the front five were rubbish."

'I never had any confidence in my hooking, my ability to strike for the ball. I knew what I had to do and I knew that sometimes I'd have to be a naughty boy and do things to make sure I got my own way. Other times I didn't get my own way because there were some naughtier boys on the other side. It all boils down, as I've been saying all my life, to the front five.

'If you're getting messed about in the scrum, you can't play as you should. If you're on top in the scrum, you play better than you ever did. That's the mentality of a front-five forward. Sometimes, when the backs were moaning about not getting a chance to score, I'd spell out the facts of life in the front five and they'd apologise for complaining.'

His sentence for the Swansea bust-up over, Windsor wasted no time climbing ever higher through the hefty list of contenders squabbling for the right to knock the incumbent national hooker, Jeff Young, off his perch. Nobody would suffer more in that respect than Roy 'Shunto' Thomas, the Llanelli hooker who spent his entire playing career sitting on the bench as a Test reserve, to first Young then Windsor, without winning his cap. Other long-term understudies at least had a few fleeting moments in the sun.

Ray 'Chico' Hopkins got 20 minutes in place of an injured Gareth Edwards against England at Twickenham in February 1970, long enough to turn an apparently lost cause into an improbable victory. Clive Shell, the Aberavon number 9 who stepped up after Hopkins had gone north to Swinton rugby league club, had no more than 90 seconds out in the middle to show for his years of shadowing Edwards.

Windsor's rise from one of the least fashionable clubs to a place among the all-star cast of the global game began when a letter arrived at his home in Newport from the Welsh Rugby Union.

Dear Sir,
First Welsh trial – Bridgend, 11th December, 1971. Kick-off 2.30 p.m.
 I am pleased to inform you that you have been selected to play for the WHITES in the above match against the REDS. Please report to the dressing-rooms, Bridgend RFC, not later than 1.30 p.m.

Kit: Please bring your own white knicks, stockings and black boots. Jerseys will be provided.

Meal: After the match a meal will be provided at the Wyndham Hotel, Bridgend. Time: 5.00 p.m.

Car parking: Car parking facilities are available at Bridgend RFC, the appropriate authority is enclosed.

Expenses: Out-of-pocket expenses incurred in attending the Trial Match will be reimbursed on the Saturday after the game. The enclosed expenses form must be returned to the Welsh Rugby Union office by Friday, 10th December.

Please complete the enclosed invitation form and return to me not later than Tuesday, 7th December, 1971.

Yours faithfully,
W.H. Clement,
Secretary

The letter came accompanied by an invitation from Ray Williams, the Welsh Rugby Union's first full-time coaching organiser, to attend a coaching 'teach-in' on the Sunday after the trial. Wales were the pioneers when it came to coaching, blazing a trail which the rest of the world would follow, but not before countries like Scotland raised objections to what they saw as an early step towards something which the reactionaries on their Union perceived as the ghastly horrors of professionalism.

Young may have kept his Wales place for the 1971 Grand Slam campaign, but his opposite number made enough of an impression in an outgunned Whites team to be earmarked for promotion. From that trial match onwards, Windsor's capping as the next Wales hooker was nothing more than a matter of time.

He finished that season rubbing shoulders with established internationals as a member of the WRU President's XV against Neath to mark the club's centenary. By then, coaches like former Abertillery hooker Brian Wilkins were recommending him for immediate promotion to the Wales team, and even referees began to praise the textbook quality of Windsor's striking for the ball in the set piece.

He started the following season on the highest rung of the ladder leading to the promised land of the full international game, for Wales B against France B, the crème de la crème of uncapped players at Cardiff Arms Park, Saturday, 21 October 1972. It was to be the start of a perennial duel with the French in which he would be repeatedly singled out for some gruesome treatment, almost as if he had done something to offend Joan of Arc in a previous incarnation.

Windsor went into the front line of the trenches as one of a pack captained by a flanker from Pontypridd, Tommy David, whose job was to provide decent ball for an international sprinter on one wing, J.J. Williams, and a bearded young warrior on the other who was in constant need of reassurance, Ray Gravell. Before being put to the sword to the tune of 35–6, the French had been acclaimed in a glowing, full-page article in the match programme as 'a joy to behold', a description which still makes Windsor laugh and point to the scars on his face.

'The Froggies always seemed to target me, from the first game to the last,' he says. 'Their tighthead prop was biting all the time in the scrum. Glyn Shaw was alongside me in the front row at loosehead. He was a handful, Glyn. He'd play his guts out for you and he was as quick around the pitch as any openside and ferocious with it. Against a really good scrummager, he could have problems because he was a bit too long in the back.

'I was onto him about this bastard prop coming across and I couldn't get under him. He'd grab hold of your ear in his mouth so that you couldn't pull away. I'd aim the top of my head at the side of the face of the opposition tighthead to stop him coming in at an angle, to push him away from his hooker.

'Glyn said to me, "I'll have the f****r." I said, "If you're going to start a scrap, make sure you let me know first, otherwise I could be in trouble with my ear in his mouth." He didn't say anything, and in the next scrum this prop came across and grabbed my ear, as usual. Glyn hit him straight under the chin, which caused the French fella to clamp his teeth on my ear. Sixteen bastard stitches.

'I tell you, it hurt. Everyone started fighting then and Gerry Lewis, the physio, took me off, stitched me up and I came back. We got stuck into their tighthead and he ended up in hospital. Can you believe that not a single committee member of the Welsh Rugby Union said anything about it? Not a dicky bird. Nobody saw anything so nothing was done. It was swept under the carpet "till the next time".'

That the newspapers were full of it made officialdom's neglect all the more damning. Tom Lyons, the veteran sportswriter who thought he had seen it all down the years, from Bruce Woodcock winning the British heavyweight title to lunching with Sir Matt Busby and his famous Babes shortly before many perished in the Munich air disaster, came up with a tasty line in the *Daily Mirror* the following Monday: 'Windsor's ear – *à la carte.*'

At least Windsor knew what to expect from the annual fixture the following season. Despite the stitches, he was back at the happy hooker lark the following Wednesday, for Cross Keys against Pontypool, which brought him into direct conflict with Alan Talbot. If a rival could ever be a friend, then Talbot, the fellow steelworker who was always ready to give the younger man the benefit of his technical advice, fitted the bill.

'Before the game, Alan and I had a photograph taken and I was there wearing a white headband. Believe it or not, there were people that night who asked me, "Why you wearing a white headband?" Because I had 16 stitches in my effing ear.

'I always wanted to play because I loved the game. Whenever a club match was called off because of bad weather, I'd be straight on to Newport Sarries and ask them how they were fixed for players. This one Saturday they said, "We're short of one second row for the thirds down at Tredegar Park." I said, "I'll play." I was off down there like a shot even though I was playing for Wales at the time and somebody might fancy taking a shot at me. That's what rugby football meant to me.'

Pontypool romped off with the Welsh club championship that season and by the end of it Windsor had joined them, encouraged by Talbot to fill the front-row vacancy left by his friend's retirement after Pooler had seen London Welsh off to clinch the title. The Welsh selectors, alias 'the Big Five', who occupied a status in Welsh society somewhere between the Royal Family and the Pope, decreed that Windsor's pre-Test apprenticeship required one more exposure to France in the annual autumn B match. This time, down in the relative warmth of the November sunshine in Toulouse, he would be subjected to an even worse form of brutality.

'The scrum goes down and I'm there looking up with my arms pinned. Their number 8 looks at me and I can tell right away what he's going to do well before he does it. He looks around to see where the ref is and then he kicks me straight in the face. What a bastard. What a mess. When I get up, I can't see out of one eye. I try the other one, but I can hardly see out of it because my nose is broken and pushed so far over that it's affecting the eye.

'That was them saying, "Welcome to France." That was only the first boot in the face. They kicked me in the face virtually every time I went to France. The All Blacks would ruck ruthlessly and if you were on the floor you got a trampling. They weren't dirty, but the French packs I played against showed a violence, especially to me, which I never experienced anywhere else.

'It was so bad that every time I left to play France, I'd say to Judi, "Take a good look at my face, love, because you might not recognise it when I come back." I must have played nine or ten times against them and they broke my nose every time except for one.

'Terry Cobner – "Cob" – was captain that day in Toulouse. He comes up and says, "Are you OK?" I tell him, "No, I'm f****d." So he says, "You've got to stay on. Don't let them see you're hurt."

'I felt so bad it was like I was running in the sea, going up and down with the waves. I picked the ball up to throw it into a lineout and I thought everyone was moving. I don't know if I threw it to one of the forwards or the full-back. After I came off, they pulled my conk across to its original position and stitched me up.

'Nobody likes a hard game more than I do, but you draw the line at someone booting you in the face. The ref missed it because the ball had been passed out and he's following it. The touch judges then didn't have a clue. For all I knew, maybe one of them was the French team's bus driver. The clubs used to supply their own touch judges and some of them were so bent that at some grounds a home player could run round behind his touch judge and he still wouldn't put his flag up.'

Despite the injuries, Windsor still turned up for the after-match dinner. The local president stood up to utter the usual platitudes about the sporting nature of the match capturing the essential spirit of the *entente cordiale* when he spotted the patched-up Welsh hooker with blood seeping from his wounds. 'We have a man here called the Duke,' he told the assembly. 'I call him the Iron Duke.'

It was as close as he ever got to being given the *Croix de guerre*. A bitten ear and rearranged face from successive matches against the uncapped French left him in no doubt about what to expect in subsequent years from one of the meanest, roughest, toughest bunch of hombres ever to be welded into a Test pack. They could also, when the mood took them, give a more than passable impression of a gang of thugs.

'I had so much respect or fear, or a combination of both, for those French forwards of the '70s that I could name every one of them, all eight of the bastards – Paparemborde, Paco, Cholley, Palmie, Estève, Skrela, Rives and Bastiat. Palmie and Estève, in particular, gave me a dog's life. We had to go in and punch and boot like mad and even then it was touch and go whether we'd beat them by pure violence. They always kicked shit out of me.

'Estève would try to kill you on the field and then kill you with kindness afterwards. The first scrum was always the worst. We'd go down and I'd hear this voice calling, "Bo-bee, Bo-bee." Then this almighty fist came through from the second row and smashed me in the chops. You had to meet fire with fire. If you didn't, if you sat back and took it, they'd destroy you.

'The amazing thing about those matches in Paris was that once the game was over, Estève suddenly became my best buttie. He was a fearsome sight with his big black beard, but he'd insist on taking me to the poshest nightclubs like the Folies Bergère. It was 60 quid to get in, but Estève would walk right up to the main door, they'd greet him like a long-lost son and he'd wave us through. He'd go straight down the aisle and up onto the stage among all the dancing girls. The singer would stop singing and say, "*Ah, le Pays de Galles.*"

'Then as the night wore on, he'd take us to other places in Pigalle which looked as though they were about to close. All he had to do was knock on the door and they'd crack open a bottle of champers and arrange a table and chairs. Every so often Estève would put his arm around me, "Bo-bee, *mon ami.*" I didn't know whether he wanted to boot me again or what.'

The archaic amateur regulations, as framed by the English public schoolboys who invented the game, were never designed for the blue-collar brigade from those parts of Britain, primarily South Wales, where the working class embraced the game. Had they been, they would have made allowances for those from humble backgrounds who were paid piecemeal and who therefore lost money whenever they had to take time off work to meet the increasing demands of being an international player.

When Windsor first reported for Wales duty in Cardiff the day before the England match in January 1973, he soon discovered a few harsh realities. 'The first time I turned up on a Friday night at the Angel Hotel,

I wore a three-piece suit, waistcoat, shirt and tie. I walked in and they said, "F*****g hell, it's the Duke of Windsor."

'They were all lounging round in shell suits, which were all the rage. I'd been brought up to look smart, blazer and tie, and to be polite, especially to the selectors. It was always Mr Jones, Mr Bowcott, Mr Stephens, Mr Rowlands and Mr Young, never Cliff, Harry, Rhys, Keith and Jack. They were the Big Five.

'Jack Young was related to Jeff Young, the No. 1 hooker. Jeff was a smashing bloke. I was after his place, but he was really good to me. He'd look after his place, of course, but he was never unfriendly. He'd had a stack of caps and been on a Lions tour, so it would have been easy for him to have stayed with the big boys and left a newcomer like me out in the cold. Instead, he always made me welcome.'

By then, a few eyebrows had been raised at Young keeping his place despite conceding some of the five penalties against the All Blacks at the Arms Park the previous month, when a twenty-one-year-old full-back of Lebanese background, Joe Karam, outkicked Phil Bennett in a 19–16 away win. Nobody articulated the call for Windsor's immediate elevation against England better than Mervyn Thomas in the *Daily Mail*: 'Windsor, travelling reserve against New Zealand, would add industrial gristle and skilled mobility to an over-scholastic pack.'

Soon, he would have first-hand experience of one of the so-called scholars, Mervyn Davies. Having sat and watched the entire Five Nations championship without being asked to break sweat despite defeats in Scotland and France, Windsor at least made the end-of-season trip to Canada. It turned out to be another eye-opener.

For reasons best known to themselves, Wales put out most of their front-line players for a nine-try romp against Canada in Toronto when they would have been better off using the non-cap match to blood a few of tomorrow's men. Jeff Young's impending retirement made it all the more difficult to understand why they still picked him. Windsor, therefore, began his breakthrough season, 1973–74, continuing to understudy Young, as reserve for East Wales against the touring Wallabies at Rodney Parade.

'I thought Jeff played well that day, well enough to keep his place for the international against Australia,' Windsor says. 'I went into the clubhouse and after a while Robin Davey of the *Argus* came up to me and said, "Congratulations. You've been picked against Australia." I said,

"Bugger off." He said, "No, there's just been a press conference and they've announced the team. You're in."

'The first thing I did was to contact my great friend John "Paddy" Burke, who started me off. He was there watching the game, and as soon as I gave him the news he fetched his car and took me straight to our dad's house. We went straight over to the St Julian pub and had a pint there. He was chuffed to bits and so were the people at the steelworks.

'They had a great tradition. The first hooker from Whitehead's to play for Wales was a really famous fella, Bill Travers, who went on the last Lions tour before the war. They called him "Bunner". The next one to be picked for Wales from the steelworks was Vic Perrins of Newport. So when I started work on the Monday, I was asked to go up to personnel and they all said how proud they were of me.

'They wanted to present me with a watch to mark the occasion. They asked me to pick it so they could inscribe it. I was made aware that the amateur regulations prevented me from picking any watch if it was a penny over £25. The steelworks' gesture was marvellous, because I never thought I'd get to the higher levels.'

Nobody was entitled to feel more satisfied at the new hooker's arrival on the Test scene than Hedley Rowland, the schoolteacher who had put him on the road to rugby fame, if not fortune, some 15 years earlier. Rowland always thought he would play for Wales at full-back or outside-half, a judgement based on Windsor in his early teens, before he filled out.

'Although small, he was completely fearless and shone at most sports,' Rowland told Brian Wall of the *South Wales Echo* at the time of his ex-pupil's Wales debut. 'He was good at baseball and he could swim like a fish. On top of everything, he was a nice boy. Bob grew taller and put on weight after leaving Brynglas, but when he started to play in the pack I never thought of him as a future Welsh hooker.

'Yet it soon became clear that as a front-row forward he had retained all the football qualities that made him so good behind the scrum. This is the reason he scores so many tries. Bob is always thinking. He can anticipate situations and get into the right place at the right time. He will do well for Wales.'

Hedley was not wrong there. In typical Windsor fashion, he began by taking a strike against the Australian head followed by the almost obligatory kick in the face, this time of a purely accidental nature. For good measure, he scored the last of three tries in a 24–0 win, clicking into overdrive to finish off a five-man handling move with a touchdown any wing would have been proud to call his own. It left nobody in any doubt that the new boy had taken to Test rugby as if he had been there for years, a point made by the former Wales great Ken Jones in the next day's *Sunday Express*.

'From a Welsh point of view,' Jones wrote, 'the most satisfactory feature was a tremendous display by the forwards where Allan Martin and Bobby Windsor fitted in with the confidence of veterans.'

International rugby was all very well, but it came at a price. The emphasis on sartorial elegance meant hiring a dinner suit and the demands of pre-match training meant writing off any overtime at the blast furnace on Thursdays and Sundays.

'It was a bit of a killer because in good times you'd miss two days' pay. So I went to see Bill Clement and explained to him that, like Charlie Faulkner, I had to miss double shifts. Sixteen hours' work was a fair bit of wages, which I couldn't afford to lose.

'I said to Bill, "Any chance I could get some sort of reimbursement?"

'"No chance, Bob," he said.

'"I can't afford to come down on a Sunday for training."

'"If you can't come down on a Sunday, you don't play for Wales. You've got a choice."

'The invitation to play Australia came with instructions to bring a dinner suit for the black-tie banquet. This was money I just didn't have. To make it worse, you had to have a pair of black patent shoes. Roll on! So there was only one thing to do about that, back to see Bill Clement.

'"Bill," I says, "you want us to go to the dinner in all this fancy gear. I can hardly afford to hire a dinner suit and there's no way I can hire or buy black patent shoes. And before you suggest it, no, I can't buff up my best pair of black shoes, because the soles are hanging off them and I haven't got the money to get them fixed."

'With that, Bill gave what I thought was a sympathetic look, put his hand in his pocket and brought out a large wad of notes tied with two elastic bands. I thought, great, I'm going to get a few quid for a pair of shiny black shoes. And just as I'm thinking I'm quids in, he gives me both rubber bands and says, "Tie those around your shoes until the next pay day."

'When you got into the Welsh team, you had to have a medical before every game. You'd go and see Gordon Rowley, the team doctor, but Charlie, because he was sensitive about his age, was half frightened to death about what they might find.

'I went in before him and all the doc asked me was, "What will happen if I covered over your left eye?" I said I'd be partially blind. "And what," he asked, "would happen if I covered your right eye?" I said I'd be totally blind.

'When I went out, Charlie asked me about it. So I said, "Easy. Just say 'partially blind' to the first question and 'totally blind' to the second. You can't go wrong."

'Charlie sat down. The doc said to him, "What would happen if I cut off your left ear?"

He said, "I'd be partially blind, sir."

"What would happen if I cut off your right ear?"

"I'd be totally blind, sir."

The doc said, "How do you make that out?"

Charlie said, "My hat would fall over my eyes."

'You'd give your right arm to play for your country, but over the years losing wages because of time off for training became a bind and it became a bind for Charlie as well. We were in the same boat. One thing which really peed me off about playing for Wales was the boot money, not because it broke the amateur rules but because for a while I didn't get my full whack of the readies.

'Kit was an untapped area then. Derek Tapscott was a former international footballer for Wales who was working for a company called Gola. One day he said to me, "How would you feel if I gave you all the kit, tracksuits, trainers and boots, all buckshee?"

'I said, "Lovely, Derek. Thank you very much."

'He gave me all the gear, so at the next squad training I'm there in my Gola tracksuit. The other boys always seemed to have nice shell suits and now, at last, I was up with them instead of wearing the usual scruffy training stuff. One of the senior players came up to me and said, "What are you doing wearing that?"

'When I explained that Derek Tapscott had given it to me, the senior international said, "It's all Adidas down here. Tell him you can't wear that."

'"Adidas?" I said. "I've got bugger all from Adidas."

'So he said, "You wear their boots, you get 20 quid."

'I said, "Bloody hell, do you? Why did nobody tell me about this before now? Why have I had to be in the squad for this long without being told anything about boot money?"

'"Ah, well," the senior international said, "the cake is only so big. And the more slices you take out of it, the smaller the slice gets." I said, "From now on, every time a new player comes into the squad, I'll tell him that he'll get a nice bit of gear and 20 notes for wearing the boots. I'll let them know what the score is right away, which is more than anyone did for me."

'We'd get our money on a Friday night from Arthur Young, the Adidas rep who used to be my teammate at Newport Saracens. You'd go to his room and get paid. Arthur's activities didn't go down well with the bigwigs in the Union, but he was only doing his job and, as far as I was concerned, a very good job. That £20 made up for the money I had to fork out on a dinner suit.

'It also made up for a big hit which I once took – drawing about eight players on top of me – so that Arthur could have the glory of scoring a try under the posts for Newport Sarries. Some international players would be glad when bad weather gave them a Saturday off because it meant they didn't have to run the risk of being injured. I never gave it a thought and when I was at a loose end after Pontypool's match had been called off, I got straight in touch with the Sarries at Newport.

'They were playing Cwmtillery and they were glad to give me a game because they were a bit short in the front row. The game was in full flow when Arthur dummied to pass to me. Fortunately for him, the entire Cwmtillery pack bought it. Unfortunately for me, it seemed as if all eight of them hit me at the same time, leaving Arthur to stroll through the barn door for his try.

'The Adidas boot scandal caused a rare old stink when the word got out, but it had been going on well before I found out about it. Some players couldn't wear one or other of the Adidas boots because they didn't feel comfortable or whatever. So they'd wear a different boot and then go to a lot of trouble to paint it black with the three white stripes of the Adidas trademark and make it look like an official boot. I was annoyed because many of those established players were a lot better off than me and they left me to find out about the arrangement by accident.

'It made you realise how slow the Welsh Rugby Union were to exploit the commercial value of going to a company like Adidas and doing a deal which would have been for the benefit of the whole game from the grass roots up. It was a stupid thing not to do. If they'd done a deal, they could have had enough free beer to last all night at the dinners after internationals. Instead, I'd be praying that the free beer wouldn't run out because I couldn't afford to buy a round.

'You'd claim your bus fare or mileage, but before you could do that, Bill Clement sent you a sheet telling you the exact mileage from your front door to the Arms Park or the training ground at the Afan Lido in Port Talbot. You could never really put one over on Bill. For example, the late John Bevan – "Bev" – God rest his soul, had sixpence knocked off his expenses claim because Bill decided he had overcharged on the bus fare by a tanner, the equivalent of two-and-a-half pence.

'He was a great bloke, Bill, even if sometimes he gave the impression that he ran the WRU from his front room. He would help you out just as long as you weren't breaking any regulations. I hated flying, so did Terry Cobner, and Bill would arrange for us to go to Scotland by train, up on the sleeper, which was good crack. He wouldn't give you anything, but he was a gentleman.'

The players were amateurs who were expected to take time off work to meet the professional demands of training. Apart from two complimentary tickets, they got nothing in return beyond the glory of playing for their country if they won and, more often than not, a fair bit of abuse from an unforgiving public if they lost, especially to England. Windsor discovered even before he won his cap that the Welsh Rugby Union was not in the business of giving away any kit, that a player keeping his jersey or swapping with his opposite number would be made to pay for doing so.

Six days after his first match as a non-playing reserve, against England at Cardiff Arms Park on 20 January 1973, a letter from the Welsh Rugby Union dropped through Windsor's letter box:

Dear Mr Windsor,
I have been informed by Mr Gerry Lewis [team physio] and Mr Clive Rowlands that you kept your reserve jersey from the Wales v England match last Saturday. Reserves are only entitled to ONE jersey during a season and your jersey for the Wales v New Zealand match was not returned.

It is, therefore, essential that you bring this jersey with you to Scotland as another one will not be allocated you.

Yours sincerely,
W.H. Clement,
Secretary.

With his career taking off for the heights at 26, Windsor knew he could hack it because he had been grounded in what he considered to be the toughest school of all, in his native Monmouthshire.

'They go on about the Turks and the Jacks, Llanelli and Swansea and the rivalry between them,' Windsor says. 'With respect, they didn't know what a local derby was. In the valleys of Gwent, there were seven of them in the first-class league. There wasn't a valley club in Monmouthshire which didn't have a good front row, so, wherever you went, you had to battle for every inch. And if you weren't up to it, you got turned over.'

Soon Wales would find a front row housed under the same club roof with the capacity to win two Grand Slams in three seasons, four Triple Crowns on the bounce and four Five Nations championships. The 'Viet-Gwent', as the troubadour Max Boyce would call them in one of his more celebrated ballads, were about to step out of their familiar stamping ground into the deeper jungle of Test warfare . . .

4

....

THE VIET-GWENT

In the pantheon of British rugby, they will have to find a place some day for a humble man who would be horrified at the mere thought of anyone singing his praises. Ray Prosser, a fixture in the Wales team of the late '50s and a Test Lion in New Zealand, would probably top any list reserved for those who never got full recognition for their achievements.

As a manager-coach, he was more Bob Paisley than Brian Clough and yet, for all Prosser's aversion to the limelight and loathing of self-promotion, there was a touch of the Cloughs about him. Just as 'Old Big 'Ead' was the best football coach England never had, so Prosser, especially in the admiring eyes of his players, was the best rugby coach Wales never had.

At the height of his playing career, Prosser had been a cornerstone of Pontypool's Welsh Championship-winning team in 1958–59. When that team disintegrated and age overtook them, the redoubtable old prop watched his home-town club slide so far down the table that they could go virtually no lower. Ten years after finishing top of the pile, they ended up second from bottom of the old eighteen-team Welsh Club Championship.

Prosser returned by popular demand in 1969 and began applying his own variation of Sir Isaac Newton's law of universal gravitation, that what goes down must first go down a little more before it can go up. Pooler ended the 1970–71 season rock bottom of the Welsh table, losing 32 of their 45 matches. There was only one way they could go now, not least because by then they had put into harness a coach–captain duo, Prosser and Terry Cobner, whose alliance would send waves across the oceans of the rugby world.

In a change of fortune extraordinary by any standard, they went from last to first in two seasons, overtaking London Welsh in the final weeks of the season to leave Cardiff second, Swansea third and the much-fancied Exiles down in fourth. The new champions lost only nine of their forty-three matches and when the celebrations were in full swing at Pontypool Park, Prosser did what he always did when there was a bit of glory on offer. He disappeared, resurfaced in the least raucous corner of the clubhouse and bought himself a beer.

Any Fancy Dan considered a viral danger to the ego-free zone around the dressing-room was given a dressing-down or told to get on his bike. Cobner's less than ecstatic response to winning the championship said everything about the work ethic and no-frills culture fostered by Prosser: 'We are just a good, workmanlike side. We have won the title without any stars. Now we've got to try and do it again next season.'

And, just in case anyone thought it was nothing more than a flash in a valley pan, they did win it again, albeit two seasons later, this time losing even fewer matches, five out of forty. By then there were stars galore, all of them in a pack fronted by an all-Wales front row then in the process of earning themselves legendary status and backed by Cobner, who typified the collective indomitable will of a team welded together by Prosser.

He drove a bulldozer for a living five days a week and spent Saturdays watching his forwards bulldoze allcomers into submission, strictly for the fun of it. As the daddy of them all, he could empathise with the fact that Wales kept Cobner waiting until he was 28 before granting him his cap. Prosser knew only too well how his protégé felt, having been detained by the Big Five until he was a few weeks short of reaching 29 before they picked him against Scotland at the Arms Park in February 1956. The match marked the official opening of the new South Stand, which raised the capacity to 12,800 seated and 60,000 overall.

Unusually, Prosser was a club second-row forward who became an international prop. When they restored him to the side for the concluding match of that Five Nations series, at home to France when Rex 'Tarzan' Richards made his fleeting appearance on the other side of the front row, Prosser stayed there for the next five years, ending as he began with a home win in Cardiff, 9–0 against Ireland in March 1961.

By then, he had achieved the distinction of proving himself the best in the British Isles as a member of the 1959 Lions in Australia and New Zealand. A wretched combination of injury and illness conspired

THE VIET-GWENT

to restrict him to one Test, the last against the All Blacks, before the largest crowd ever seen at a match in New Zealand, 63,000. Prosser's presence coincided with the Lions avoiding a blackwash, three Lions tries trumping two All Black penalties for a 9–6 win.

If the tour did nothing else, it eventually brought the lawmakers to their senses, illustrating that there was something wrong with the points system when a team could outscore their opponents 4–0 on tries, as the Lions did in the opening Test, and still lose, to six Don Clarke penalty goals, 18–17. Prosser, ever the pragmatist, would no doubt have questioned the point of throwing the ball about and creating a stack of tries only to lose the match.

The '59 Lions consisted largely of company representatives, schoolteachers, insurance inspectors, sales executives, a civil engineer and an industrial consultant. Apart from the Abertillery back-row forward, Haydn Morgan, who was a mechanic, and the Scot, Hugh McLeod, who was listed as a warehouse worker, Prosser was the only other Lion with a blue-collar job, an excavator driver.

No less distinguished a critic than Sir Terry McLean, the globe-trotting doyen of New Zealand journalists until his death in 2007 at the grand old age of 94, acclaimed Prosser as 'one of the great personalities of the Lions team'. McLean got a revealing response from Prosser when he asked him to compare the standards and attitudes of New Zealand rugby with those back home. The Welshman's verdict was that there were 'not enough working-class boys in this team', a mistake he would never be in danger of making at Pontypool.

Having followed the Lions bandwagon wherever it rolled around New Zealand and Australia from mid-May to mid-September and mixed with the players socially, McLean cast an educated eye over them all as rugby players and human beings in his book of the tour, *Kings of Rugby*. Of Prosser, he wrote:

> He was a homely chap and never pretended to be anything else. Though comparatively ill-educated – the only university he had attended was the University of Hard Knocks – he had a dramatic fluency in both the Queen's and Billingsgate English. His descriptions of the effect upon the human frame of various types of excavator and/or bulldozer driving were classical in their bare, terse phrases.
>
> When the mood was upon him, he could strum a pretty lay upon

the piano. He was, in a word, inimitable. Prosser suffered the agonies of the damned from homesickness when a muscle injury restricted his appearances in Australia and when he later suffered a severely broken nose, a heavy dose of influenza and a discharging ear, all within a day or two, he literally convinced himself that he was going to die.

Perhaps he would have, if a hotel manager and his wife in Invercargill, not to mention the hotel staff, had not shown him extraordinary kindness. Within a week or two, Prosser had to be shunted into a Christchurch hospital, again with a discharging ear, and once more he became convinced that he was going to die.

But here, too, the staff was wonderfully sympathetic. Money changed hands in wagers among the nurses when Ray escorted one of the principal figures among them to the third Test and hereafter he made such rapid progress that at the end, so far as could be judged, no one was sorrier to leave New Zealand than he.

And what a fine forward he proved to be in the last matches of the tour. He was tremendously good at tidying up, especially in the lineout. Prosser was one of the very finest of the Lions' forwards and the team was unlucky not to have had him on call throughout the tour.

No player can expect to get to the top without a little luck along the way and Windsor will readily admit that he had his share. The luckiest break of all, in the early summer of 1973, took him from Cross Keys to Pontypool. The short journey from one Monmouthshire valley to another opened up horizons he never imagined, stretching far beyond the town to South Africa, Australia and New Zealand.

To paraphrase Neil Armstrong, it was a case of one small step for a Welsh hooker, one giant leap for the Lions. At Pontypool, Windsor became the best hooker in the British Isles thanks to Prosser.

'As Wales coach, Clive Rowlands was at the Cross Keys annual dinner at the end of the '72–'73 season as guest speaker,' Windsor says. 'There'd been a lot of talk about whether I was going or staying. He was on to me about it and I told him I didn't know and that I might well decide to stay. Then the time came for him to speak.

'"I can tell you all now," he said, "Bobby Windsor's staying." A week later I signed for Pontypool, which made the timing of Clive's comment a bit unfortunate, but that was just the way it worked out. The move had been at the back of my mind for a while, ever since I got into the Welsh set-up.

'My good friend Alan Talbot took me aside one day at the steelworks and told me, "You've got to go to Pontypool. I'm finishing and if you want to get on in the game, Pontypool is the best place. They've got a good pack of forwards and you will really enjoy playing there." Alan was talking from personal experience, because he'd made the same move a few years earlier and now he was at the end of his playing days.

'Shortly after that, Ray Prosser came to my house with Ivor Taylor who was helping Pross out on the coaching side. We went to the local pub. I said to Pross, "How much do they pay?"

'He did not look pleased and sounded even less so.

'"We pay f*** all."

'And that was nearly the end of the conversation. Then he said, still not looking at all pleased, "If you're really lucky, we'll give you a game and that's all we'll be giving you." That was the end of the conversation. He got up and left.

'I went back and talked it over with Judi. Don't forget I'd been playing Saturday, Wednesday, Saturday for Cross Keys and they'd slipped me a fiver every time. Over a season, that was a tidy sum and we were in no position to turn anything down. As I said to Judi, "It's going to be a bit of a struggle if I do go because I won't be getting a bean."

'Even so, it was too good a chance to miss. Cross Keys were a great family club, but sometimes it was a real struggle to raise a team, especially for the midweek games. Half the time you'd be going to places like Neath, you'd look around the dressing-room and there'd be half a dozen players there you'd never seen before and some of them you'd never see again. That's just the way it was, but after a while it got me down.

'Cross Keys got me on the ladder and I shall always be grateful to them for that. But, career-wise, going to Pontypool was the best move I made. It meant I was playing for the best coach in the world. That's what he was. My respect for Pross was so great that he's been like a father to me for years.

'Pross knew more about the technicalities of forward play than anyone I ever met – the positions of your feet, positions of your body, when to bind, when not to bind. He'd always give you a few options, so that if the opposition did this, then you did that. If it didn't work, then you switched to Plan B or Plan C and one of them would always work. You were never stuck.

'He'd had a ferocious time in New Zealand with the Lions. All he ever really saw of New Zealand was hospitals; he'd be out of one and into another, mainly thanks to the booting they gave him. He used to joke about going into the scrum in that last Test arse first, so they could kick him there for a change, instead of in the mouth. If you couldn't take that, you were soft and he never had any room for softies.

'Pross never lied to you, never gave you any bullshit. He was just an ordinary, down-to-earth bloke who had this genius for winning rugby matches. The success of the team was built on the father–son relationship with Terry Cobner which existed throughout the ten years when Cob was captain.

'Win or lose, Pross would come into the changing-room after the match. If you'd won by 50, he'd never praise you. If you lost, no matter by how many, he'd never bollock you. He'd tap you on the head, ruffle your hair a bit and say, "Right-o, boy. Training Monday night. Don't be late."

'Then he'd walk through the park to the clubhouse. As players, we went upstairs for our grub and free beer. Pross never did. He always stayed downstairs in the bar there. He'd always be mindful that there'd be people saying, "Look at Pross, upstairs having free food and free booze" – even though he had earned the right to eat and drink as much as he wanted.

'Many's the time we begged him to come upstairs and have a drink with us. He'd always find an excuse not to and I can see now that he was being clever, that he felt he couldn't get too close to the players, that his bollockings would carry more weight if he stood back a bit and kept his distance. He'd put us through the hardest training any of us had ever known. You had that steep hill behind the pitch and he'd have us running up and down there. We'd train for an hour and forty minutes without a break.'

Nature had provided a picturesque form of torture to help in Prosser's quest to raise his players' fitness levels to heights not touched by other clubs during the amateur era. The Shell Grotto had been perched atop a hill rising some 700 feet above the club's ground since long before William Webb Ellis picked up the football at Rugby School and invented the sport. The Grotto, built during the late eighteenth century, is said to have numbered among its visitors the Prince of Wales, later to become King Edward VII.

Local folklore has it that His Royal Highness stopped there for a picnic during a hunting trip. Any player caught stopping on the way up to catch his breath, never mind have a picnic, ran the risk of being bawled out by the omnipresent Prosser. The sound of his master's voice booming across from a vantage point on another hill is seared into Windsor's brain.

'We'd do four laps of the pitch to start, then up the hill, down the other side, then up the next hill and down again. Pross would be on top of the second hill so he could see you across the valley as you went up the first hill. Any slacking and he'd have you. I wouldn't want to go back up to that Grotto on a motorbike, never mind run up to it.

'But that superior fitness was a big part of our success. It often made all the difference in the last ten minutes or quarter of an hour. You only had to see the look on the faces of some of the opposition forwards to know what they were thinking. Sometimes they'd be muttering it under their breath: "For Christ's sake, ref, blow up. We're knackered."

'In practice matches at Pontypool under Pross, you didn't want the ref to blow up. You wanted another ten minutes and then another ten after that. That's how much we enjoyed the game, same as with the Welsh team. We'd work and work and work so hard in training that 90 per cent of the teams we played against didn't have anything left in the last ten minutes.

'On the Monday night before training, he'd call you into his little room under the stand and go through Saturday's match. Then he'd pick one or two things from the match and ask you, "What the hell were you thinking of then? Why didn't you do this?"

'Nowadays, they have laptops and earphones and all kinds of technological stuff. You see them during the matches writing things down and looking at screens. Pross had the best computer of all, his brain. He could go through every single minute of every match without the aid of any videotape and see things that nobody else could see. Brilliant – but then he always said it was a simple game.

'The All Blacks showed him that in 1959, when they had a storming pack of forwards and a scrum-half, Sid Going, who kicked it into the box. The easiest way to gain any ground is a steady scrum, accurate box-kick and the blindside wing up flat so that whoever catches it knows he's going to be flattened, that's if he doesn't drop it first.

'If we'd had the Cardiff or Llanelli or Swansea backs, we'd have been world champions. Unfortunately, we didn't have the backs. The *Western*

Mail used to slam Pontypool for ten-man rugby, so backs wouldn't come there, even though in one particular season our winger, Goff Davies, scored more tries than anyone else in Wales.

'I used to pull Pross's leg and say to him, "Why the hell do you pick a pack of forwards who win 99 per cent of the ball and a defensive back line?" Martin Parry was outside-half for Newport when they won two championships and he won two more after he came to Pontypool. Martin couldn't kick a rugby ball from my front door to the garden fence, and that's not because I have a big garden. But he could knock down a raging bull and he could play a bit of football.

'Pross loved anyone who showed a bit of guts. He'd forgive them other failings in return for some bravery. Another great thing about Pross was that even though we had as near an all-international pack as damn it, he was always on the lookout for someone better. As soon as he heard of someone half useful, he'd shoot off and watch him play. If he was good and he happened to play in your position, then he'd be in and you'd be out.

'He brought in so many good players, all local boys from the feeder junior clubs like Talywain, Garndiffaith and Cwmbran, that he created a squad which was so powerful that the second team, Pontypool Athletic, would have beaten most of the first-class first teams. When he brought a batch of new players in for a practice match, the blood would be flying about because they all wanted to get into the first team and we all wanted to slap them down.

'And then Pross would call a halt: "That's enough, boys. Time for a cup of tea and a bite to eat. Everyone together."

'That way, he kept everyone on their toes. You never dreamt of coming the big "I am", because you'd have been made a laughing stock, and rightly so. Nobody knew more about the game than Ray Prosser and that's still the case today, now he's in his 80s.'

When The Duke reported for pre-season trials at Pontypool, the other two-thirds of the Viet-Gwent were *in situ*. While Graham Price had joined his home-town club straight from West Monmouth Grammar School, the senior member of the trio got there before Windsor and via the same route.

Anthony George Faulkner, known the rugby world over as Charlie, had stood shoulder to shoulder with Windsor for Whitehead's, Newport Saracens and Cross Keys. The temporary parting of the ways, according to Windsor, was over the small but highly irregular matter of £1.50 in appearance money.

'Charlie was getting £3.50 and I was on £5. Before my first season as captain, I was invited into the committee meeting to discuss plans. Charlie says to me, "Tell them I want a fiver, same as you. If they don't agree to that, I'm f*****g off."

'When I came out of the meeting, he said, "What's happening?" I said, "You're f*****g off."

'They wouldn't pay him the fiver. Charlie left and applied for a trial at Newport, where they had a massive number of trial matches because so many wanted to play for them. I've always suspected that they didn't want Charlie there in the same way they didn't want me there. I don't know, but there was a feeling that we wouldn't fit in. The good thing that came from that was that Pross picked him up and that was the best thing that ever happened to Charlie.

'The next time I ran into him was at Pontypool during the pre-season trials. Charlie caught me on the head, which meant five stitches, one for every note I used to get at Cross Keys. Maybe that got the aggravation out of him, because nothing ever came between us from then on.'

Price, five years Windsor's junior and ten years younger than Faulkner, would claim a unique niche in Lions history as their only forward to prop the scrum through twelve successive Tests on three tours spanning six years – New Zealand 1977, South Africa 1980, New Zealand again in 1983. Always the strong, silent type throughout his marathon career, his introspection offered a sharp contrast to Windsor's extrovert, cheeky-chappie persona.

By keeping himself to himself and speaking only when he felt it necessary, the monosyllabic tighthead might have evoked memories of Calvin Coolidge, the 30th President of the United States of America. When his death was announced from the White House, Dorothy Parker, the celebrated wit, said, 'How can they tell?'

There were times in his early days when Price would have made Coolidge seem like a bundle of laughs. 'Charlie used to say in our playing days that sharing a room with Graham was like sharing a room with a corpse,' Windsor says. 'Sometimes he'd never say a word for hours on end. He'd lie on his bed so you weren't too sure whether he was sleeping or whether he was dead.

'There were some places he didn't like going. The bar was one of them, any bar. If there was one thing that frightened him to death, it was the thought of being caught at the bar. And that is the truth. I don't think anyone in Pontypool ever saw him buy a pint in all the years he played there.

'Very quiet, Graham, although he has been speaking more since he got the MBE. Charlie doesn't miss a chance to tell him that it stands for Me and Bobby's Efforts. Mind, Pricey was some player. Fit as a fiddle and could scrummage all day long. He was the first of a new breed of front-row forward.

'Before he came along, the old tighthead always struck like a hooker, putting his backside out. Graham never struck for a ball in his life, but he was the new scrummaging prop who drove the scrum and ran around the field like a stag. He showed the tremendous value of having a prop on the tighthead who didn't budge. If Ireland had one, they'd win the World Cup. The guy they've got there, John Hayes, is terrible. Everyone's a handful for that man.

'I'd known Charlie since the early days at the hot mills in the steelworks. He didn't know what the hell he was doing when he got there, same as me. And I'm talking about the rugby, not the job. Charlie was Welsh judo champion, but he'd never played rugby before. I was the last person to help him because I didn't know what was going on myself.

'People used to say that a member of his family called him Charlie because he was a proper Charlie. That's a bit of fun, but the name stuck. I've known his wife, Jill, for 40 years or so. Sometimes when she answers the phone, just for a laugh, I'll say, "Hello, Jill. Charlie in?" And she'll say, "Tony, it's for you."'

There had never been a triumvirate in any team sport quite like the Pontypool front row before they began pounding scrum machines in 1973. As if their reputation as outstanding practitioners of their craft was not intimidating enough, Windsor reinforced it with his own fiery brand of psychological warfare, which he based on the famous histrionics of the then Cassius Clay before he fought big, bad 'ugly bear' Sonny Liston for the world heavyweight championship at Miami Beach on 25 February 1964.

On the eve of the fight, Clay went to Liston's home and shouted verbal abuse at the 'ugly bear' before being led away. Undaunted, the young challenger then recited a poem which he had composed for the occasion and which went as follows:

THE VIET-GWENT

Clay lands with a right, what a beautiful swing,
And the punch raises the bear clean out of the ring.
Liston still rising and the ref wears a frown
But he can't start counting until Sonny comes down.
Now Liston disappears from view, the crowd is getting frantic
And our radaring stations have picked him up somewhere over the
    Atlantic
Who on earth thought when they came to the fight
They would witness the launching of a human satellite?

At least one psychoanalyst dismissed his antics and his poetry, and pronounced that his actions were those of a frightened young man. The next night, he was so afraid that he stopped Liston in six rounds.

'Liston was a destroyer of men, but they reckon he went into the ring thinking that Muhammad Ali, as he became, was crazy,' Windsor says. 'The trouble with that is that you don't really know how to deal with someone who you think is off his rocker. I used that tactic whenever I felt the need for a bit of extra help, like when I first came up against someone I rated, like the England hooker John Pullin, playing for Bristol against Pontypool.

'Pullin had been pictured in the papers a few days before carrying a sheep under each arm on his farm near the Severn Bridge. That gave me loads of ammunition to fire at him. So I'd keep chipping away at him, "Why haven't you brought the sheep? You'll wish you'd brought them by the time we've finished with you."

'He must have thought I was a nutcase. I'd have been disappointed if he hadn't, because that was my plan, to needle him and throw him off guard. I terrorised scrum-halfs at the lineout on the opposition throw. I'd stare at them and tell them, "Next time, I'm really going to get you."

'It didn't always work and there were times they got me instead. Alan Williams of Bridgend hit me two or three times on the earhole during one match. He didn't give a monkey's. Ian Lewis of Tredegar was another who gave as good as he got. I was giving him a hard time one Saturday and the next thing I know, everything's gone black. I could see out of one eye, but the other one felt as though it had been separated from my face by a couple of feet.

'After the match, I went into their dressing-room to see Ian. I wanted to tell him, "That was a cracker." They said he'd gone. For all I knew, he might have been hiding under the shower. Maybe he thought I was upset. So I said to one of the other players, "When you see him, tell him Bobby said well done. I'm not taking the piss – I mean it." The terror tactics didn't bother some people, and good on 'em.'

By the time the front row broke up, their act had withstood the heat generated in the severe theatre of Test rugby and, for one match only, with the Lions in New Zealand, but it wasn't, as Windsor points out, always a bed of roses.

'People go on about us being the best front row ever and it's very nice to be remembered for what we were, but there were times we got turned over. I remember when the three of us played against Argentina for East Wales at Rodney Parade. What a shocker that was. For the first time in our lives, we were up against a team whose hooker didn't hook.

'They had an eight-man drive on their ball and ours and we couldn't cope with it. Brian Wall, a reporter on the *South Wales Echo*, asked me after the game what had gone wrong and I told him straight, "They took us to the cleaners." The next day, when it appeared in the paper, Charlie and Pricey said, "You shouldn't have said that." And I said, "What do you mean I shouldn't have said that? It's f*****g true and 20,000 people in the crowd know it's true."'

Prosser's regeneration brought more spectacular results when Pontypool claimed their third Welsh club title in April 1984 as reward for a consistency of performance which no club can realistically expect to emulate – played 46, won 42, drawn 2, lost 2. Of the Viet-Gwent, only Price still commanded a first-team place, with Windsor, the fires still burning, if a little less brightly, at 38, providing a competitive back-up to the new hooker, Steve Jones, and Faulkner making his way into coaching.

The rejuvenation of Cobner's pack worked such a treat that Prosser saw his team lose only twice, by one point at home to Cardiff on 19 October 1983 and by two at Neath on 2 March 1984, which was no way to mark the old coach's 57th birthday. They scored a grand total of 220 tries, and David Bishop – a multidimensional scrum-half with the skills to double up as the nearest thing to a one-man team, and who simply has to be the best one-cap wonder of them all – accounted for 36 of them.

In a season when Peter Lewis kicked 171 goals from full-back, tries came from all over the place. Chris Huish got 24 from the back row,

THE VIET-GWENT

Goff Davies 22 from one wing, Bleddyn Taylor 11 from the other, Lee Jones 19 from centre, Eddie Butler 13 from number 8 and John Perkins also finished in double figures from the second row. And this from a team accused of playing ten-man rugby.

'We had players who never got the recognition they deserved,' Windsor says. 'Brian Gregory's a good example. For my money, there was a time when he was the best blindside wing forward in Europe and yet he never got a Welsh cap. We had Ron Floyd and Big Bill Evans in the second row and Mike Harrington at number 8 long before Eddie Butler and Mark Brown took over the position.

'Martin Parry was an outside-half ahead of his time. He couldn't kick the ball any distance, but he'd tackle a runaway train – and that, remember, was in a time when outside-halfs didn't tackle. Martin had something which can't be coached, a footballing intelligence which meant he could see things before they happened. It didn't matter that he wasn't a goalkicker because we had Robin Williams at full-back for a while and he could nail penalties from all over the field, left or right.

'Peter Lewis took over and kept the tradition going. Goff Davies must have been the best wing in the British Isles never to get a cap. Ivor Taylor, whose son Mark played for Wales in the 2005 Grand Slam team, was another vital part of the team in the centre, alongside David Cornwall.'

By the time Prosser stood down in 1987 after 18 years in charge, he had almost certainly won more matches than any other club coach, so many that it would take Sir Alex Ferguson the best part of 20 years to beat his record.

5

NIGHTCLUB BOUNCER

The surviving members of England's World Cup-winning football squad of 1966 may beg to differ, but a powerful case can be made for calling the 1974 Lions the international team of the twentieth century. During a three-month trek all over South Africa, they played 22 matches, won the first 21 and drew the last, the final Test for a record of invincibility which put them right up there alongside Sir Donald Bradman's 1948 Australian cricketers on the very short list of touring unbeatables.

The '74 Lions reduced the Springboks to such a shambles that their redoubtable president, Dr Danie Craven, became embarrassed at having to present the traditional green-and-gold-lined Test blazer to an ever-lengthening number of players swept away by the best of British and Irish. 'It hurts me to be giving these to you,' he said after the Lions had wrapped up the series in the third Test at Port Elizabeth, 'because you have not earned them.'

The non-white population cheered every victory and long before the end the acclamation had extended to Robben Island, where Nelson Mandela, then in the tenth year of his incarceration, had asked a friendly guard to keep him posted on the score during the Tests. For some, campaigning against the evils of the apartheid system then enshrined in South African law, the only shame about the tour was that it had taken place.

In a desperate last attempt to prevent the Lions giving what they saw as succour to a racist regime, Peter Hain and approximately one hundred fellow anti-apartheid demonstrators gatecrashed the touring team's hotel at Heathrow on the eve of their departure for Johannesburg. Hain, who became chairman of the Young Liberals after moving to Britain from his native Nairobi with his family in 1966, failed to divert the rugby men from their destiny, despite mounting a concerted campaign.

NIGHTCLUB BOUNCER

His message did not fall entirely on stony ground. One player, John Taylor of London Welsh, declared himself unavailable as a personal protest against apartheid. 'Were I to play, I would be helping to condone and perpetuate a government of the sort that is in existence in South Africa,' he said at the time. 'I went there on the '68 Lions tour and the moment I got there I realised it was a mistake.'

Where Taylor spoke out, another Welshman, Gerald Davies, maintained a discreet silence until many years later over the fact that he, too, had had no wish to go because of the political situation. Hain did at least force the Lions high command to address the issue, which the captain, Willie John McBride, did when he spoke to the troops in the privacy of their hotel's conference room.

'I know there are pressures on you and there must be doubts in your minds,' he told them. 'But if you have any doubts, I would ask you to turn around and look behind you.'

There, at the end of the room, two huge doors were then pulled symbolically open. Once that had been done, he spoke again: 'Gentlemen, if you have any doubts about going on this tour, I want you to be big enough to stand up now and leave this room. Because if you do have doubts, then you are no use to me and you're no use to this team. There will be no stain on your character, no accusations if you do so, but you must be honest and committed.'

Not a soul moved.

The Lions' sensitivity to the whole operation in the light of Hain's widely publicised anti-apartheid campaign can be revealed for the first time in a strictly confidential letter, dated 5 April 1974, which Windsor received at his home in Newport from the tour manager, Alun Thomas of the Welsh Rugby Union. The warning about South Africans being 'sticklers' for the laws referred to those governing the game, but the same could have been said about those which enforced the racial segregation of apartheid.

Dear Bob,

A quick note of much congratulation on your selection. It is a great honour and I know you will take full advantage of it. You will be hearing soon from my assistant manager, Syd Millar and from our captain, 'Willie John' on what we require from you between now and the day of departure. Please read, mark and digest what they will be asking you as the success of our tour will depend on it.

Their suggestions and instructions are the most important priority for the moment. In the meantime I am enclosing copies of:

1. An interview with Syd, the message of which it is vital we all understand and appreciate that South Africa is a harder tour than New Zealand.

2. An article of the laws sent over from South Africa which gives you an idea of their interpretation and what sticklers they are for the letter of the law.

The prime object of our tour is to win the Test series. We start now thinking and planning for this to happen. May I also remind you of two other vital facts underlined in the memorandum you have received from Mr Albert Agar (Hon. Secretary of the Four Home Unions Tours committee).

1. To treat as highly <u>confidential</u> our assembly hotel and departure details.

2. Cessation of playing prior to commencement of the tour. Be firm, definite and lay down clearly that you do not wish to play more than once a week and not at all after April 20th.

Finally would you please let me have per return:

a) name of wife or intended with date of birth if between May 6th and August 1st.

b) names of children with dates of birth if between May 6th and August 1st.

c) size of shoe. I am hoping to 'scrounge' a pair of Dunlop greenflash shoes. No half sizes available and also a pair of Norvic Chukka 'Scallywags' (leisure wear), half sizes available.

d) I am giving notice that I require within 14 days or sooner from everyone three stories – clean, dirty, sporting, religious, political etc. I will not take no for an answer and they had better be good as you will be listening to them many times on tour.

e) Could I recommend you read *The Lions Speak*, which describes brilliantly the attitudes behind the success of the '71 Lions. If you were on that tour, read it again and any general book on South Africa, e.g. Alan Paton – *South Africa and Her People*.

f) Would you write to the South Africa Tourist Corporation, Piccadilly, London W1 telling them who you are and they will send you a marvellous map and tourist guide. It is important you do this.

g) Left to the last for obvious reasons. Anyone unduly troubled by Mr

Peter Hain or [who] has 'a conscience about coming' do ring me first before doing anything. Reverse the charge if you must.

I mentioned in a letter to all potential Lions at the beginning of the season that it would take special players to win in South Africa. You are going to be one of those and I know you will not fail in your resolve to live up to that challenge. My warmest congratulations again and let us get down to it now.

Sincerely,
Alun Thomas, manager.

Windsor saw the demonstrations but is adamant that he did not have a clue what they were demonstrating about. 'I had never, ever heard this word apartheid before in my life,' he says. 'Discrimination? Racialism? I worked on the motorways with all colours and creeds. I was living in a council house in Bettws, Newport, with a family and I was flat broke. What the hell was happening or not happening in South Africa did not concern me. I didn't give a stuff.

'Whatever happened in South Africa was never going to affect my life. I had enough problems at home to worry about. When it came to going to London to meet up with the Lions, a friend gave me a lift because I didn't have a car. We saw all these people outside the hotel with placards carrying the word apartheid. I didn't know what it meant. Maybe I was a bit dull, but I said to my mate who took me up, "Apartheid? Is that Welsh for all the best?" I thought they were giving us a pat on the back.'

Once he had checked in, officials of the British Isles Rugby Union Touring Team, to give the Lions their full, unwieldy title, directed Windsor into the kit room, where each player helped himself to all manner of gear, a veritable treasure trove of goodies which were too much to resist.

'Laid out on tables in a big room were all kinds of shirts, roll-neck jumpers, V-neck jumpers, ties, towels and all sorts of souvenirs, all with the Lions badge,' Windsor says. 'It was all lovely gear, loads and loads of it. I went round once and no one seemed to notice so I went around again. And again. Whatever I didn't need, I shoved into bags. Nobody was watching us on the inside because they were too busy watching the outside and all those protestors with the placards.

'As a thank you to my mate for driving me up, I gave him some stuff so he could sell it when he got back to Wales and give the missus some money to help her pay the bills while I was away. Nobody was any the wiser. I found out later that there were more people wearing Lions gear in Pontypool than in the whole of South Africa!

'I'd gone to London with 40 quid in my pocket and I was worried about how I was going to manage. The gear was an early bonus. I had an inferiority complex, not because I was in awe of being surrounded by so many great players but because they were almost all collar-and-tie chaps. They all had a few bob. I had nothing.

'My pay at the steelworks was based almost entirely on how much steel we produced. The more you put out, the bigger the bonus. It was all piecework, so you worked your nuts off. You had to get permission for time off. If you were on, say, £20 a week, the majority of that would come from bonuses. Whitehead's said they would pay me a basic wage while I was away, which wasn't much.

'It was never going to be enough so, as soon as the word came through that I'd been picked, I got a job as a bouncer at the Stowaway nightclub in Newport. Charlie Faulkner started at the same time, along with Eric "Goopy" Phillips, the Newbridge second row, and my good friend John "Paddy" Burke.

'So I was in good company, even if there were times when Eric might have caused more trouble than he prevented! We needed a good team because you'd get a lot of valley rugby sides who'd play in the Newport area on the Saturday afternoon looking to let off steam in Newport on the Saturday night. The boss would never let a squad of 20 or 25 rugby players pile into his premises mob-handed. If that lot caused any trouble, we bouncers would be hopelessly outnumbered.

'When the teams got turned away, we'd tell them to use their heads, have a couple of pints in town and come back in twos or threes. The only problem then was that they all wore blazers with the same club badge, which was a bit of a give-away. But you never had the kind of trouble then that you get now. No knives, no bottles, no glasses in the face.

'There'd be enough punch-ups to keep us busy. Most of those we chucked out took it in good part. They'd pick themselves up, dust themselves down and say, "Where's the nearest curry house?" There were some very funny incidents.

'Goopy was having a spot of bother one Saturday night downstairs at the disco in what they called the cabaret room. Being outmanned, he gave us a shout and we piled downstairs. There was a fire-exit door at one end and the usual drill was to grab the troublemaker, run towards the door, hit it open and out he'd go. This particular night, we were grabbing them and chucking them out one after another.

'Charlie grabbed this one kid and ran to the fire exit in the normal way, except that he ran outside by mistake and the door clattered shut behind them. We knew when we chucked people that they'd be banging the door to try and get in so we didn't pay any attention, even when you could hear the banging above the disco noise.

'The shouting outside the door went on until someone said, "Where's Charlie?" When we eventually realised that he must have locked himself out, we opened the fire door to go looking for him and found him standing there, covered in blood. As bouncers, we were easily identified by our dicky bows. All the yobs we'd thrown out had ganged up on Charlie, and when we got to him he had his false teeth in one hand because they'd kicked him in the mush.

'An even funnier thing happened to Charlie on another night. At the bar in the cabaret room they used to serve chicken and chips. The bouncers had to stand in certain positions to make sure the singer got the best of order. Charlie would position himself by the food bar, where he'd put his hand round behind his back and grab a chicken when he thought no one was looking.

'Any food we wanted had to come out of our fiver, so it was smart on Charlie's part to get some grub for nothing. Anyway, what we didn't know was that the girl in charge of the food had been given a rollicking because too many chickens were disappearing. Because of that she had moved the chicken tray from its normal place and put the deep-fat chip frier there instead.

'The female singer that night was in full voice belting out one of the hits of the day when Charlie puts his hand behind his back thinking he'll nick a few chips only to go straight into the deep-fat frier. All you could hear was a big bellow all over the nightclub: "Aarrrgh!" It was like something straight out of *Monty Python's Flying Circus*, Charlie with third-degree burns on his fingers and the rest of us doubled up with laughter.'

Their moonlighting at the nightclub ended with the owner putting on a celebration evening in honour of Windsor's selection for the Lions tour. What ought to have been a pleasant, trouble-free night with his confrère Faulkner finished up in another misadventure, which resulted in two-thirds of the Pontypool front row appearing before Newport Magistrates' Court. The outcome, only days before the Duke's initiation into the Lions' den in London, added a touch of hilarity to proceedings.

'We had a very good party and left about half past five or six o'clock in the morning,' Windsor says. 'We were driving home, me, Paddy and Charlie, and as we got near Charlie's house in Malpas, Paddy turned the corner and clipped the tail of a car parked at the side of the road. We dropped Charlie off and drove away, not thinking any more about the slight accident.

'As luck would have it, somebody had seen it happen and called the police. We ended up in court on a charge of failing to stop after an accident, which meant we had to work out what we were going to say about the accident. The story we agreed on was that as we turned the corner, a cat ran out in front of us and, in swerving to avoid the cat, we clipped this stationary car. It was too early in the morning to wake the people concerned and we had intended to come back and tell them what had happened.

'Paddy gave evidence first. When he mentioned the cat running out in front of us, the prosecuting solicitor asked, "And what colour was the cat?"

'"Black," says Paddy.

'A little while later, it was Charlie's turn to be cross-examined. "Mr Faulkner," says the solicitor, "we have heard from Mr Burke about this cat. What colour was the cat?"

'"Grey," says Charlie.

'"Very interesting, Mr Faulkner. Your co-defendant said it was a black cat. You said it was grey. How do you explain that?"

'"It was a frosty morning, sir," says Charlie, without batting an eyelid.

'I'm not kidding. The true stories are the best ones and I think even the magistrate tried to get under the table so nobody would see him laughing his head off. It was brilliant by Charlie. The whole court went deathly quiet because everyone was trying to keep a straight face. We were found not guilty.

'Nightclub bouncing was hardly the ideal way to prepare for what was going to be the rugby experience of my life, but it had to be done – seven o'clock in the evening until one o'clock the next morning, five nights a week. I had two kids by then, Joanne and Ricky, and every penny went on making sure they were looked after.

NIGHTCLUB BOUNCER

'We had nothing, but Judi would have made me go anyway even if she had to get a boat and row me to South Africa. She'd have lived on bread and margarine rather than have me miss that tour. Unbeknown to me, my darling first wife went ahead and arranged for us to buy the council house. Instead of paying rent, we were paying a mortgage. I only found out about that after she passed away.

'One of the marvellous things about Welsh rugby is that the junior clubs in the area, like Talywain, Blaenavon, Cwmbran, Garndiffaith and the rest, would put on a bit of a do for you in honour of your selection. They were delighted a local boy was going off to play for the Lions and they wanted to show their appreciation. They would invite you up to their club and make a presentation. They'd also give you a little wallet with some money in it – £20 here, £25 there.

'It was strictly against the regulations. If anyone had found out, we'd all have been for the high jump, but these were wonderful examples of the local community rallying round one of their own. I was going to be away for three months and I don't know how the family would have managed without those little gifts.

'That first night with the Lions, the management took us all out to a pub for a good piss-up, which is the best way for people to get to know each other. Almost overnight, I became big butties with two Irishmen, Dick Milliken and Tommy Grace. I got on with the Irish and the English, especially the likes of Fran Cotton, Roger Uttley, Mike Burton and the magnificent Andy Ripley. What warriors they were. You could go anywhere with those men and face the most fearsome foe anytime without being afraid.

'You'd have taken on Al Capone with them around. Some Welsh people go on about the English being this and that. On Lions tours, the best men in the world are the English. Englishmen are like oaks, strong, dependable types who never let you down. Really good blokes to have around you, on and off the pitch. There wasn't a nicer bloke than Ripley. What an Adonis, and what a tragedy that he died so young, at the age of 62.

'The worst people on tour? Welshmen. As soon as some of them get on the plane, they're complaining about being homesick. Unbelievable. There are more bad Welsh tourists than good ones. The Scots were fine, especially "the Mouse" – Ian McLauchlan – and "Broonie" – Gordon Brown. Even though it was like putting your arms around your missus in the scrum, the Mouse was a warrior. Broonie would have been the love of my life if I hadn't met Judi first! With men like that, you could hardly fail.'

They took off from Heathrow for the overnight flight to Johannesburg on Monday evening, 6 May. By early on Tuesday morning, before the plane began its descent into Jan Smuts airport, Windsor had become the first casualty of the tour. The pre-departure rooming list had Windsor sharing with the other hooker, Ken Kennedy, and soon the Irishman, a consultant geriatrician at a London hospital, would be summoned to an emergency 30,000 feet over the African continent.

'My mum and dad had come up to see me off,' Windsor says. 'We had lunch on the Lions and, for starters, I had a prawn cocktail. I've always had a hatred of flying so I didn't feel good when I got on board. I deliberately sat next to J.P.R., a doctor and an educated bloke. Up we go and down come bottles of gin. Being a beer drinker, I never drank shorts.

'They said, "Get it down you and shut up. It'll make you sleep." A few hours later, after they put the lights out on the plane, I began to feel really bad. The stewardess came along and asked if I was all right. "No," I said. "I'm burning like hell and weak as a kitten."

'She called someone else up and they had to help me out of my seat to the back of the plane. They laid me flat out. A woman who was a nurse came over and on her advice they got some ice cubes to try and bring my temperature down. Then they called Ken Kennedy up and he put a thermometer in my mouth. He pulled it out and looked at it.

'Someone asked, "How is he, Ken?"

'Kennedy said, "According to this, he's dead."

'I was in a bad way. We'd been advised to wear leisure gear on the way out, shorts and a red polo shirt. When we landed, they reckoned there were hundreds at the airport to see us arrive. Everyone else stepped out of the front of the plane to a hero's welcome and there was me being carried out the back on a stretcher, all on my own apart from the two fellas carrying me.

'They shoved me in the back of this ambulance. Off they went, ding-a-ling. Unfortunately, they hadn't bothered to secure the stretcher so every time the driver stopped at traffic lights, the stretcher shot up towards the front of the ambulance and almost cracked my head. Then when the driver drove off, the stretcher shot back the opposite way and smashed into the door. After a while of being clattered on the head one minute and hurled into the door the next, I was so far gone I began to wonder if this was the end.

'Then they got me into hospital and when they took my red T-shirt off, it looked as though I still had it on. I'd sweated so much that the dye had run. They carried out tests and told me that I was suffering from food poisoning but that I'd made it an awful lot worse with the amount of alcohol I'd poured down my neck.

'I was there for six days and I overheard some of the hospital staff joking that I'd caught a condition called "Bok fever" and having a laugh. I asked them what they meant and they said that Bok fever was a condition suffered by those who were shit-scared of what the Springboks would do to them. After losing a stone and a half in weight, the only thing that bothered me was whether the Lions would send me home before I got the chance to do anything about the opposition.

'As soon as I was well enough to leave, four of the boys, including Gareth Edwards, picked me up and we headed for the Lions base not that far away at a place called Serfontein. We stop at this roadside restaurant for a bite to eat and the waiter comes round for the orders. I look at the menu and ask for an omelette. Now, bear in mind that I've never had an omelette in my life.

'The waiter says, "What sort of omelette would you like?"

'I say, "An omelette omelette."

'The waiter's getting a bit funny by now.

'"Yes, sir. What kind of omelette?"

'And I say, "One with egg in it."

'With that, the rest of the boys burst out laughing and it became a standing joke. I didn't realise that the waiter meant whether I wanted mushrooms or tomatoes or whatever.'

After his unscheduled stop in Hillbrow Hospital, a few Naas Botha drop kicks from Ellis Park, Windsor was too concerned with making up for lost time and lost weight to pay any notice to the political storms raging back in Britain over their arrival. Harold Wilson's government, annoyed that the rugby authorities had refused to bow to pressure and abandon the tour, instructed the British Embassy in Pretoria to boycott the Lions.

The Foreign Secretary, James Callaghan, Minister for Sport Denis Howell and the Prime Minister himself had spoken out against the tour and advised the Lions to stay at home, while conceding that they did not have the power to intervene and prevent it taking place. Now the team was not to be entertained at any formal function, nor was the embassy to have any contact with individual players.

Eldon Griffiths, Minister for Sport in the previous Conservative government, condemned the move as 'illogical'. 'South Africa's racial laws, of which I disapprove just as strongly as any Labour minister, apply with equal force to industry, trade and the arts,' Griffiths said. 'Yet visiting British businessmen, bankers, water engineers, teachers and painters have all been received by the British Embassy in Pretoria, many of them since Labour took office.

'What is so different about the British Lions? On the face of it, this looks like rank discrimination against rugby players.'

The Lions management described the embassy boycott as 'a stab in the back', while the players regarded it as a personal snub. In contrast, South Africans had given them a rapturous welcome. A gathering of fans estimated at 200 waved banners and sang 'For they are jolly good fellows' as the Lions filed through the arrivals hall.

Dr Piet Koornhof, sports minister in the apartheid government, headed the reception committee alongside the distinguished president of the South African Rugby Board, Dr Danie Craven. Neither doctor could contain his delight that at least one team had arrived in defiance of the sporting boycott.

'The Lions tour is a great breakthrough for rugby and sport in general,' Koornhof said at the airport. 'We should like to call them a very courageous team.'

Craven, presiding over a game in a country where the abhorrent constitution made it illegal for blacks to play in the same team as whites, was hardly going to waste any time discussing the morality of the issue. 'The Lions have taken a stand which I hope the rest of the world will follow, to show that nobody must interfere with sport,' he said. 'Naturally, this is a very great moment for all of us.'

The thousands of black rugby players denied the opportunity to play for the Springboks because of the colour of their skin would have shaken their heads in utter disbelief at the reference to political interference. Apartheid had ensured that their sport had been interfered with from birth. But that was another story for another time. The Lions, as Alun Thomas pointed out, had come to play rugby, not to attend embassy cocktail parties.

McBride shrugged it off, promising that all the politicking would have a unifying effect on his squad. Meanwhile, Windsor had more trouble when he began training under the unsympathetic direction of Syd Millar, an old-school prop-turned-coach who knew the game inside out after three Lions tours as a player. Despite periodic bouts of vomiting and being some way short of his fighting weight, the Welshman was pitched straight into the opening match, Western Transvaal in the heartland of Afrikanerdom on the Highveld at Potchefstroom.

The Lions began with a clear declaration of intent, thrashing the home team 59-13. Nine tries backed up by ten goals from Phil Bennett made it the biggest win achieved by any British and Irish international team in the Republic, a record which would be smashed a fortnight later. The sheer quality of their first performance not only set the tone for what was to come but made nonsense of pre-match warnings that the macho men of Western Transvaal would soften them up for the Springboks.

'Their papers were full of stuff about this tighthead prop being the strongest man in South Africa,' Windsor says. 'This bloke was supposedly able to go round his farm carrying two cows at a time and he was going to mangle the Lions front row. He was up against the Mouse and, being a short-arsed bloke, his great asset was an ability to get really low and under the opposing tighthead.

'The lower you go, the harder it is for the hooker to do any hooking. We only had a couple of practices and during one of them, I said, "Look, Mouse. When you go that low, try putting your head between your knees and then try to put your feet up. It's a physical impossibility, even for a contortionist."

'At one of the earliest scrums in that first game, I told the Mouse to drop the tighthead and slip out. Then I gave that South African heavyweight champion or whatever he was a boot in the chops. There was a bit of a dust-up and they had a bloke in the second row called Johan Tromp. I could see him taking a big swing at me, I ducked and he hit Tommy David instead. Tommy went down like a sack of spuds.'

His temporary lowering to a horizontal state was nothing compared to the flattening of every South African obstacle put in the Lions path. The domino effect began with the 59–13 destruction of Western Transvaal and continued ad nauseam until the fourth and final Test, by which time it was too late to make a blind bit of difference to the Lions' enshrinement in the history books and Windsor's part in it as a permanent member of the indestructible Test pack.

THE IRON DUKE

A fortnight after rewriting the history books in Potchefstroom, the Lions did it again at sea level in Mossel Bay, easing past South Western Districts 97–0, and that at a time before the try had been upgraded from four points to five. McBride's team touched down 16 times. J.J. Williams led the way with six, followed by three from England centre Geoff Evans, two from J.P.R. Williams and the remainder distributed among five others, including Alan Old.

The English stand-off converted all but one for a personal haul which took some working out in those pre-calculator days. His 37 points, without precedent in the annals of the Lions, has stood the test of time ever since, and yet the competition for Test places had reached such a level of ferocity that not even the most monumental of field days was enough to get Old into the line-up for the start of the series ten days later.

The prize was so great that, when push came to shove, the Lions even fought among themselves. During one scrummaging session early in the tour, Fran 'The Chin' Cotton disengaged himself and punched Sandy Carmichael in sheer annoyance at failing to make the Scotland prop yield as much as an inch. 'I immediately regretted it,' Cotton said. 'Not only because he was a fellow player but because the cameras began to click at what was thought to be a crack in the unity of the Lions. I apologised to Sandy and we were pictured shaking hands to demonstrate to the rest of the world that we were all still very much together.'

Old found himself in good company amongst those on the outside of the Test team looking in. Andy Irvine, Tom Grace, Geoff Evans, Johnny Moloney, Mike Burton, Chris Ralston, Stewart McKinney, all of whom would have been automatic choices for just about any international team bar the All Blacks, all missed out by varying degrees of whiskers. So, too, did Ken Kennedy, ousted by the fearless, indomitable, irascible Windsor.

It was as if all those years sweating buckets in the hot mills had prepared him for an expedition which, when the fur flew at its thickest, could have been mistaken for a re-enactment of the Boer War. In that respect, Windsor had convinced the tour management and the cabal of senior players headed by McBride that his over-my-dead-body attitude was exactly what the Lions wanted.

'Ken Kennedy was a very good hooker and an even better looking bloke,' Windsor says. 'He was also very clever, all the more so when compared to a dull twit like me. But, without wishing to sound big-headed, I was more abrasive and that's what it came down to – letting them know I was around. At least that was the impression I got and I suspected that some of the old hands, like the Mouse, might have put in a word for me.'

Abrasive is a word to cover a multitude of sins. The stony-broke Welshman with his invisible armour of steel was about to turn up the heat on the Springboks in the blast furnace of the scrum.

6

. . . .

BLASTING THE BOKS

When the Lions began planning for the psychological warfare of their 1974 South African tour, one match from the recent past dominated their thinking. The suffering inflicted by the infamous Canterbury Butchers in New Zealand three years earlier was burnt so deep into the psyche of those who witnessed it that, long before touching down in Johannesburg, they had vowed that, come hell or high water, there would be no repeat.

Never again would the Lions play it by the book like gentlemen, not when it meant standing there and taking it as their front row had done against Canterbury in Christchurch. No Test prop has ever been subjected to as systematic a beating as Sandy Carmichael took that day at Lancaster Park, where the New Zealand referee was, ironically, a doctor, Humphrey Rainey, who, needless to say, failed miserably to send anyone off.

Despite the brutality inflicted upon Carmichael and the presence of a replacement prop on the bench, the unflinching Glaswegian refused to leave his post and kept scrummaging to the end, displaying a bravery which puts to shame the uncontested scrums of the professional age. X-ray examination showed that Carmichael's skull had been fractured, in addition to five other fractures of the left cheekbone.

Far from showing any remorse, the Canterbury forwards were reported to have sneered at the '71 Lions as 'soft Pommy bastards'. Willie John McBride had caught the ball from the kick-off against Canterbury during the previous Lions tour in 1966 and what happened next taught him a very painful lesson: that there was not much point turning the other cheek to New Zealand forwards other than to give them another soft target.

'They got hold of me and took me 30 or 40 yards downfield towards my own line, the blows raining down as we went,' McBride wrote of the kick-off in his autobiography. 'What maddened me was that not one of my fellow Lions players came to my aid, to help me hold onto the ball and give the New Zealanders some of their own treatment.

'"Where the hell were you bastards when I needed you?" I shouted at them. And their reaction? Well, they laughed and one of them said, "Why the hell didn't you let go of the ball, you bloody fool?" I knew then that we had no hope of winning the series.

'There were days when you came off the rugby field with such aches and pains that you didn't know whether to sit down, stand up or stand on your head. But, as far as I was concerned, I would never bow the knee to any assailant or opponent.'

McBride and his fellow Ulsterman, coach Syd Millar, imbued every forward with the same take-no-prisoners mentality, having taken painstaking care in the selection process to pick only those with the stomach for a fight. They wanted the best, but each and every one of them had to prove they were immune to intimidation.

On the eve of their first match of the tour, McBride told them, 'I am not prepared to take any intimidation and we should not accept any such rubbish. Tomorrow, if anything happens, we are all in it together – and I mean all. You belt the guy nearest to you as hard as you can.

'Whether he has been the one guilty of the illegal act has nothing to do with it. If that doesn't stop it, you haven't hit him hard enough. Hurt one of us and you hurt all of us so we'll finish it. Then, once you've done that, it's all over and we are back playing rugby.'

As their supreme commander-in-chief embarking on an unprecedented fifth Lions tour, McBride had ensured that if any opponent started any trouble, the Lions would make them wish they hadn't, that any team of Springboks or budding Springboks would 'learn a very painful lesson and that message would go out right across South Africa – mess with these Lions and you end up in a mess yourselves'.

To achieve that aim, McBride devised an internal alarm system, a coded alert which would be a call to immediate arms. His first suggestion, 999, was deemed a trifle unwieldy by the majority of the troops before they settled for a marginally abbreviated version and one digit fewer, 99. One nine less would, presumably, avoid wasting one-hundredth of a second when time was of the essence.

It was so far up Windsor's street that he would often make a point of starting the aggravation himself and beating the South Africans to the punch, so to speak. To him, rugby was like war without the fatalities, the pitch a battleground where every inch had to be won by blood, sweat and clenched fists as well as clenched teeth. By welding him at the very tip of their assault force, the Lions had found the perfect man for the role.

Windsor also knew that the home-grown referees were not about to change the habit of a lifetime and that the Lions could dispense their own rough justice on the hoof without any risk of anyone being ticked off for being a naughty boy, let alone sent off. It would make an already lethal player all the more so, granting him a licence to put a veritable arsenal of primitive weapons at his disposal.

With officialdom happy to turn a collective blind eye and no live television cameras to expose the skulduggery, the law of the Wild West, the outback and the ancient highway ruled. If the Lions had their very own Butch Cassidy, Ned Kelly and Dick Turpin in their pack, then there was never any doubt that Windsor was their Jesse James.

'There was at least one punch-up in every game,' Windsor says. 'I didn't want anyone to start punching or booting me. I punched and booted them at every opportunity and you never had to wait very long for the opportunity to present itself. In my position, with one arm around each of my props in the scrums, I was an easy target. I was advised by those running the tour to put the boot into the opposition as soon as I could.

'The management and senior players consisted of people who had been on previous Lions tours when they had lost the series. Worse still, they had lost the fight. And one of the central themes of this tour came over loud and clear: "We may lose the series again, but we are definitely not going to lose the fight." That's why they picked hard men.

'So I went out into every match thinking to myself, right, I'm going to start putting it about here as soon as I can just to let you bastards know that I'm not going to stand and take it. I'm going to boot, bite, butt and do anything to anyone who starts messing me about. That was my attitude from the first match to the last and it never changed.

'You realised very quickly that you could do anything and that anything could be done to you. We had South African referees for all the matches and I learnt right from the start that the referees weren't going to give you any protection. We had to send for more kit because the stuff we had kept getting ripped and we got fed up wearing jerseys that had to be knitted together to repair the stud marks. In one match we had sewn-up jerseys and holes in our socks. Afterwards Willie John told the management, "We're ambassadors for our countries out here and this kit is a disgrace. Unless we get a new set of jerseys we're going to tell the papers about it."

'A lot went on in nearly every match, but only once did a referee stop a match because of foul play, against Boland when I got caught belting the scrum-half. I was afraid he was going to send me off. I said, "Sorry about that, ref, an accident." And that was that, so I went back to my job of terrifying the scrum-half, knowing the ref wasn't going to stop me. Apart from that, they never did sweet FA about it. But we felt good because we had so many good people around us. Look at that pack – Fran Cotton, Ian McLauchlan, Willie John McBride, Gordon Brown, Roger Uttley, Mervyn Davies and Fergus Slattery. You'd have gone to war with that lot. They were brilliant.

'As the hooker, I was the point of the spear of the Lions scrum. A spear which is bent will never stick in a door, but a spear being driven upwards by sheer scrummaging power will blast through the door. The French knew that, which is why they tried to take my head off every time I came up against them with Wales. Whenever I got in a position in any scrum where I wasn't able to drive up, I'd tell the rest of the pack just to lock it out and not waste their energy scrummaging.

'After one match when there'd been a particularly big punch-up, Willie John was doing a press interview and I happened to be standing beside him at the time. A South African reporter asked, "How come when there's any trouble you all pile in together?"

'And Willie John said, "We shout 99."

'I laughed. I thought it was a load of bollocks, but I also thought it was not a very clever thing for McBride to have said. Not all the Springboks were stupid so once it had been plastered all over the South African papers in Afrikaans and English, they knew what was going to happen the next time they heard the call. For all I knew, they might have retaliated by shouting "98" and getting stuck into us before we could get stuck into them.

'I always thought "99" was what you said when you wanted one of those ice-cream cones with a chocolate bar sticking out of the middle. Now I've been to many, many dinners given in honour of the '74 Lions. I've sat there alongside people like McBride and, God bless him, my best buttie, the late Gordon Brown and I've said to them, "Tell all these people here tonight, that this '99' business is a myth." And they said, "Get stuffed, Bobby – we're making a fortune out of it.'"

The war machine was in full swing as early as the second Saturday of the tour in what became the Battle of Boet Erasmus, the stadium in Port Elizabeth where the Lions socked it to Eastern Province. It would have been another Canterbury had the tourists not been ready to take what they had been given and hit back with twice as much. McBride sat that one out, but what had happened in Christchurch three years before was at the front of his mind when he addressed the team before kick-off.

More than 35 years later, Mike Burton remembers clearly the captain making a direct reference to the 1971 game. 'McBride said, "They've got the same colour of jerseys as Canterbury,"' Burton says. 'Then he paused for effect before adding, "Remember that." I couldn't remember it because I wasn't on that tour, but everyone had read about Canterbury and I thought, bloody hell, this is going to be some game . . .'

And so it was. The Lions, galvanised by warnings that Springboks captain Hannes Marias expected his provincial team to strike a psychological blow before the Tests, won 28–14 but only after they had reacted to a prolonged brawl involving four forwards from each side by beating the provincial team up in the process. The *Star* in Johannesburg felt moved to address the subject in an editorial the following Monday: 'It could be just coincidence that in the last decade or so both Transvaal and Eastern Province sides have been involved in a disproportionate number of unpleasant displays of temper and limbs snapping. Their records are bad and even if both local sides were largely innocent, it takes two to fight.' The authorities did what rugby authorities always did and mouthed platitudes. Dr Danie Craven said, 'This sort of thing must be eradicated.'

As Lions coach, Syd Millar took a more philosophical, almost pragmatic view. 'On any tour like this one, we expect some hard, tense matches and in the heat of the exchange it is not unnatural for tempers to flare,' he said. 'What happened at Eastern Province was, however, regrettable, especially in view of the many schoolchildren who watched.'

And so the dust-ups went on, unabated, like the one against the Leopards, an all-black team, at East London after the second Test. The scratch team lost by a street but not before they had done something which had been beyond the power of the all-white Springboks, who had failed to cross the line against the Lions in two Tests. When the Leopards scored their only try, the largely black crowd reacted as though they had won the Test series and the World Cup in one fell swoop.

'Hundreds of them ran onto the pitch and carried the scorer off shoulder high,' Windsor says. 'We never saw him again, even though there was still a fair amount of time left on the clock. That was the match when one of their tribal chiefs came out before the kick-off with two leopards in chains and walked them round the pitch. It was also the day when Mike Burton – "Burto" – began putting some nonsense about. He was standing in a lineout when one of their forwards took a big swing at him, Burto ducked and Chris Ralston caught it flush in the face.

'I didn't play in that match so, for once, nobody was trying to boot me. Ralston was a great bloke, an upperclass Englishman with a posh accent to match. When he came into the dressing-room with this gash down his cheek, I said, "How's it going, Chris?"

'"Oh, Bob," he said, "the pain is ex-crooooooo-ciat-ing."

'I said, "Well, Chris, it can't be that bad if you can think of a big word like that."

'The great thing about the tour was that for all the matches against the white teams, the black spectators always cheered for us. We'd come out and run to the end where they were standing behind fences about 40 feet high. It was against the law to mingle with the black people. Well, we broke all the laws because we got on great with those people. After one night out, Andy Ripley got back on the bus wearing nothing more than a leopard skin. We'd gone out in our number ones and he'd given all his gear away, which was typical of the man.

'Outside the grounds they'd sell bags of oranges for a few bob and the white Springboks fans would pelt us with them. I went to take a throw once and suddenly a pair of binoculars landed beside me.'

On their journeys criss-crossing the length and breadth of South Africa, the Lions knew all about one-eyed fans, but they had never heard of a one-eyed second-row forward until they bumped into Johan de Bruyn the day they came closest to losing their unbeaten record. Orange Free State before a crowd of 60,000 at Bloemfontein on the Saturday after the second Test would have been a step too far had the Lions pack not produced an eight-man shove against seven Free Staters which allowed who else but J.J. Williams to dash over for the winning try in the second minute of stoppage time.

The time had been added on because of an injury to the Free State lock, Stoffel Botha, who emerged from a ruck with a badly cut ear. Earlier his second-row partner, de Bruyn, had caused a stoppage while the players searched for his glass eye. 'He was a fearsome-looking fella,' Windsor says. 'We all wondered why the rest of the Free State came running out of the tunnel like bats out of hell. Johan was the last one out, some way behind the rest, and I'd asked Gareth Edwards why the rest of them came flying out. When Johan appeared, Gareth said, "They're running away from that bloke because they're all scared of him."'

Nobody was too sure how de Bruyn came to be separated from his false eye, although Burton's recollection of his half-time instructions from the skipper about how to blunt the Free State lock's threat to the tourists' invincibility might have had something to do with it: 'McBride said to me during the break, "Mickey, you're going to have to stoop to the lowest of the low. You're going to have to hit him in his good eye."'

Windsor recalls, 'I don't know what happened, but when everyone's looking for his eye, I thought he'd lost the real one. Broonie found it and Johan stuck it back in with a little piece of grass sticking out of the side.'

The Lions knew that they would stand or fall on their tight forwards. By the start of the series, they had identified a front five good enough, brave enough and bloody-minded enough to lay the foundations for the series. The five picked themselves – McLauchlan on the loosehead, Windsor at hooker, Cotton on the tighthead, McBride and Gordon Brown in the second row. Others behind the scrum may have monopolised the glory, but nothing would have been possible without the five at the coalface.

The Springboks prided themselves on their reputation as big, hard men who never took a backward step. Long before the Lions had finished with them, their macho image had been pulverised. The McLauchlan-Windsor-Cotton-McBride-Brown quintet didn't merely dominate their Springboks opposite numbers, they destroyed them, and no matter how often Craven and his despairing selectors changed the personnel, they kept destroying them.

The cringing Craven and his embattled cohorts made nine changes for the second Test, eleven for the third and just three for the last, presumably on the basis that by then they were scraping the bottom of a deep barrel. The Lions won the opening Test in the mud and rain of Cape Town, their pack imposing themselves to such an extent that

BLASTING THE BOKS

Johan Claassen, the Springboks coach, disappeared from his seat in the grandstand 20 minutes before the end.

The Lions had them from the very first set piece. 'We went into that first scrum and squashed them,' Windsor says. 'I had a good feeling from then on. Their front row was screaming for help. When you're down there and you've got the upper hand, the best sound in the world is to hear that *aaawww* from the other lot because it tells you they can't take the hit. They were gasping a lot in the Tests and it was music to our ears.

'We took them so low that at times I used my head to hook the ball. Then we'd drive over them. That was perfectly legal because there was no law then saying you had to keep your shoulders above your hips, as there is now.

'On their put-in, I didn't bother with the hooker, I'd come across on the opposition tighthead. We shoved Hannes Marias up so high sometimes that if there'd been a spotlight above the scrum, he'd have burnt his arse and been taken to hospital. I thought, if we keep this up, we're in with a chance.

'We were doing this to a team renowned as the best in the world for their scrummaging. Their wing forwards always had a free rein. They could rely on the six other big men to do the business in the tight so they could save all their energy for roaming around the field. You'd have Jan Ellis running around with the ball in one hand. But it's a very different game when your scrum's going backwards.

'It hurts physically and mentally because the pressure is severe enough to crush even the fittest and strongest. On your side, you've got five good men around you and eight good 'uns coming at you. If you're not careful, you end up with a broken back. If you're getting stuffed, you're praying that nobody drops the ball because every knock-on means more murder in the scrum. But if you know you've got their front row, you can't have enough scrums because you want to get in there and bust some ribs.

'That was my job and the team suffered if I didn't do it. I wasn't a dull rugby player. I'd seen in matches and on the training field how good our backs were. I knew the South Africans had nobody to touch them. That strengthened my mentality as a front-five forward. It drove me to batter them up front and give the backs the ball to finish the job.

'It makes my blood boil when people today belittle the scrum and its influence on the game. Stuart Barnes once said on Sky TV, "I don't think scrums count for much these days in international matches." That's what you get from an outside-half who wouldn't tackle his granny. I remember Mr Barnes when Pontypool played Bath at the Rec and we shoved them around so much I don't think I saw him the whole game.'

The first Test won 12–3 with four goals, three from Phil Bennett, the Lions headed for the Highveld amid dire warnings that in the second Test, at Loftus Versfeld in Pretoria, the Springboks would leave them clutching at thin air. By then, however, *die Bokke* were already clutching at straws. The heavy conditions in Cape Town, bad enough to resemble the old Cardiff Arms Park mud heap in decent condition, had worked for the Lions and against the hard-ground Springboks, or so they claimed.

'We have no excuse,' said South Africa's captain, Hannes Marias, before proceeding to trot one out. 'But the heavy pitch helped the Lions more than it helped us.'

As an exercise in kidology, it took some beating. The Anglo-Celtic mix of the Lions front five did such a ruthless demolition job that poor old Chris Pope on the South African right wing never saw the ball. In the Ostrich Room at Newlands Stadium during the after-match dinner, Dr Craven had to perform the ritual presentation of green-and-gold blazers to the six new caps in the ranks of the vanquished. He sounded more than a bit embarrassed. Rising to his feet, 'The Doc' let rip: 'It hurts me to be giving you these, because you have not earned them,' he said, before singling out the hapless Pope for 'creating a record as the first Springbok to play for his country without touching the ball'. Peter Whipp in the centre 'did better than Pope because he touched the ball once'.

The most withering comments were reserved for the newcomers in the pack. Nobody at that time had seen a Test forward as big as Kevin de Klerk, a giant weighing in at almost 18 stone. 'He looks a big man in here,' Dr Craven said before pointing towards the pitch. 'He wasn't a big man out there.' Then it was the flanker Boland Coetzee's turn to take his oil from the medicine man. 'He is the old man of the team,' the Doc said. 'And today he played like one.'

The Lions could not have wished for a finer tribute, and the best of their rugby had still to be unleashed. A fortnight after losing in Cape Town, South Africa had lost again. This time they were thrashed, dismantled bit by bit on the burnt grass of their very own citadel. This time, the Lions scored tries galore, engulfing Marias and his much-changed team with five of them, two from the electrifying J.J. Williams and the rest distributed among Bennett, Brown, the inimitable 'Broon of Troon' and the

Ulsterman in the centre, Dick Milliken. Five tries against three penalties added up to 28–9, an unprecedented winning margin. So much for the altitude factor.

'It did take a session or two to get used to the air,' Windsor says. 'You couldn't go anywhere without people telling you, "You'll get murdered at Loftus." The phone in your hotel room would be going all the time – anything to upset you. They were so fanatical about their team that they'd do anything if it helped the Boks.'

Back at sea level for the third Test in Port Elizabeth, the Lions staged another dazzling exercise in the fine art of obliteration. In many respects, it was an action replay of Pretoria: 26–9 instead of 28–9, two more tries from the meteoric J.J. and a repeat of the starvation diet of three goals and no tries. A joke doing the rounds captured the sheer futility of the South African predicament: they would be asking the referee if they could bring their own ball because the Lions wouldn't let them touch the one that mattered.

In a last, forlorn throw of the dice, the South Africans changed both their locks, picking de Bruyn on the strength of his performance for the Free State and putting him alongside Moaner van Heerden, reputedly the toughest hombre on the African continent. 'We knew why Moaner was there, and he was bouncing around as if he was going to sort the Lions out,' Windsor said. 'Edwards fired an up-and-under, and as their scrum-half caught the ball, I hit him. I don't know whether he called a mark. I was going to hit him anyway and down he went.

'Moaner walked back from the lineout and hit me right at the back of the ear-hole. I thought I'd been hit by a hammer. I tried to clear my head, and as I looked round, my old buttie Broonie was giving Moaner both barrels. Everyone had a go. When it stopped, Willie John said to Frannie, "When you see Moaner coming at you from the next kick-off, stand back and just sledge him."

'They kicked off and we all made sure Frannie had a bit of cover. Moaner came steaming through and Frannie went *whooff* and laid him out. Moaner got up and walked towards the halfway line, but he didn't know what day it was. The hardest man in South Africa was out of it. They took him off and in the papers on Monday they said it was because of a damaged shoulder. A load of rubbish. The real reason he'd gone was that Frannie hit him with a humdinger.'

By then, Windsor had proved himself by far the best hooker in Wales and the best in the British Isles. He was also the best in the world, a status acknowledged by those who went to the front behind him, like Fergus Slattery. 'South Africa's biggest strength was their physicality, but it was also their biggest weakness because they couldn't use it once they were going backwards,' he says. 'They brought all the gorillas out of their cages for the third Test. We knew we were going to get it, that physically we would be beaten up unless we met fire with fire. As a result, they were as much beaten up as we were. You hit before you got hit.

'The referee only had one pair of eyes and they were focusing in one direction. The general theme was to smack early and not wait until someone smacked you. It would be fair to say that made Bobby feel at home. He was always a shoo-in as the No. 1 hooker on that tour because he was the undisputed No. 1. The great thing about Bobby was that he shot from the hip, so you always knew what he was thinking. What you saw was what you got, and he remained throughout a very popular guy.'

The series won, the Lions celebrated as only they could, reassembling on the Monday for a flight from Port Elizabeth to East London. 'Willie John said on the Saturday night, "We can all die happy now that we've won the series." On that plane we very nearly all did,' Windsor says.

'I deliberately sat next to Tommy David because he worked for British Aerospace back home at Nantgarw, so I figured if there was anything untoward, he would have the inside knowledge to put me right. We took off with the usual roar from the engines, and in a matter of seconds there was nothing but a deathly silence.

'Tommy was next to the window and he looked out. "Bloody hell," he said, "we're only about 50 feet above the water."

'Then the pilot came over on the tannoy, explaining there was a technical problem and that we'd have to go back to the airport. He asked us, very calmly, to put our pillows in our laps for the brace position. The dead silence was broken by Mike Gibson saying, "I wish now I'd remembered to send off these postcards."

'I was never so glad to get off a plane in all my life. When we stepped down, we could see that the blades in one engine of the 737 had been smashed to bits. The pilot explained that they'd sucked in a flock of birds and that had shut the engine down. Anyway, they said they'd have another plane ready in a few minutes.

'I said, "F**k that lark. No more planes." So they arranged for a chauffeur to take me, Chris Ralston and Stewart McKinney to East London. Instead of a forty-five-minute flight, it was six hours, but I'd still have gone by road even if it had taken six days. And for the first time, we could sit back and see the country.

'After a while of driving along dirt tracks, the driver stopped so we could buy some melons from a woman selling them by the roadside. All these kids were running round barefoot in the tall grass, which got me worried about my other pet hate: snakes. I hate them as much as I hate flying. So I said to one of the locals, "Do you get any snakes here?"

'And he said, "Yes, sir. Very bad area for black mambas."

'The only snake more dangerous than a black mamba is a cobra. Snakes usually go away when they hear noises, but the mamba goes on the attack. He wasn't going to get old Bob, because I was back in that car like a shot, with the doors shut and the windows wound up.

'After that third Test, Syd Millar made one of the biggest mistakes of his life. "Right, boys," he said, "you can all disappear into the jungle and do whatever you want to do." That wasn't the smartest thing to say to that mad bunch. Some of them were crazy, and one or two were a bit mental. The 1968 Lions were called "The Wreckers" because of the damage they did to hotels, but with this lot there were times when the hotel manager was lucky that his hotel was still standing.

'They played hard on and off the pitch. If you messed any of them about, they'd come to your room and turf everything out: the bed, wardrobes, tables, chairs. When they left, there'd be you and the wallpaper. One time, in Port Elizabeth, they got hold of a piano and shoved it out onto the canopy directly above the entrance to the hotel.

'I just happened to be the one walking out of the hotel when a photographer took a picture of me, not realising that I could have been brained at any second by this piano dangling a few feet above me. It could have killed anyone.

'Another time, we're in the team room getting stuck into boxes of beer to celebrate a win. Then a few of them start tearing the boxes into bits and stacking the cardboard on the table. Some idiot then sets light to it. They're all sitting around and the fire's beginning to burn, so I go outside and come back with the fire extinguisher and a hosepipe.

'I put the fire out and a few of them got wet. The manager of the hotel and his wife happened to come in at that moment. They didn't like us and so they started giving off. I'm standing at the top of the stairs with the hose in my hand and he started shouting at us, so I squirted him with a bit of water. That was when he said to Willie John, "I've had enough. I'm calling the police."

'Willie just puffed on his pipe and said, "Tell me, will there be many of them?"

'Don't forget this was a bunch of fit young men who loved Syd and Willie John like they loved their fathers. If they'd told us to go and jump off the Victoria Falls, we'd have done it. We could let our hair down on a Saturday night, but we gave them blood and sweat every day of the week on the training ground.

'We trained the way Pontypool trained, I think, because the Lions were smart enough to realise that the way Pross trained us back home put him ahead of the rest. We'd have two sessions a day: half past nine till noon, a break for a bowl of soup, nothing else, then back at two o'clock for two hours' scrummaging, fierce scrummaging.

'We didn't practise against a machine but against the eight non-Test forwards. They all had points to prove about not being in the Test team. We'd do 40 scrums, one after the other. You had 30 men all desperate to play in the Tests. Three years later in New Zealand, on the next Lions tour, there were men there who didn't want to play in the Tests, which was a sad comment on that tour. There'd always be a dust-up during those scrum sessions in South Africa, and hardly a day went by without someone having a real ding-dong.

'The one between the Chin and the Scottish prop Sandy Carmichael was a classic example. Frannie got a bit overheated and hit Sandy because he wasn't able to shove him back. A couple of photographers got shots of the incident, and the Boks then tried to make a big deal of it, trying to say that we were too busy fighting amongst ourselves to be much of a threat. What a load of old bollocks.'

With those hungriest of Lions, fighting for a Test place was meant literally.

'Nobody fought harder than Burto, a really good man to have on the pitch and off it,' Windsor says. 'On the rare occasions when morale needed to be lifted, Mike was your man. He and I did a party piece which got a lot of laughs, Mike as the ventriloquist and me sitting on his knee as the dummy.

'Any differences in training were forgotten once we finished. Nobody held any grudges or, if they did, they kept it to themselves. For me,

BLASTING THE BOKS

Gordon Brown was the forward of the tour. Nobody ever heard of a try-scoring lock before. He got nine of them. Unbelievable.

'One of the reasons for the success of the '74 team was that we all got on really well. The tour wasn't built on 15 players but 30. The big difference about being on tour was that you could live virtually like professionals. You didn't have to go out and do a day's work, then go training and grab a few beans and chips when you got home.

'You'd go into the finest hotels in South Africa for dinner and it wasn't a case of whether you'd have a fillet steak but how many. I was 16 stone when I left and 17 when I came back. The extra stone wasn't fat but muscle. We bulked up not through going to the gym but through training hard and eating good food.

'We had some terrific athletes. Ripley, the English number 8, and the Irish scrum-half Johnny Moloney were the best of all. In training, it was almost as if they had to go head to head on the running track. Andy could run like the wind, but Johnny would be up there with him all the way. He didn't smoke, didn't drink, didn't swear – lovely chap. Rippers was a great player in anyone's book, and a lot of people thought he'd get into the Test team instead of Mervyn Davies. I think Merv got the nod because he was more of a tight number 8 whereas Andy was more suited to a looser, running game. Tony Neary was another great forward who couldn't quite get into the back row, which only goes to show you how fantastic the back row was.

'A lot of players were unlucky, but I think Billy Steele, the Scottish wing, was the unluckiest. He played the first two Tests, did absolutely nothing wrong, but someone had to drop out for the third Test because Phil Bennett – "Benny" – had ten stitches in his ankle and therefore couldn't take the place kicks. We couldn't go without a specialist kicker, so Andy Irvine came in on the wing and Billy was the one who had to give way.

'Everyone had a good word for Billy because, apart from anything else, he was the choirmaster. He was the one who taught us to sing "Flower of Scotland", which we adopted as our battle hymn along with "We Shall Overcome". When the bus parked outside the front entrance of Loftus Versfeld for the second Test, the flunkeys opened the door and couldn't understand why nobody came out.

'We were halfway through "Flower of Scotland" and we all sat there for what seemed like five minutes until we had sung the last verse.

Nobody was going to make us budge. South African fans queuing up to get through the turnstiles stopped and stared at us. They must have thought we were mad. We were a bit, but that was what the song and the spirit of one-for-all, all-for-one meant to us.

'You gave everything you had and then you tried to find a bit more. I didn't drink during the week and neither did anyone else. If we played well on the Saturday, Syd would give us Sunday off, so we'd really give the booze a hammering, but he'd make you suffer on the training ground Monday if he thought you weren't up to scratch.

'Sometimes, if people complained about some of the things we got up to, he'd tell us to calm down. He treated us like grown men, even when some of the so-called grown men took part in the lark about nude scrummaging. That got into the papers at home, about how the boys stripped off, so everyone was getting calls from his wife or girlfriend, all asking, "What the hell are you up to over there?" You can guarantee that all 30 got the same answer from the 30 players: "Not me, love. You'd never catch me doing a thing like that."

'It did go on, but it was only a bit of fun. Some of them were so mad they'd scrum down starkers in the bar.'

In contrast to the rough stuff on the pitch, the South African Rugby Board bent over backwards, with a generosity which drove a horse and cart through the rigid amateur regulations forbidding payment or anything in lieu of payment. 'When we arrived, one of the liaison men who was sent to look after us said, "South Africa is yours,"' Windsor says. 'So I took him at his word. Whatever wasn't nailed down, I rolled into a box and sent home.

'Carpets, springbok skins, vases, lovely animal figures, copper trays which were engraved – all went home. They also gave us a stack of stuff which they offered to wrap up and post home for us, which was just as well because otherwise you'd have needed a removal van to cart it all around. They said, "We'll supply the boxes, the brown paper and send it home airmail. All you've got to do is let us know."

'I was the first Lion to start a car boot sale when I got home. With the amount of goodies we all sent back, it must have cost the South African Rugby Board a fortune. I realised very early on that a successful Lions tour off the pitch depended on two tools: a screwdriver and a pair of pliers.

'We started the tour and finished it in the same hotel in Johannesburg. Checking in there for the first time, I noticed that they had a beautiful painting of the two hemispheres of the world hanging behind the reception desk. I thought, with a bit of luck, I'll have that at the end of the trip.

'On our last night, I got up at about two in the morning, went down to the front desk and to my delight there was nobody around. I got the screwdriver and pliers to work, took the painting down and spirited it up to my room. They'd given us loads of brown paper to wrap up the prezzies, so I wrapped this one up and walked out of the hotel with it the next morning onto the coach for the airport. The staff must have known it was missing, but nobody said a word.

'I was still carrying it under my arm when we reached the departure gate at the airport. A few more steps and nobody would be any the wiser. At that point, the liaison man who was seeing us off said, "Bobby, give that parcel to me and I'll have it sent home for you. Save you the bother of carrying it and risking any damage."

'I said, "That's very nice of you, but no, honestly, it's no trouble. No trouble at all."

'I was just about to walk through security when a familiar voice from one of the Lions called out, "Bobby, do as the man says." I did what I was told, even though I thought I'd never see it again.

'They said they would post it home to me in Newport, but it never arrived. I often used to wonder what became of it, until I went on a rugby tour a few years later. During the trip, we had a bit of a do at the house of the bloke who'd persuaded me to hand over that painting and there it was, hanging above his fireplace!

'I consoled myself with the knowledge that we'd all got a fair bit out of the tour, including one big cash payment. Before the game against Transvaal, one of their top officials invited me to his cattle farm for a bite to eat. The bulls had horns that were about six-foot wide. Anyway, he's showing me around and he says, "You know, Bob, we want to get the Lions a present." I said, "We've been given so many prezzies, so why don't you give us some money? Give us the cash and let us buy our own presents."

'He said, "Do you think the boys would like that?"

'I said, trying not to sound overexcited, "I think they would. You won't be getting any complaints."

'After the game, he came into our changing-room with a big briefcase. I'd told the boys that I'd fixed it up with this fella and he was going to give us some money, so they were expecting him. As soon as the boys saw him coming down the steps towards them, they started singing, "Jingle bells, jingle bells, jingle all the way."

'We opened the case up and there were bundles of notes inside. It was doled out – 300 rand each, which, from memory, was not far short of £300, because the exchange rate then had the rand worth almost the same as the pound. It was all strictly against regulations, but I didn't worry about it because nobody else did. And you could do a lot with £300 in 1974.

'If the Unions had known anything about that, we'd all have been stuffed. Under the rules, we'd have been declared professionals and kicked out of the game and maybe the tour would have been seen in a different light. We put the money in our pockets and kept shtum. If anyone in the Unions was any the wiser, they must have turned a blind eye. Better to let sleeping dogs lie than declare all 30 of us dirty professionals and make the whole game a laughing stock before the eyes of the world.

'I bought Judi two beautiful opal rings, but, stupidly, I turned down the chance of being given some gold krugerrands. I don't know what I was thinking about. I needed money for bread and coal, so it didn't occur to me that these krugerrands would be a good investment. How daft can you be?

'We got about 100 rand a game from the pool for selling our complimentary tickets, which came in handy. I came back with a case full of goodies and more money than I went out with.'

He came back with something else: a reputation as a sort of latter-day Robin Hood. At one point during the tour when some of his colleagues decided that the Lions manager, Alun Thomas, failed to match the South African generosity in one specific area of the freebie front, Windsor swept into action.

'Alun was very mean when it came to giving out the golden lion lapel badges,' he says. 'They were lovely and very sought after. We knew Alun had loads of them in his room. One day, I went up there with another player, first making sure Alun wasn't in. We had no key, so I just gave the door what I thought was a gentle kind of shove. It nearly came off the hinges.

'Inside, there were two bags full of badges. We each grabbed one and scarpered. Next morning, the manager calls a big meeting. He starts off, "I want to know who stole the badges."

BLASTING THE BOKS

'Fair play to Syd and Willie John. They spoke up, saying that it had to be South Africans, because why would any of the boys want to break into your room? The next day, we're at the airport. My teammate's got his badges in a shoulder bag, I've put mine in my suitcase. Suitcases went through on the big trolley, shoulder bags had to go through the magnetic detectors.

'My teammate went straight to the back of the queue, worried that he was going to be caught. As luck would have it, the suitcases were going past on the trolley, so I dumped his shoulder bag on top, out of harm's way. And nobody ever said another word about the badges.'

The series having been lost, a bemused Craven turned to the Lions in the hope of finding some sorely needed inspiration. What he found served only to increase his overall bemusement. 'Dr Craven came to Syd Millar and asked if he could have permission to come into the dressing-room to see what we did before a game,' Windsor says. 'At this particular ground, you had to walk down steps to get into the dressing-room, and I was sitting next to Chris Ralston.

'Chris had one leg up on the bench, tying his bootlace. He had a big cigar in his mouth and was blowing smoke all over the place. Dr Craven couldn't get over it. The Springboks had strict rules – no smoking, no drinking, no sex, like they were a bunch of loonies. He walked out.

'After the series was won, Syd tried his best to rally the boys. He'd keep saying, "We've got a job to finish here." It never occurred to any of us that we could go through the tour unbeaten, and we were never able to reach the same level of mental strength for the last Test as we'd done for the other three. It wasn't for the lack of trying, and maybe that's why we only got a draw.

'And, then, at the final whistle, the most amazing thing happened. The crowd came onto the field and carried the Springboks off. You'd have thought they'd won the series.'

When their plane climbed into the sky above Johannesburg, the homeward-bound Lions could look back at a trail of destruction stretching as far as the eye could see. Their opponents had gone through six props, two hookers, five locks, seven back-row forwards and three pairs of half-backs and still lost by a country mile.

The most telling verdict on the '74 Lions came from Phil Jones, a Welsh journalist who had emigrated to South Africa from Cardiff some years earlier. His words, in the *Rand Daily Mail*, a courageous opponent of apartheid, had a prophetic ring to them: 'McBride had done what he set out to do – crush the Boks on what could be the last tour by a Lions team of South Africa under present race conditions in this country.'

By the time the Lions returned 23 years later, having abandoned the tour scheduled for 1986, apartheid South Africa had been transformed into the Rainbow Nation by the incomparable Nelson Mandela.

7

ON YOUR BIKE

They came home to receptions fit for conquering heroes. In many corners of the British Isles, the neighbours put the flags up and the red carpet down to give the Lions a right royal welcome in honour of what they had done for the sporting morale of the United Kingdom and the Republic of Ireland.

The news agenda during that summer of 1974 had been dominated by the IRA bombing campaign in London, Turkey's invasion of northern Cyprus and the Watergate scandal, which ended Richard Nixon's presidency of the United States despite his famous declaration, 'There will be no whitewash in the White House.' Lord Lucan had not quite got round to disappearing when an unbeatable rugby team began commanding its own share of the national spotlight.

In the village of Pontlliw, on the outskirts of Swansea, the locals drove Mervyn Davies around in a vintage coupé flanked by little girls in Welsh national dress. Twenty members of Pontarddulais Town Band, all of whom had cancelled a rehearsal for the following week's National Eisteddfod, led the procession to the stirring sound of 'Men of Harlech', and so many turned out that the 1926 open-top Austin carrying the local Lion had to stop at the bottom of a hill until the crowd cleared.

When J.J. Williams returned to Nantyffyllon, near Maesteg, what seemed like the entire village stood beneath their hoods and umbrellas in defiance of a wet summer evening for a glimpse of the wing whose four tries in two Lions Tests had never been done before or since. In an old mining village at the gateway to the Rhondda Valley, the Rhydyfelin Non-Political Club put the finishing touches to a 'buffet and cabaret' in honour of their most famous member, Tommy David.

Meanwhile, a little further east, in Monmouthshire, the only player from that large county on the trip arrived home to a rapturous greeting from his wife and, by now, three children.

For Bobby Windsor, there were no bands, no fanfares, no cavalcade round the streets of his native Newport. While Willie John McBride had his photograph taken with the Conservative Party leader, Ted Heath, and others rushed to bask in the glow of the best combined Great Britain and Ireland rugby team to leave these shores, Windsor's primary concern was to get back to work. As a latter-day professional, the trip would have earned him more than £50,000 in fees and commercial opportunities galore, from advertising to sponsorship and newspaper columns to television interviews.

Rugby back in the mid-'70s gave its best players the opportunity to appear on the international stage and play for nothing more than the love of the game. The Unions wielded such power that a player could be excommunicated on the merest suspicion of having been approached by a rugby league club, which, in a supposedly free world, was rather hard to avoid when the occasional mogul from the north of England came knocking on your door with a bag full of readies.

When the late George Parsons climbed on board the train at Newport station to join the rest of the Wales team en route to play France in Paris in 1947, the Welsh Rugby Union had him kicked off it as it was beginning to puff its way out of the station, or so legend has it. A policeman in Pontypool, Parsons had been suspected of negotiating terms with a rugby league club, and that was deemed sufficient reason for the sort of high-handed treatment which ought to have been exposed as a national disgrace but which, like so much else in those days, seemed to have been swept under the carpet for fear of challenging the Establishment.

Windsor could not afford to buy a car before he went on the tour, and he was even less able to afford one when he came back. Within a couple of days of touching down at Heathrow, he was clocking in at the local steelworks, and that entailed a round trip of some eight miles from his home. The scourge of the Springboks, who had literally put his neck on the line at least 20 times every time he played in South Africa, went to work on a bicycle.

To win an international cap demanded a level of excellence which could be reached only by making sacrifices, often financial ones, which was certainly true in Windsor's case. In return, the game rewarded players for their talent, dedication, perseverance and courage with the honour of representing their country, and woe betide anyone caught fiddling expenses or putting as much as a pound note in his pocket as payment for playing.

Union players who cashed in their chips with the League were considered guilty of treason and were treated accordingly. The International Board regulations on amateurism demanded that they be shunned, and many a famous player was refused entry to his old union clubhouse. Regulation 2, Section 7 of the amateur principles, as applied then, spelt it out in all its draconian pomposity: 'No person shall knowingly accept or allow to continue in membership anyone who is not an amateur and shall expel anyone it subsequently ascertains was ineligible when accepted.'

Any player who wrote an autobiography or had it ghostwritten for him could not take a penny of the proceeds and stay in the game. Many lost their amateur status as a consequence, a counterproductive measure which meant that for long periods outstanding Lions like Fran Cotton and Phil Bennett, to name but two, were on the outside looking in, unable to give the game the benefit of their vast experience.

Luckily for Wales, Windsor was happy to play the game he loved for nothing, and if Cross Keys had slipped a fiver into his pocket after every match, it certainly wasn't going to change his lifestyle. He may have been a newly minted British Lion, the best hooker in England, Ireland, Scotland and Wales, and an integral part of a Lions team which had won a lottery of sorts, but he still had to get on his bike, ride to work and mend his own punctures.

When a local car firm with a sharp eye for a bit of marketing approached Windsor with a view to updating his rustic form of transport, the heavy hand of the Welsh Rugby Union came down on him like a ton of bricks.

'I'd just got home from work one day shortly after I'd got back from South Africa when the phone rang,' Windsor says. 'The caller said he was Brian Lewis from Howell's car dealers in Newport. "I'd like you to come to our garage," he said. "We'd like to show our gratitude for what you've done and we hope you won't be disappointed. Something to your advantage. In fact, it's very much to your advantage."

'So I went to the garage on Corporation Road and saw Mr Lewis. When I got there, he pointed to a brand-new Allegro car in a lovely mustard colour. "There you are," he said. "All yours, with our compliments.

I'd heard that you've been riding a pushbike to and from work and that ain't fair after what you've done for the sports fans of this country. All the other players have got cars and now you've got one too. All we ask in return is that you come to one or two company dos during the year. Come down Saturday and we'll have it all taxed and insured for you. You can drive it away."

'I thought, what a lovely man. I'd taken the bag of badges that I'd acquired during the tour and gave them to him. Those gold lion badges were like gold dust, so Mr Lewis was well pleased, but he couldn't have been as pleased as I was.

'You have to remember that it was a constant struggle to make ends meet, feed and clothe the kids and pay the bills. Buying a new car was so far out of my reach that I didn't even dream about it. The springbok skins which I'd be given as souvenirs during the Lions tour weren't framed or put on the wall. We used them to cover the holes in the carpet in the front room. That's how tough it was.

'So when they gave me the keys to the car on the Saturday, I felt like I'd won the pools. It was probably the first brand-new car on the estate. I pulled up outside the house and blew the horn: "Beep, beep." The missus and the three kids jumped in and we drove round the estate. I felt like an emperor on a tour of inspection. I was chuffed to bits and so were the kids – Joanne, Ricky and Mandy.

'The next day, Bill Clement rang up from the Welsh Rugby Union. "We hear you're driving round in a nice new car," he said.

'I said, "That's right, it's great. The kids love it."

'He said, "Well, Bob, you take it back to the garage in the morning, otherwise you will be banned from rugby union for life."

'"What? Say that again."

'"Take it back to the garage in the morning, otherwise you will be banned from rugby union for life."

'That was how it was. You either accepted it or you went north to play rugby league. I took it back and got the bus home. It was obvious someone had squealed on me. I felt awful. Apart from everything else, I'd made a fool of myself. Everybody saw me in the shiny new car. Next day they saw me on the old pushbike, in my overalls and wellies, pedalling to work. I felt a proper f*****g twit.

'I was riding to Whitehead's on my bike one day and waiting at the traffic lights when a kid going to school with his pals recognised me.

He seemed to have some difficulty convincing the rest of them that it was me. It was as if the other kids were saying, "Don't be stupid. That's not Bobby Windsor. Bobby Windsor wouldn't be going to work on a bike. He's a millionaire."

'I found situations like that a bit embarrassing, but now that I look back I feel proud, proud of being maybe the last of the breed of old sportsmen who went out and fought for the honour of Great Britain, then went back to work as if nothing much had happened. Charlie and I were just about the last of the breed. It doesn't happen like that any more.

'I suppose I could have kept the car, told the WRU to stuff themselves and gone to play league. I'd had a few offers after the Lions tour and one of the clubs sent their chairman to the house with a briefcase full of money. This would be a down payment, they'd find me a job and give me more next season.

'League then was a dull game. It was before they brought in the six-tackle law which meant they then had to do something with the ball and play some rugby. If you had the ball, you kept it until you dropped it. I was in love with rugby union. I'd have played it seven days a week if I could, so there was never any question that I'd turn my back on it.

'They don't realise how lucky they are today, being paid to play the game. What a wonderful world it must be when someone comes along and gives you £200,000 a year for doing something which I willingly did for nothing more than the love of the game. Apart from the fiver in my top pocket at Cross Keys, I was never paid a penny to play. Throughout the early years, I paid to play, as did everyone else at junior level. There was a £3 annual membership subscription at Newport Saracens.

'On top of that, you paid £1 a week to have your kit washed and provide a bite to eat for the visiting team. You always hoped they wouldn't eat all the nosh and there'd be a few scraps left for us. Stumping up for that every week was never a problem. One of the "perks" of joining Pontypool was that I no longer had to pay an annual subscription.'

While other Lions were feted, Windsor's return was unusually low key by comparison. For the first time in his rugby life, he felt jealous of those teammates who enjoyed a higher public profile.

'I was the only Lion from Monmouthshire, which is a big part of Wales,' he says. 'I'd switch on the television when I got home and I'd see the likes of Merv, Gareth, Benny and J.J. all being driven around in open-top cars. I was back in Bettws and nobody outside my family and a few friends seemed to know I was home.

'I looked at the others being given the big treatment on the telly and it hurt. For the first time in my life, I was jealous. I wanted to be driven round in an open-top car as well, to be given some sort of public recognition. In other parts of the country, people were falling over themselves to make a fuss of the Lions.

'When we got back to Heathrow, Ted Heath, who was then the leader of Her Majesty's Opposition, was there to welcome us. Now, one of Tommy David's best friends at the time was David Bailey, the photographer. Tommy loved cameras, or at least he loved being photographed by them, and when we got back to Heathrow, Tommy jumped in front of Mr Heath in the arrivals lounge and got splattered by a bag of flour from one of the anti-apartheid people. I laughed so much I needed treatment for my ribs.

'After I'd been home for an hour or two and unpacked, I said to Judi, "Come on, we're going to the Merry Miller to have a pint of beer." I walked in and there weren't many around because it was early in the afternoon.

'The barman said, "Hello, Bob. Haven't seen you this long time. Anything up?"

'He obviously wasn't a rugby bloke, so it wasn't his fault. Perhaps it was because I was a Newport boy playing for Pontypool. My old club, Newport Saracens, were very good. They put on a dinner in my honour at the King's Head and, because I always rolled my own cigarettes, they got Rizla to sponsor it.

'Miss Rizla was there, a girl called Helen Morgan. Not many knew of her then, but the whole world did not long afterwards because she won Miss World. Then she had to give it up when they found out she was an unmarried mother, and if anyone still hadn't heard of her, they had after that.'

The episode over the car was one example of Windsor falling foul of the amateur rules. On tour with Wales in Japan the following year, 1975, when the visitors ran in twenty-four tries during the two uncapped mismatches, he was allowed to keep a gift despite it having exceeded the piffling maximum sum as laid down in the regulations. This time, another potential embarrassment arose, over the players having to return gifts presented to them in honour of their visit to the Imperial Palace in Tokyo.

ON YOUR BIKE

Les Spence, the genial Cardiff president who had last seen Japan in very different circumstances as a prisoner of war, averted another petty row by using a little common sense rather than insulting his hosts by handing back the goodies and trying to make them understand why they were unacceptable.

'We were invited to the Emperor's palace by one of the princesses, who wanted to make a presentation to us,' Windsor says. 'We went to a banquet and we were all given a silver pocket watch, specially engraved and worth a lot of money. Les Spence was a great bloke and I remember looking at the watch and saying to him, "Isn't that lovely?"

'We thought nothing more about it until the next day. Two members of the Welsh Rugby Union committee had flown out on a free trip. The next thing, we were told, "You've got to give those watches back."

'We told Les. He said, "Hang on, boys, leave it to me." He came back an hour later and said, "You can keep the watches, boys. Just don't say anything about it."

'On the plane home, I asked him how he'd managed to talk the WRU people out of kicking up a fuss about the watches when they got home. "Easy," he said. "I made sure they were given one each."

'The tour allowance was something like 35p – enough to buy a postcard but maybe not the postage. Phoning home was always a bugbear – you had to pay for those calls out of your own pocket unless you could come up with some way of making sure someone else paid. In Japan, Charlie Faulkner and I hit on an idea between us.

'John Dawes, or "Sid", as we called him, had finished playing then and taken over as coach. Charlie says to me one day, "Sid can ring home from his room and the cost of the calls are taken care of by the Japanese Rugby Union. They pick up the tab for every call."

'We decided that when he next went out of the hotel, we'd go up to his room and ring our wives back in Newport. Phone calls were expensive, but we reckoned that even if it was £500 they weren't going to say anything to him. All we had to do was get into his room, pick up the phone to the hotel operator, give her the international number and wait for her to put it through. I'm standing at the door keeping a lookout, Charlie asks for the number, puts the phone down and then picks it up when it rings.

'The operator said, "Phone call for Mr Dawes."

'Charlie said, "I'm sorry. He's not here." And he put the phone down.

'I said, "Charlie, you stupid so-and-so."

'He said, "It wasn't for me. It was for Mr Dawes."

'I reminded him, "Charlie, we're in Dawesy's room. They're bound to say that."

'They were so stingy with the daily tour allowance that one phone call home would make me skint. My pride wouldn't let me borrow a tenner, so I lived on my wits. I liked it when it came to my turn to be duty boy, especially on Lions tours, because one of the duties was to go to the hotel reception and ask for the players' bills just before we checked out.

'The receptionist would put them all on the counter. I knew which one was mine so I'd put it in my pocket along with the duplicate and then dole out the others. On one particular morning, when we were leaving Cape Town, I was caught out. The bus was about to pull out of the front of the hotel when the manager came running out. Syd Millar, the coach, stopped the bus and had a word with the manager.

'Then Syd stood up and said, "Who hasn't paid his bill?" Nobody said a word. Then Syd said, "This bus isn't moving until someone owns up, and if that means sitting here all day, that's what we'll do."

'Then he read out the number on the bill, which started with the code 0633. That's a Newport number and I was the only Monmouthshire player on the tour, so that really stuffed me. I stood up in the middle of the bus, trying to sound very angry, and said, "Right. Which one of you bastards has been phoning my wife?"

'Syd laughed his head off, along with everyone else. The manager got off, we drove away and that was the last I heard of it. Unless the Lions footed the bill, someone somewhere is still waiting to be paid. If I ever win the lottery, I suppose I could always go back to Cape Town and settle the account, if the hotel is still standing.'

By New Year 1975, a new force had been unleashed on the sporting world – the Pontypool front row, the 'Viet-Gwent'. Windsor having got there first 14 months earlier, Faulkner and Graham Price completed the unholiest trinity for the opening match of the 1975 Five Nations, against France at the Parc des Princes. The Big Five had dropped Phil Bennett, the fulcrum of the Lions machine in South Africa the previous summer, as a punishment for his having failed to turn out in the annual pre-Christmas trial.

John Bevan of Aberavon took his place, one of six new caps in a team that proceeded to score very nearly one try for each of them. Steve Fenwick, Gerald Davies, Terry Cobner and Gareth Edwards had all scored when Price joined them by doing something nobody had seen a tighthead prop do at that level – gallop 75 yards in support of a last-minute attack and score in the corner. Windsor remembers what happened the following Monday night.

'When Pricey got back to Pontypool and reported for club training, Pross said to him, "That prop you played against last Saturday must have been f*****g useless."

'"Why's that?" says Graham.

'"Because if he had been any f*****g good," says Pross, "you wouldn't have been able to run that far at the end of the game."

'Pontypool didn't get where they were by giving you pats on the back. One of the unsung heroes of that game was John Bevan, who did brilliantly to prevent a French try when the game was still in the balance. He tackled a Frenchman in the corner and turned him over, which took some doing. The decision to drop Benny caused a big controversy, but he wouldn't have been able to stop the French scoring the way Bev did.

'People were slagging them off for daring to drop a star of the Lions tour, but the selectors were quite right. Benny and I have been great mates for a long time, but there was no doubt in my mind that he got a bit above his station, as if playing in a trial was beneath him.

'The selectors probably thought, who do you think you are? If Charlie or I had ducked out of a trial because we didn't fancy it, neither of us would have been seen again, and rightly so. I never cried off a Welsh trial because of flu or anything else. I never took my place for granted and I didn't want to give anyone else the opportunity in case I ended up being dropped. I used to take a swig of Benylin on a Saturday morning, especially when I had a bit of a cold. If they took it today, they'd probably be done for being drugged up.

'The impression the selectors would have been left with when Phil dropped out of that trial would have been that he was saying, "You know what I can do." They felt they had to nip that in the bud. Too right they did. They couldn't let one player get away with it, otherwise all the other established internationals would do the same. The Big Five had to make an example of him. You learnt very early on that you didn't mess them about.

'When I first played for Wales B at the Arms Park, I was at the after-match dinner at the Angel in Cardiff with maybe the best uncapped back in Wales. We came out of the dinner and stood on the top step of the entrance to the hotel. This player had a glass in his hand and he threw it out onto the road. And who was standing round the corner? Three of the Big Five. That bloke never got a cap.

'Years after I finished playing, the captain of Wales, Paul Thorburn, gave a V-sign to someone in the crowd at the end of a match against England at the Arms Park. The Prince of Wales was there and at the dinner, Thorburn made a verbal attack on a well-respected member of the press who happens to come from my home town, Stephen Jones of the *Sunday Times*.

'Thorburn should never have captained Wales again. What he did was a disgrace. He abused a very privileged position and never apologised. The Welsh Rugby Union made it a bigger disgrace by ducking out of their responsibility to show the world that rugby union wouldn't tolerate such behaviour. They should have been charged with bringing the game into disrepute, along with Thorburn.

'It was a sign that the old standards were not what they used to be. In my time, you'd never have dreamt of giving a V-sign to the crowd, even when they were asking for it in hostile places like the Parc des Princes. The size of that win the first time I played there in 1975 meant there was no way Benny would come straight back in for the next game, England at home. We won that, so Bev was bound to stay at outside-half for the game after that in Scotland.

'If it hadn't been for injuries, you wonder how many more games Benny would have missed, because we didn't lose many. In the end, two injuries got him back in. David Richards, then a kid at Swansea who had been put on the bench, did his hamstring during training at Aberavon on the Sunday before the Scottish game. And when Bev dislocated his shoulder in the first half at Murrayfield, Benny was back where he would have been all along but for missing the trial.'

There appears to have been another, more pragmatic reason for Bevan being picked. As coach, Dawes considered the Aberavon number 10 a better fit for the tactical game he wanted Wales to play.

'There are two kinds of stand-off half,' Dawes told David Parry-Jones, author of *The Dawes Decades*. 'Bevan was in one category, his awareness of opportunities and what was "on" meant that matchwinners in the back division saw plenty of the ball in space. In contrast, Benny's game was always instinctive, reacting like lightning to the ghost of a chance to make breaks himself. It was noticeable, too, that he disliked being on the bench with the prospect of having to take the field as a replacement. When Bevan was injured at Murrayfield, Phil came on to play in a wholly unconvincing mood.'

Windsor sensed that too. 'I didn't know this until Mervyn Davies told me so 35 years after the match, that Benny had refused to take a penalty kick,' he says. 'Swerve was captain that day, so he would know and I have no reason to doubt him. Fate is a very strange thing and it makes you wonder what would have happened if dear old Bev had not bust his shoulder when he did.'

Despite a narrow loss at Murrayfield, where the last non-ticket international generated a then world record attendance estimated at 104,000, Wales won the Five Nations title. Had Allan Martin, one of the last goalkicking second-row forwards to use the toe-end torpedo style, managed to convert Trevor Evans' try from the touchline with the last kick of the match, they would have been unbeaten champions.

Soon, Wales would turn themselves from a very good team into a great one. The first of two Grand Slams was only just round the corner, starting at Twickenham on 17 January 1976 with a win over England which had almost become routine. J.P.R. embroidered arguably his finest Five Nations match with two of the three tries in a 21–9 victory. Wales followed that with a comfortable home defeat of Scotland before polishing Ireland off in Dublin with the grandstand finish to top them all – eighteen points in the last five minutes through converted tries by Gerald Davies, Gareth Edwards and Phil Bennett.

'The win at Twickenham was one of the best of the lot,' Windsor says. 'There was no such thing as a bad England pack, not with proven props like Cotton and Burton, Tony Neary in the back row and new players, like the Leicester hooker Peter Wheeler, who were beginning to come through. They were hard games.

'When we went to Dublin, because of the bombings on both sides of the border at the time there was heavy security all round the Shelbourne Hotel, where we stayed. The Irish were always fantastic, the way they looked after you off the pitch. On it, they'd rip into you for an hour and then they'd begin to run out of steam. We had world-class backs and we made sure we gave them good ball. You gave them enough, they were bound to score.'

Only France at the Arms Park could prevent Wales sweeping the board. In the end, it came down to one tackle, by J.P.R. on Jean-François Gourdon. In the finest 'they-shall-not-pass' tradition, the granite full-back smashed the powerful Gourdon off the pitch with a shoulder charge which today would have cost him a yellow card, at the very least, and his team the greater catastrophe of a penalty try.

'I have never been more relieved in all my life to see someone make a tackle, because if that big French wing had scored, I'd have had to live with it for the rest of my life,' Windsor says. 'Do you know how he came to be running away down the touchline? Because I lost a strike against the head. Can you imagine what I felt like?

'I hooked it, but somehow it bounced back on their side. I got my head up out of the scrum and all I could see was Gourdon racing clear. I was almost screaming at myself in agony because I could see him ending up behind the posts to give them the easiest of conversions and level the game at 19 all. If J.P.R. had tackled him the way the law says you must these days, not even the great man himself could have prevented him scoring.

'He smashed Gourdon into touch with a shoulder charge. Today, he would probably have been sent off for an illegal tackle – no use of the arms – and they'd have been given a penalty try between the sticks. Instead, we had a lineout, which we managed to win, I passed the ball back to Edwards and he booted it into touch. All over, and if anyone heard a long hissing sound, like the air coming out of a punctured tyre on my old bike, that was me.

'There was no World Cup then so the Grand Slam was the biggest thing you could achieve. Outside that, the only prize to come anywhere close to it was beating the All Blacks, and on the one day when we had them beaten, they cheated us out of it. But that's another story, for later.

'This wasn't any old Grand Slam. We'd scored 102 points in the 4 matches and nobody had ever scored that many in the course of doing the Slam. Another record was that we'd only used 16 players all season. It would have been 15 had Graham Price not had to go off because he'd been gouged by one of the Froggies, which meant he was walking round like Blind Pugh.

'Mike Knill came on for his only cap. It was great that he got it, because Mike was a terrific tighthead who deserved a stack of caps. He could lock a scrum up as well as Fran Cotton. I was talking to Gérard

Cholley, the French prop, at the dinner and he paid Mike the biggest compliment of all. Cholley said, "Whoever put Price off the field made a mistake, because the replacement was better."

'In South Africa, during the Lions tour, Harry Secombe had sent champagne down for the players, and when we got back to the dressing-room after the French Grand Slam game, there was another crate of the stuff, sent with the compliments of Spike Milligan and that well-known flanker from Aberavon Richard Burton. The stuff is being sprayed all over the place when there's a knock on the door and the bloke who looked after the changing-rooms came over to me.

'"Bob," he said, "there's a chap here says he's your father."

'I said, "Our dad?"

'I asked Clive Rowlands, the coach, if it was OK for me to bring him in and I went to the door. I said, "Come in, Dad, and have a drink." He was quite a shy man, my father, but that day he had tears of joy in his eyes. He sat down in the corner with a glass of champagne in his hand and I felt so proud. That was one of the best moments of my life, our dad there in the middle of the Grand Slam team sharing in the celebrations.

'I could see by the look on his face how proud he felt also. He was probably thinking back to all those early days and how he'd got me out of the odd scrape and how he could never have thought then that one day his lad, Bash, would be part of what Mervyn Davies always reckoned was the best Welsh team he ever captained.

'He went straight back to Newport and the Centurion pub to tell all his mates about it. He must have enjoyed himself, because the next time I called in, our mam said, "I hope you don't let him into the dressing-room again . . ."

'He'd have found it a very different place had he gone in there before a game. As coach, Clive was a great one for pulling the heart-strings, for reminding you who you were playing for – your families, your communities and all those Welsh people who'd have given their right arm to have been in your position. If that kind of thing suited some players, that was fine by me, but I was never one for that kind of stuff.

'Most of that was drummed out of us at Pontypool. Because the dressing-rooms were so close together at Pontypool Park, we'd hear the other team trying to psyche themselves up by shouting at the top of their voices. Pross would hear them and shake his head. "Listen to those howlers," he'd say. "Like a bunch of Red Indians."

'With the Wales team, you'd always have Ray Gravell singing the patriotic songs. "Grav", God rest his soul, was a great bloke, but after a while he'd get on my nerves and I'd have to tell him to shut the f**k up. Then you'd have Geoff Wheel, the big Swansea lock, who'd holler a bit when he got nervous, but he couldn't help that. Brilliant bloke, Geoff.

'Pricey would always get on the table and have a rub-down for half an hour from the physio, Gerry Lewis. He'd come off looking as pink as a salmon. What I wanted was to hear someone crack a good joke to ease the tension. That close to the kick-off, all I really wanted to do was get out onto the pitch.

'Once the whistle blew, I was absolutely ruthless in making sure I did my job. As a front-five forward, my philosophy was pretty basic: do it to them before they do it to you. Without that kind of mentality, you would never be much use at international level. We had to beat bigger packs by skulduggery and there were times when we played like a gang of thugs.

'We had to go in and punch and boot like mad. Sometimes, against bigger sets of forwards, the only way we could beat them was by pure violence. We'd do things the other home countries wouldn't do. We'd rip into them, intent on causing injury. You wore the longest studs you could find, knowing that you'd get away with it because, more often than not, none of the officials bothered checking them. Stud inspections just before kick-off never happened.

'The Irish boys would punch you and give you a nibble on the ear and a kiss afterwards. The French were different from Ireland and the other home countries. They were mean and vicious. The French would rip your head off, if they could, and chuck it over the fence. With them, it was always war.

'You stamp on someone's head, he goes off, has some stitches and comes back. Stamp on his ankle, he doesn't come back. A lot of players who did things like that wouldn't dream of admitting to it, but that was how the game was. The darker parts, like the scrum, could be very nasty and you had to be nasty to survive.

'You were playing for your country and you were desperate to win at all costs. That meant going out with the deliberate intention of intimidating the other side by whatever you could get away with. Some referees gave the impression they would only send you off if you committed murder. Even then, they might have thought twice about it!

'Our job was to win good ball for the backs and with a back line like ours, that meant we'd win. We had to get them the ball any way possible, fair or foul. You were so wrapped up in doing your bit that you didn't stop to think of the consequences. It was all part and parcel of the game, and when it was over you had a few beers with the man you'd been punching and kicking.

'I never gave it a thought until one incident during a club game for Pontypool put the fear of God in me. We were playing Oxford and we had a young guy playing his first game for us, Steve Sutton, who would go on to play for Wales. Steve then was a bit of a lightweight in every sense and he was up against a really dirty bastard in the Oxford team who started to give him some real stick.

'After a while, we decided to do something about it. When this Oxford player pulled Sutton down in one lineout, I booted him in the chops. He went off on a stretcher to hospital and I forgot all about it until the phone rang at home at six o'clock on the Sunday morning. It was Pross.

'He said to me, "That boy is still in hospital. I think you could have killed him."

'Even now, those words send a shiver down my spine. I cannot express the relief I felt when I was told later in the day that the Oxford bloke had made a full recovery. It made me stop and think – until the next time I had to fight my corner against the French.

'Their pack never failed to give the impression that they didn't give a stuff if they did kill you. That worries even the toughest, but at least you know what's coming. Every time I played against France, I'd have their two second rows, Michel Palmie and my old sparring partner Alain Estève, kicking me in the face.

'Once, at half-time, I was in a mess. I said to Charlie Faulkner, "F**k this. The next scrum I'm going to get even with Estève. I'm going to kick the bastard."

'I bided my time, knowing I'd get my chance. When it came and he was on the ground, I booted him in the mush as hard as I could, and that started a fight. At least I thought that we'd seen the back of Estève. How wrong can you be? Once the ref had calmed everyone down, I saw Estève get to his feet and walk back.

'Then he turned round in my direction and gave me a wink. And I thought, "Oh, f**k me. There's going to be hell to pay any minute now."

'Imagine how I felt. I said to Charlie, "He's given me the wink. What am I going to do now?"

'Charlie said, "Try kissing him. If that doesn't work, tell him he's wanted on the phone."

'After the match, Estève was my big pal who took me out on the town and couldn't do enough for me. Everyone at all the night clubs in Pigalle knew him – with the fuss they made of him it was almost as if he owned the place. It was the same wherever he took me. He'd go from being my worst enemy to my best friend, all in the same day and night.

'Estève was a brute on the field but nice off it, which was more than I could say for his sidekick, Michel Palmie. Nobody was that surprised when they heard that he had been banned for something that happened in a club match. I don't know about that, but I do know that French pack was the best I have ever seen. They had men in every position who always got the job done, legally or illegally.

'I will go to my grave with the names of all eight engraved on my heart – Gérard Cholley, Alain Paco, Robert Paparemborde, Michel Palmie, Alain Estève, Jean-Pierre Rives, Jean-Claude Skrela, Jean-Pierre Bastiat.

'In a way, it was only right that my last international was against France, at the Parc des Princes in February 1979. They didn't show the match on television in Wales, not because they were afraid of any X-certificate stuff but because of a strike by technicians in Paris. Some of the old foes were missing that day, like Cholley. Instead they had another tough guy on the loosehead, Armand Vaquerin, who was such a headcase that he ended up blowing his brains out in a game of Russian roulette at his bar in Béziers. How mad can you get?'

The heavy mob, with the sole exception of Estève, who was replaced by another mighty lock, Jean-François Imbernon, had all been there at Cardiff Arms Park for the Grand Slam finale three years earlier. It was to be the last time Windsor, or anyone else for that matter, ran out in the national jersey behind a team led by Mervyn Davies, then within a few steps of reaching the zenith of his career.

He had already been identified to captain the Lions to New Zealand the following year, 1977, due reward for his pragmatic approach to winning rugby matches. Where John Dawes, ever the perfectionist, wanted Wales to win in style, Davies, ever the realist, wanted them to win 'at all costs'. Something of a myth has grown up of the '70s team as the supreme entertainers, but in fact that aspect of the team's play tended to be kept in check until the game had been driven beyond their opponents' reach, which often restricted exercises in cutting loose to the final minutes, as evidenced by that most purple of patches in Dublin.

For all the matchwinners at his disposal behind the scrum, the number 8 in the ubiquitous white headband knew they would be useless unless the forwards gave them the ammunition. 'As captain,' Davies said, 'I believed the game could be divided into three phases: confrontation, consolidation and domination.'

Twenty-two days after winning the Slam, on Sunday, 28 March 1976, he captained Swansea in a Welsh Cup semi-final at the Arms Park club ground against, ironically, Windsor's Pontypool. Not quite half an hour into the match on a sunny afternoon, Davies went down with the ball nowhere near him. From that dreadful moment onward, the only question that mattered was whether the neurosurgeons could save his life.

'Because of the reputation Pontypool had in those days, some people were left with a suspicion that Merv had been caught in a ruck,' Windsor says. 'That was hanging around until it was proved that the brain haemorrhage was not the result of any physical contact, that he was just as likely to have had it sitting at home in his armchair watching television. It came out subsequently that he'd had two blackouts playing for London Welsh, and after a while everyone realised that it was nothing to do with Pontypool.

'We were down straight after the match because we had lost with a place in the cup final at stake. We had pushed them off every scrum. We won everything and still lost. Alan Mages, my opposite number, who was a policeman and a very good player, said to me, "Bob, we just won a game of rugby without the ball. Work that one out . . ." Keith James had a nightmare for us at outside-half. Swansea and Llanelli had backs with pace. We never had that. At home to Cardiff in the cup once, they won four balls all match and scored four tries, every one of them by Gerald Davies.

'Everyone hated Pontypool in those days, especially Llanelli and certain sections of the press. Llanelli would win the cup, as they often did then, and they'd be the best club team in the world on the basis of winning six cup finals. Pontypool won near as damn it 50 games for the championship and never got the accolades which Llanelli did. Neither did many of the players.

'Kevin Moseley, another second-row forward from the club who played for Wales, is one example. He was sent off for allegedly stamping on a Frenchman and they banned him for thirty-two weeks. Thirty-two weeks! I think that was the longest ban slapped on any player at that time, apart from for eye-gouging. If he'd been playing for some club other than Pontypool, you wonder whether he would have got the same suspension.

'David Bishop is another example of a player whose reputation went before him. He was, by any standards, a fantastic, unbelievable rugby player and he only got one cap. That was the most unbelievable bit of all.'

Rarely can Welsh rugby have been viewed as a more formidable force on the playing fields of the world than on that first Saturday in March 1976. Asked to identify the next peak of excellence as the country began celebrating its status as the best in Europe, Davies said, without a trace of bombast, 'Three Grand Slams in a row.'

It would be the last interview he gave as captain of Wales.

8

BOOZING LIONS

No history of the twentieth century can ever be complete without reference to the earth-shattering news of 16 August 1977 of the passing of the rocker in the blue suede shoes. By a strange quirk of fate, it happened to be the day the Pontypool front row lined up en masse for the Lions in an international match against Fiji in Suva after a four-month journey around New Zealand overflowing with misery from start to finish.

Charlie Faulkner and Bobby Windsor had made it all the way from their local steelworks team into first-class rugby at Pontypool, via Cross Keys, on to the international arena with Wales and now, in tandem with their junior partner, Graham Price, to the global role of representing the best of the British Isles. An event later that same day revolving round a place on the far side of the globe called Graceland had a shrinking effect on the column inches generated back home by the Viet-Gwent for an achievement still unique in the annals of the world's most famous touring rugby team.

Elvis Presley's death, announced that afternoon at 3.30 p.m. Central Standard Time from the Baptist Memorial Hospital in Memphis, overshadowed everything else on the planet, as the Lions discovered when they eventually landed home after touching down in what seemed like every European capital because of a baggage handlers' strike at Heathrow. While they had been away, Britain had basked in a sporting summer par excellence.

Some, like Virginia Wade, Lester Piggott and Geoffrey Boycott, rolled the years back as if they had never been away. Wade marked the Queen's silver jubilee by winning the women's singles title at Wimbledon; Piggott, who had won his first Derby in 1954, guided The Minstrel round Epsom Downs to win by a neck and Boycott ended three years of self-imposed exile from Test cricket by making his hundredth hundred against Australia at Headingley.

Tom Watson and Jack Nicklaus went head to head in the last round of the Open golf championship at Royal Turnberry, the famous 'Duel in the Sun', which the younger American won. Elsewhere, new stars took their places in the firmament, headed by a cricketing phenomenon, Ian Botham, and a brash New York kid with a caustic line in on-court dialogue, John McEnroe.

A third successive series win for the Lions would have fitted perfectly into fond memories of a British summer of blue skies. One of the wettest and coldest New Zealand winters on record turned the 26-match tour into a prolonged test of endurance. The Lions spent 94 days criss-crossing both islands and swore that it rained on at least 91 of them.

Torrents of the stuff descended day after day as if following the Lions around wherever they happened to hang their hat. In Westport, for example, the deluge forced both teams to change in their respective hotels, and the sight of whole teams caked in mud told a story of paddy fields and paddies, as in the rows and wrangles which the tourists, to some extent, brought upon themselves with their management's almost contemptuous attitude towards public relations.

Something had to go badly wrong for the Lions to lose the series. They were pulverising the All Blacks in the scrums to such an extent that their opponents resorted to the ultimate admission of their own inadequacy: they reduced their scrum to a front row and nothing else, making a mockery of a fundamental element of the game. And still the Lions contrived to finish second best. They paid a heavy price for their carelessness, never more so than in the first of the four Tests.

They ought to have been able to overcome the considerable handicap of losing a number of senior players who would have formed the high command of the tour. Mervyn Davies, the captain-designate as soon as he had led Wales to the Grand Slam the previous year, had been cruelly removed by a brain haemorrhage. The next in line, Roger Uttley, the iron-willed English flanker who had been a permanent member of the Test back row in South Africa alongside Davies, damaged his back badly enough to be declared another non-starter.

Phil Bennett took the captaincy and has long accepted that decision to have been arguably the worst of an otherwise glittering career. 'I should never have accepted the captaincy,' he said in his autobiography. 'I have no desire to appear ungracious, ungrateful or play the role of the unlikely hero but I've spent many a wistful hour thinking of what could have been achieved had the leadership gone to someone far better equipped than I . . .'

His hand was further weakened by the unavailability of Gareth Edwards, J.P.R. Williams and Gerald Davies, who had played starring roles in South Africa and, in Davies' case, in New Zealand in 1971. If appointing Bennett was a mistake, then it was widely accepted that the selectors had made another by picking a few too many Welshmen, despite the absence of the aforementioned trio.

The tour was managed by George Burrell, a Scot from Galashiels who was wounded at Normandy in 1944 while serving with the King's Own Scottish Borderers. He recovered to play four times for Scotland at full-back in 1950–51, then completed a rare double by refereeing two Tests eight years later.

John Dawes, the most astute of captains when the Lions had won their only series in New Zealand six years earlier, had won everything there was to win as a player and now he was hoping to repeat the feat as a coach. His feuding with journalists during the tour, including old teammates like Mervyn Davies, who was there for a national newspaper, contributed to a sour atmosphere.

Burrell, 'Dod' to his friends, showed his sensitivity to comparison with the '71 Lions tour on one bizarre occasion, as outlined by Fran Cotton, when the manager saw a player reading a magazine about the previous Kiwi tour. According to Cotton, whose captaincy credentials were clearly not considered good enough, Burrell 'snarled, "Put that bloody thing away." Carwyn James, the wonderfully successful coach of the previous tour, was shunned and Dawes asked his friend and fellow tourist of 1971, Mervyn Davies, to leave the room where we were having our farewell party.'

Another version of the same incident, referring to Burrell giving the Welsh lock forward Allan Martin a flea in his ear for inviting Davies to the reception, revealed a disturbing depth of hostility in the sour relationships between the Lions and some fellow travellers. What made it worse was that Davies and Dawes had spent years together playing for club and country.

'It was the last night of the tour and I was invited to attend the official closing function by the New Zealand RFU,' Davies said in his autobiography *In Strength and Shadow*. 'I only had minimal contact with the team up to that point . . . But many of them were my mates and by the end of the tour I thought it wouldn't matter who I spoke to. I remember bumping into Derek Quinnell and Bill Beaumont, and Bill warning me that they – the players – weren't allowed to speak to me. These men were my friends and I couldn't understand what they were referring to, until they said that Burrell had decreed there would be no contact with the press. But, I insisted, I wasn't press.

'What hurt me most was that it was left to John Dawes – my dear friend and mentor – to ask me to leave the function. I told John that I was the guest of the NZRFU and not there in any press capacity. A few choice words passed between us and I took my leave . . . The man I admired most in rugby had humiliated me. I was heartbroken when I left.'

What a shocking state of affairs. Cotton was far from enamoured of Dawes the coach, especially in relation to the first Test. 'Dawes succeeded in burning-out the Test team, who went on to lose 16–12 in a strange game in which the Lions were lethargic, uncompetitive and totally lacking in energy and zest,' Cotton remembered in his autobiography. 'It was an abysmal performance which in no way reflected the overall talent within the party. Dawes was a complex man. Although he usually seemed arrogant and self-assured, he bitterly resented criticism. He regarded all criticism either of himself or players by the British press as disloyalty and at one stage instructed the team to stay away from all journalists. This only served to place the team under unnecessary pressure.

'It all smacked of a man who had been enormously successful as a player and coach but had failed to keep his feet on the ground. In one of their frequent heated exchanges, conducted through the media, Jack Gleeson, the All Blacks coach, observed, "Perhaps John has not lost enough." I am inclined to agree.

'My biggest disappointment with Dawes was his coaching, particularly with the three-quarters, who started brilliantly but by the end of the tour it was an event if they managed to pass the ball down the line without dropping it.'

As if the foul weather and internal disenchantment were not bad enough, the Lions had to contend with the inevitable attempts by sections of the Kiwi press to demoralise the tourists by indulging in the traditional pastime of playing some dirty tricks. It was thus that Wanda from Wanganui, a game girl by all accounts, gave the trip a little titillation via the front page of a weekly newspaper which specialised in a bit of scandal, the *New Zealand Truth*.

Under a headline proclaiming the Lions to be 'lousy lovers', based on a claim that she had slept with four of them, the energetic Wanda issued a suitably damning verdict: 'I found them boring, self-centred, ruthless, always on the make and anything but exciting bedmates.' Dawes' dismissal of it as 'all lies and invention' failed to prevent the story being given enough legs to carry it back to Britain, which ensured that the players would be fielding calls from wives and girlfriends.

Whatever the truth of *Truth*, there was an overt hostility towards the Lions which made them wonder, as amateur players, whether the trip, taking a quarter of a year away from their families and their work, was worth the candle. Dawes, taken aback at the general unfriendliness shown towards the British and Irish players, made a revealing comment in Christchurch after the Lions had won the second Test: 'If there was a DC-10 leaving here for London tomorrow, the whole of my team would choose to be on it.'

How different it had all been in the first half of the season leading up to the tour and the Lions' defence of their title as the best international team on the rugby planet. For Bobby Windsor, busting a gut as usual every Saturday, and sometimes every Wednesday too, in defence of his title as the best hooker in Europe, certainly, if not further afield, it began with a letter dropping onto the mat of his council house in Bettws, dated 25 November 1976. In the quaint ways of the Establishment, the squad was referred to not as the Lions but by their long-winded title, the British Isles Rugby Union Team. At a quick glance, the addressee could have been forgiven for wondering if the Lions were changing direction and heading for Beirut. It read:

> To all those who may be contenders for places on the B.I.R.U.T. to New Zealand 1977.
>
> Dear Bobby,
> May we introduce ourselves as the management of the 'Lions' team to tour New Zealand during 1977. George Burrell, chairman of the Scottish Rugby Union selectors, and John Dawes, coach of the Welsh international team.

It gives us great pleasure to write to you as a leading player with the potential to take part in this tour. For the first time ever we will go abroad as a winning side following the magnificent efforts of the "71 Lions' in New Zealand and the "74 Lions' in South Africa. It is hard to reach the top but a lot harder to stay there. This saying will never be truer than in May to August next year when all the fitness, skill and character we can muster will be required.

New Zealand Rugby Footballers by nature hate to be beaten, especially on their home grounds and by the 'Lions', facts they have not been allowed to forget by their supporters. To try to remedy this there have been several short tours in New Zealand culminating in their tour of South Africa. Clearly they intend to be well prepared for the "77 Lions'!!

There it is then. The Committee and Management will provide the planning and preparation. YOU THE PLAYERS WILL PROVIDE THE SKILL AND COMMITMENT TO WIN THE GAMES.

We hope you will be with us.

Good Luck.

Yours sincerely,

George Burrell, John Dawes.

'In South Africa, we had beautiful weather, loads of places to visit and the Lions were lauded wherever we went,' Windsor says. 'The world was our oyster. In New Zealand, we had non-stop rain, very few places to visit and there was a hostility towards the Lions which we found hard to understand. It was a shambles.

'We were so well looked after in South Africa that if we wanted an extra bottle of wine with a meal, we got it without any questions being asked. In New Zealand, we were down to a choice of chicken or fish and one bottle of wine between four. Russ Thomas, our liaison officer, who later became president of the New Zealand Rugby Union, kept putting the Lions down all the time. Whether he didn't like the job or he didn't like us, I wasn't too sure, but we didn't like his attitude.

'He would talk down to us and tell us what we could have and what we couldn't have. The most disappointing part of it all was that our management sat around and allowed him to do it. We'd go to restaurants, sit in a roped-off area and when you asked for a steak because you were

Victor Windsor before his
son's birth in 1946.

Little Robert and big sister Sally.

Bobby's parents, Connie and Victor, with Sally.

Whitehead's Steelworks RFC, *circa* 1965, with two future British Lions in the middle row: Charlie Faulkner, second from left, and Bobby Windsor, second from right.

Bobby and Judi on their wedding day, September 1964.

The Iron Duke, forged in the furnace of his workplace.

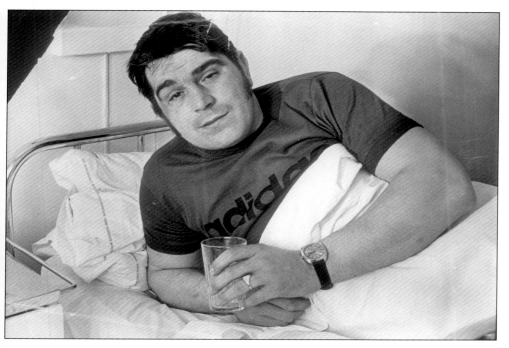

Day one of the greatest Lions tour of all, in his sickbed in a Johannesburg hospital, May 1974. How the Springboks wished they could have kept him there . . .

The lull before the storm: watching a club match before the tour began. From left, pipe-puffing Willie John McBride, Ian McLauchlan, Windsor, Tony Neary and Gareth Edwards.

The Front Row Union, South Africa 1974. From left, Mike Burton,
Ian 'Mighty Mouse' McLauchlan, Windsor and Fran Cotton.

They'd call them Wags these days, but nobody did back then. The wives and girlfriends
behind the invincible 1974 tour, with Judi Windsor on the far left of the top row. Mike
Gibson and Willie John McBride are the Lions among the Lionesses.

Ready to smash into England at Cardiff Arms Park, 5 March 1977. Clive Burgess, strangely omitted from the Lions tour later that year, is on hand. England captain Roger Uttley, centre with the sideboards, and a grounded Fran Cotton fear the worst.

Heroes and worshippers. The ball-boys watching the Wales team pose for the camera before their victory over England in Cardiff on 15 February 1975 include a 17-year-old Terry Holmes, fifth from left, and, third from left, Steve O'Donoghue, who would play for Pontypool and go into business with Windsor.

An hour or so later, Windsor leads the charge against the old enemy with Allan Martin and Trevor Evans in support.

Christmas at the Windsors': Santa Claus, Joanne, Mandy and the springbok skins covering the holes in the carpet.

The most famous front row in rugby history – the Viet-Gwent in their natural habitat at Pontypool Park at the height of their fame.

And as they are now.

Windsor using his speed to support Scotland's Andy Irvine
during the ill-fated Lions tour of New Zealand in 1977.

Windsor overcoming his fear of flying, somewhere in the clouds above New Zealand,
backed by his room-mate Moss Keane. Note that the legendary Irishman is
equipped with the bare essentials for the trip – cigarette and cans of beer.

Windsor, Geoff Wheel and referee Quittenton watch Terry Holmes swoop during the most controversial of Wales matches, against New Zealand at the Arms Park on 11 November 1978. Wales led 12–10 only for the man in black on the right, Andy Haden, to rob them with his notorious dive from a lineout.
(Picture by kind courtesy of the *South Wales Argus*)

The Iron Duke with a touch of silver, shortly before his 64th birthday, among the palm trees at the marina close to his home in Majorca. (Picture by kind courtesy of Alan Walter, *Daily Mail*)

fed up with chicken or fish, they'd say, "You can't have that because that's *à la carte*."

'After a while, the weather got everyone down. The rain turned most of the training grounds into swamps and you'd come off plastered in mud from head to toe.

'I was asked to share a room with Moss Keane and Willie Duggan, the idea being that I would somehow be in charge of them. They'd come back to the hotel room after training, chuck their kit in the corner and put it back on the next morning. After a couple of days, their gear was so caked in mud that it was walking around on its own.

'A typical day with Moss and Willie had to be experienced to be believed. One of my toughest tasks of the day was always the first – to wake them up for training at about 8.15 to be on the bus one hour later. I'd wake them up with a cup of tea. Willie would open his eyes, look at you and the first movement he made wasn't to get out of bed but to light a fag. When they got up, they put their kit on, which, after a couple of days unwashed, was standing up on its own by the wall.

'Out they'd go for training. When they came back, they changed out of their kit and went off to find the roughest part of whatever town we happened to be staying in which, in this case, was Invercargill, about as close to the bottom of the world that you can get short of the South Pole. Then they'd find the roughest bar and start drinking with the locals.

'They missed a team meeting one day and John Dawes said to me, "Where are they?"

'I said, "Who are you talking about?"

'He said, "You know. Your Irish room-mates. Now, why aren't they here?"

'I said, "Oh, Mossie and Willie. I think they've gone out just to have a look around, like."

'He said, "There'll be another team meeting tonight and they'll be in trouble if they're not there. Find them. And if you've got to get a taxi, charge it to the Lions."

'I backed my hunch and headed to the docks. I looked in a couple of joints and thought to myself that I wouldn't fancy being stuck down here on my own. All the pubs were like old betting shops – a big room, a shelf round the wall, no tables or chairs, just a bar. And that's where I found them, having a great time.

'"Come on, Bob," they said. "Have a pint."

'I told them, "Hey, we've got a team meeting at six o'clock. You've already missed one."

'I could see they were in a "happy" state, which didn't make getting them out of the pub any easier. "Now," I told them, "listen to me. When you get to the meeting, just sit there, shut up, listen and at the end walk out. Whatever you do, do *not* say anything, otherwise they'll know you're pissed up."

'Fair dos, they did as they were told. They got away with it. Mossie was a big mischievous fella. The more he smiled, the more you knew that he was up to something. They went straight back to the pub downtown, back on the toot with their Maori friends.

'Mossie and Willie went out of their way to stick up for the underdog. When we went to official receptions given by the New Zealand government, they'd give their hosts a hard time and slag them off for the way the white man had treated the Maoris. They'd be on about the Maoris having had their land stolen and would it not be a good idea to give it back to them. They were unique.

'They gave everything they had in the games and on the training ground and enjoyed themselves off it. Mossie could take a drink, for sure, and when he had a few beers in him you couldn't be sure what he would be up to. J.J. in particular was wary of Mossie and, as it turned out, he had good reason to be.

'On one of the few days when it didn't rain, we were standing around a swimming pool. J.J. was there, immaculately turned out as usual. Mossie couldn't resist the temptation to push J.J. into the pool. Mossie then turned the drama into a crisis by jumping into the water himself, a daft thing to do for someone who couldn't swim.

'As he's thrashing about, he catches hold of J.J. and accidentally pulls him under. A few of us had to jump in and rescue them both, first making sure that J.J. could get out by taking Mossie away from him, otherwise the pair of them might have drowned. J.J. got out looking like a drowned rat and shouting a few obscenities. The two words which came over loud and clear were "Irish" and "bastard". My trouble was that the management, for some reason, held me responsible for them.

'Meanwhile, at training, everyone would be wearing something different, and that, to me, didn't feel like the Lions. It was a shambles from the start. New Zealand teams specialised in a rucking game, and more power to their elbow, because I've always believed in that as a vital part of rugby football. As a result, our jerseys often got ripped and they weren't being replaced or properly repaired.

'At one stage, a few of us turned round to Dod and said, "Stuff this. We're supposed to be representing our countries here and we're going out looking like a bunch of gyppos." Maybe Burrell wanted to be the first manager to come back from a Lions tour and say, "I only spent sixpence."

'If Mervyn Davies had been there as captain, none of these problems would have arisen because he would have nipped them in the bud by imposing a discipline from the start. Merv would have been every bit as good a captain as Willie John had been three years before.

'Benny and I have been butties most of our lives, but Phil was a quiet, modest sort of bloke who never sought conflict. Burrell was an abrasive Scot who liked his drop of whisky and Benny was never going to stand up to him. The management tended to be on the pop too much. I can only compare it with the previous tour. You might see them having a drink on a Saturday night, but you never saw them having a drink during the week. If they went to their rooms and had a drink there, that would have been clever. To be fair, the weather was so awful in New Zealand that you couldn't even go for a walk, so it was very hard to ease the boredom.

'The easiest way of doing that was to go to the bar. There were some who drank too much and I will admit that, during the second half of the tour, I was one of them. There were players on that tour who didn't want to be in the Test team, but I did, desperately. I was in for the first Test, which we lost, out for the second, which we won, and I knew from that day on that I wasn't going to get back in.

'I went out for a few nights on the pop. You had to use your head and make sure you didn't come in blind drunk. If there had been more discipline and control from the management, there would have been less drinking. The tour was a cock-up. We were not blameless, but it all stemmed from the top.

'Dawes made a mistake by antagonising the press, which, in turn, only heaped more pressure on the team. Reporters covering Lions tours were good lads, by and large, always willing to lob a bit into the beer kitty. I recognised that the journalists had a job to do and that their job was a damned sight easier when the team was winning, but Sid seemed to go out of his way to make enemies of them.

'If you have any brains, you use the press in the way they use you, and you all get on together. That's the way it was done in '74. The people running that tour understood the truth of the old saying about the pen being mightier than the sword.

'Benny wasn't strong enough to deal with the management we had. He didn't get the help he should have had. Looking back, there is no doubt in my mind that Fran Cotton should have been made captain, because he would have done the best job in difficult circumstances. He would have been a strong disciplinarian, he had the utmost respect from everyone and many of the off-field things which went on would not have happened under Frannie. He would have made sure of that.

'It was such a cock-up that they hadn't thought to put someone in charge of the forwards. John Dawes would take the backs and we forwards would be told to go and do some lineouts. It was a mess and it was still a mess when we played. Early on in the tour, I went to the management and said, "You've got to put someone in charge of the forwards because the way it is nobody knows what they're supposed to be doing. Designate one man and if we're doing the wrong thing, then at least we're all doing the same thing."

'They said, "Well, who do you think we should put in charge?"

'I said, "Terry Cobner has captained Pontypool for ten years. He has the respect of the players and I think he's the best man for the job." From then on, Cob ran the forwards. He did a good job, as was shown by the fact that we battered just about every New Zealand team all over the park in the scrums. We pushed the Junior All Blacks back and kept pushing them until we'd shunted them back over a distance of 30 yards. They were rubbish. The great shame was that our backs got bogged down in the atrocious weather.

'The Lions had bogged themselves down in other areas too, before we had left London. To start with, there were too many Welsh boys on the trip. It was nothing unusual for the Welsh to get homesick, but on this tour more of them did than usual. I am sure the players from the other countries looked at the large number of Welsh players, a Welsh coach and a Welsh captain and assumed that Test selection would be a carve-up.

'Only one member of the Welsh team failed to make that Lions tour, the late Clive "Budgie" Burgess from Ebbw Vale. They took Trevor Evans of Swansea instead and I don't know whether that was because

Budgie had had a barney with Dawes during the Five Nations. We had a meeting one day and Budgie expressed his complete disagreement with something Dawes had said about a certain aspect of play.

'I said to Clive afterwards, "Shut up, Budgie. He's picking the Lions squad in a little while. Don't be so daft and talk yourself out of it."

'I don't know whether that was a coincidence or not, but it makes you wonder. Why leave the man who has played in the back row all season at home and take his substitute instead?

'The conditions in New Zealand would have suited Budgie down to the ground. He was known as the dog on the floor who would snaffle the loose ball. He took so much stick from stray boots and what have you that he had a face like Frankenstein. Nothing against Trevor, who was a very good player in his own right, but Budgie was a warrior and that was what we needed.

'Despite his absence, we won all the matches in the run-up to the first Test, apart from the last one, when the midweek team lost to New Zealand Universities. My concern was to keep my Test place, to start where I'd left off in South Africa three years before and prove I was a better man for the job than Peter Wheeler of England.

'I was the better scrummager. That was my forte. My biggest concern was over the trouble I continued to get from the calf muscle I'd damaged back home, but I overcame that to get the nod for the first Test team at Wellington. We lost it because of one of the most ridiculous tries the Lions could have conceded anywhere.

'They took a penalty shot at goal and missed. We had a couple of fellas behind the posts who stood looking at the ball. Nobody caught it. The ball dropped to the ground and one of their props, Brad Johnstone, fell on it for the try. How stupid was that? The conversion put the All Blacks ahead at 10–9, Phil Bennett put us back in front with another penalty and we had the win all but wrapped up when we threw it all away.

'There can only have been seconds left on the clock when the Lions tore the Blacks to shreds. A double break put Trevor Evans clear with three men outside him and two New Zealanders to beat. Draw, pass, draw, pass, the Blacks are skinned and we're in for the try to clinch the game. Instead, Grant Batty, their fastest back, made the interception and ran the length of the pitch without a cat in hell's chance of anyone catching him.

'It was a classic example of the 12-point try, or 14-pointer under today's scoring. We'd gone into the match with the double disadvantage of being without Gordon Brown and Fran Cotton. Both were injured and we missed them, but we were more certain than ever that we had the beating of the All Blacks.

'Ironically, both were back for the rest of the series and I was out on my ear. I went into the team room at our hotel in Christchurch, where the side for the second Test was being announced, thinking I'd done enough to keep my place. They called out the names and mine wasn't there. I was out. F**k me. What a bombshell.

'What hit me like a bullet was that Terry Cobner was in charge of the forwards. He and I had been big butties. We'd been through the mill together, but he hadn't given me even the vaguest inkling that I was about to be dropped. It would still have been a savage blow, but he could have eased it a bit if only he'd have come to me beforehand and said, "Bob, this is a tough selection. Sorry, but you're out."

'At least I would have been prepared. As soon as the team was read out, I went straight to Peter Wheeler, shook him by the hand and congratulated him. That done, I went straight back to my room in a foul mood. I could have kicked the wardrobe because I was furious. Above all, I felt terribly let down by my club captain.

'Cob did come to the room to try and explain, but I was in no mood to listen. I told him straight, "F**k off. Keep away from me."

'I was the one who'd proposed that he should take charge of the forwards at the start of the tour and there he was, dumping me at the first opportunity. That was how it appeared to me. In my anger, I did not mean to decry the selection of a great player and a good friend, Peter Wheeler.

'Later, after the tour had finished, I had a word with Phil Bennett as captain. I said, "When you picked the team for that second Lions Test in Christchurch, what were the reasons for dropping me?"

'He said: "Cob picked the forwards. He had the pack he wanted."

'That only made me feel worse. Until then, I thought there was always the chance that Cob had wanted me in the side but that he had been outvoted by the other selectors.'

Bennett acknowledges Cobner's part in the agonising process that led to Windsor's omission. 'It was a massive, massive decision,' Bennett says. 'I remember thinking at the time, how can you drop Bobby Windsor? On the other hand, Peter Wheeler was playing like a man possessed. He was incredible. I had so much respect for Bobby. I also had the utmost respect for Peter. But a choice had to be made. There was a long debate. I can't recall the details because it was so long ago, but Terry, because of his special role with the forwards, would certainly have had a big say in the selection of the pack.'

Even after more than 30 years, the subject still rankles with Windsor. 'The whole business about not forewarning me stank from that day on and it still stinks,' he says. 'I accept in hindsight that I was wrong because, whatever you may think, the team is more important than anyone in it.

'What I couldn't get over was the fact that Cob and I had been old friends playing for the same club, the same country and now the same Lions. If the roles had been reversed and I had to choose between Cobner and Tony Neary in the back row, I'd have picked Cob. Under no circumstance would I have left him out the way he left me out.

'In saying that, I know I am being unfair to Peter Wheeler. It was such a sore point with me for so long that it began to fester and a lot of things went through my mind. Among other things, I remembered back to 1974, shortly before the Lions were named for South Africa.

'We'd played somewhere across the border on the Saturday before the party was announced. In the bus on the way back to Pontypool, Cob and I said to each other, "If you get in and I don't, or the other way round or neither of us get in, we're up at the club on Monday night. Right-o, that's what we're doing. See you then."

'I walked into the club at the appointed time. Pross was there with about half a dozen committee men. Nobody else. All I got from Pross was, "All right, Bob? Aye, bloody shame about Cob, isn't it?" Then he said, "Well done, Bob, you're on it." It came across as an afterthought and Pross says he regrets that to this day. I felt as though I'd been kicked in the nuts, but then I had to take into account the special father–son relationship which existed between the coach and captain, a relationship which I hope I still have with Pross.

'The Pontypool people had a great love for Cob, and rightly so, because of the fantastic job he did captaining the club for ten years. I understood their disappointment for him. When Judi died, I could not have wished for a better friend than him. As for my being dropped from the Test team, we've never discussed it.

'It was the decision which finished me for good as far as the Lions Test team was concerned. Once they had won in Christchurch and squared the series, I knew there would be no way back. J.J. Williams got the only try and a can of beer which someone in the crowd threw at him.

'There was enough aggro on the pitch without anyone needing to be hit by a beer can. The match was violent even by my standards, really violent. As per normal, Graham Price needed stitches in his head after being caught in the loose and given a few ruckings. There was the odd brawl, but the Lions really got stuck into them that day and thoroughly deserved the win.

'They were bound to pick the same team for the next Test. I was back in action the following Wednesday for what felt like a Test match, against the Maoris before 52,000 people at Eden Park. The selection of Sid Going at scrum-half and Tane Norton at hooker made it an even tougher assignment. We were in trouble, losing 19–6, when Mike Gibson pulled us through, and it ended 22–19.

'Unfortunately, my old room-mate Willie Duggan got his jaw smashed by one of the Maori back row. In the Test the previous weekend, Willie had been given such a trampling that his back was black and blue. The Lions needed him because injuries had limited their options at number 8, so they patched him up as best they could by taping a half-inch-thick sponge down his back.

'I was about to throw the ball into a lineout. There was a lot of jockeying for position and that can be a fair indication that someone is going to get belted. I told Moss Keane and the rest of the boys to be careful. I threw the ball, Willie went up for it and the bloke standing opposite him (Maori number 8 Murray West) smacked him straight in the chops. Willie went down like a barrel of Guinness.

'We thought he'd fractured the jaw, what with the blood coming out of his mouth and the medics all around him. Mossie, ever the wit, leant over him and said, as only he could, "Look on the bright side, Willie. At least you didn't hurt your back."

'Mike Gibson should have been straight into the Test team on the strength of what he did in the Maori match. Gibson is one of the best players I have ever seen, as an outside-half or a centre. He was great whatever his position and he would have been of tremendous help to Benny at a time when Phil needed help. He was at a loss. He didn't have Gareth on one side and he didn't have Ray Gravell on the other.

'Instead, the selectors went with Steve Fenwick and David Burcher as the centres. Good players, but not the fastest. When you had forwards winning so much ball, Gibbo would have been the perfect rapier to put the Blacks to the sword.'

Gibson, by common consent the most complete back to emerge in the British Isles during the amateur era, found himself caught in the crossfire between Burrell and Dawes on one side and members of Her Majesty's press on the other. Terry McLean, the leading Kiwi rugby journalist of his or any other generation, made the astounding claim that the Lions accused Gibson of 'feeding the enemy' because his wife, Moyra, stayed at the McLean family home.

'Furious rows blazed between the press, especially the British contingent, and Burrell and Dawes,' McLean wrote. 'Duels would once have been fought as a result of Dawes accusing John Reason of the *Daily Telegraph* and Clem Thomas of *The Observer* of using Gibson as a spy.'

When the Lions made their final flight from the South Island to the North and on to the last lap of their journey, Anthony George Faulkner was waiting to climb on board after making the long haul from Newport to Auckland as the replacement for his injured compatriot Clive Williams. The oldest Lion in captivity, at estimates which started at 36, Faulkner barely had time to get his feet under the table before he was straight down to business, reuniting the Pontypool front row in the red of the Lions against a combined Thames Valley–Counties team at Pukekohe on 3 August 1977.

Before making their choice between Faulkner and the redoubtable Scottish Lion Ian McLauchlan, the Lions management asked Windsor for his expert opinion. 'They called me to a meeting and explained that the two props on standby were Charlie and the Mouse,' Windsor says. 'I did as I thought Terry Cobner would have done with the choice of the Test hooker. I chose Charlie, my buttie since we were kids.

'There was more to it than pure sentiment. I justified my choice to the management by telling them, "The Mouse has been on two successful Lions tours and done it all, a winner in New Zealand and in South Africa. He has nothing left to prove. Charlie has been dreaming of an opportunity like this for most of his life and if you pick him, he will die for the cause."

'I left the meeting. Shortly afterwards, Phil Bennett came out and gave the thumbs up. Straight away, I rang Charlie. His wife, Jill, answered the phone and said he was away on a coaching course in Aberystwyth. So

I said, "Jill, get hold of him quickly and tell him, otherwise they'll pick someone else." That reminds me, those phone calls I made to him cost 60 New Zealand dollars and Charlie's never repaid me for them.

'Three of us went to the airport to meet him. The biggest thing about Charlie was always his age. Nobody really knew how old he was and whenever people asked me I'd always plead ignorance, although I did have a fair idea. When the Lions booked your flight in those days, the last thing they considered was the players' comfort or the most direct journey.

'Like everyone else, Charlie was stuck in economy and he had to make several stops. He'd been travelling for nearly 30 hours and when he walked out of the airport I thought he looked 90, and I'm not kidding. He said he was starving, so we sat him down in the cafeteria and got him a cup of tea.

'The waitress came over and Charlie ordered bacon, egg and chips. She said, "I'm sorry, we haven't got any bacon."

'Charlie said, "You've got five million sheep in this country and you're telling me you don't have any bacon?"

'We took him straight to the hotel and Dawes made him train straight away. He thought that was funny. Charlie was knackered, but he went training with his usual enthusiasm because he was thrilled to be there. I thought it was totally unfair of Dawes. But it was brilliant to have Charlie there. We'd been butties since we'd played together for Whitehead's steelworks when I was 16 and here we were, side by side, packing down for the Lions.

'He was chuffed to bits and so was I. It was great for Charlie and great for Pontypool – four Lions from the club on the same tour – and that was marvellous for Pross. The first thing Charlie said when they gave him the Lions blazer was, "Where's my badge?" He got his badge.'

Andy Dalton, in the throes of an apprenticeship which would take him all the way to the captaincy of New Zealand, led the locals as arguably the country's best young hooker. Windsor went out the night before the match for what turned into a marathon session, content in the knowledge that his services were not required the following afternoon.

'We got in at half past five that morning,' he says. 'Then Phil Bennett got woken up at nine o'clock to be told that he was playing because John Bevan had been taken ill. They woke me up about half an hour later to say I was playing because Peter Wheeler had gone down with flu. All I can say is that it was just as well that the ref didn't have a breathalyser. If I'd been in a car, they'd have asked me to blow in the bag.

'Dalton reckoned that every time he put his head in the scrum it smelt like a brewery. I was not in the best of shape. I'd become a bit of a rebel by then because I'd failed in my big objective, to play in all four Tests. They nearly caught me coming in late one other night and next morning Dod Burrell called a team meeting. He said, "It's not the enemy without we've got to be wary of, it's the enemy within." I knew what he was talking about, and, more to the point, who he was talking about.

'We'd lost the third Test and gone 2–1 down. Again, it was hard to understand why we'd lost. We'd taken numerous strikes against the head, we'd dominated possession and the backs did very little with it. In the last Test, the All Blacks gave up all pretence of trying to compete in the scrum by putting only their front row in and taking the other five out. How embarrassing was that for New Zealand? Under the current laws, you must have a minimum of five forwards to constitute a scrum.

'When they just put three in, I thought they were bound to be penalised for it on the assumption that it was illegal. If it wasn't, it should have been, but they got away with it just as they got away with a lot from the New Zealand referees. It would have been only fair if we'd won that final Test and shared the series. That was the very least we deserved and to lose the last one by a single point, 10–9, was heartbreaking.

'New Zealand isn't a bundle of laughs at the best of times, but we still had our moments, most of them when the rain stopped, which wasn't often. In Hamilton before the Waikato match, we were guests at a race meeting where every race was named after a Lion – the J.P.R. Hurdle, the Phil Bennett Sprint and so on.

'A racehorse trainer came up to me before the first race and asked me to put 300 dollars on this horse. Well, you know what they say about a nod being as good as a wink to a blind horse. I put his money on and Benny and I invested a few of our own dollars on an each-way bet. The horse finished third at 40–1 and we cleaned up.

'The trainer won three grand, Benny and I had a few hundred each. I put my money behind the bar for an all-night drinking session. The Harvey Wallbangers went round and round, but I don't seem to remember Phil lobbing in much of his winnings. Another of the few laughs the boys had on that tour was also at my expense.

'For some reason which I never understood, I had a white quiff of hair above my forehead. There was a popular television programme of the time called *The Mallen Streak*, based on a novel by Catherine Cookson, and the main character in it had a similar piece of white in his black hair. People used to say to me, "Oh, I see you've copied so-and-so on the television," which annoyed me because I'd done nothing of the sort.

'The first time I had noticed it was when we had that scary incident with the plane at Port Elizabeth during the previous Lions tour. With the fear I felt that day, it was a wonder every hair in my head didn't turn white instead of just a few at the front. By the time we got to New Zealand, it was bothering me to the point where I started trying to blacken it out.

'I put some lacquer stuff on with a toothbrush, but what I didn't realise is that you had to keep putting it on. Anyway, early in the tour, I was sitting having breakfast with Graham Price, who doesn't miss a trick. He said, "Your hair's gone pink."

'I said, "What the f**k do you mean, it's gone pink?"

'"Pink. Your hair is pink."

'I finished breakfast in a hurry and took a look in the mirror. He was right. It had gone pink. It looked like I was the first punk rocker to play for the Lions. It would have been all right if I'd kept painting it black, except there wasn't much point what with it pissing down every day in New Zealand. There was only one thing for it. I went straight out to the nearest barber's and had a crew cut. Pricey, of course, had told everyone else by the time I got back, so it took a bit of living down.

'For every good day on the trip there were too many bad ones. I didn't enjoy the tour, for two reasons: I wanted to play in the Test team and we lost the series. When we flew out of Auckland for home, everyone cheered because we'd been so cheesed off for so long. All of a sudden, there was this great sense of relief.

'We were so happy to be leaving. That outburst of joy at getting out of New Zealand was the saddest comment of all, because Lions tours were meant to be enjoyed and the spontaneous reaction showed how glad everyone was to be out of there. It wasn't just the weather or the Test series. The people weren't all that nice either.

'The teams we played against had a strange way of showing their appreciation. They didn't even give us a lapel pin badge, which is usually the least you get. The only members of the Lions party who got badges were the captain of the day, the manager and the coach.

'We thought maybe that was because they were going to give us something really nice at the end of the tour as a thank you for coming and making them a fortune. I don't wish to sound ungrateful but when the last day of the tour arrived, they gave us a foot-long stainless steel tray with a map of New Zealand on it. Wow . . .

'Landing in Fiji, we saw something we couldn't ever remember seeing in New Zealand – sunshine. We were sitting around the pool at the hotel in Suva and there were drinks all round, even though we were playing a Test match the next day. Everyone was on the piss, including the management.

'There was too much drinking on the tour, and I include myself in that, but at least I was in good company. As duty boy on one particular day early in the tour, part of my job was to go the manager's room at half past eight in the morning to get the instructions for the day, starting with training.

'Dod Burrell said, "We'll have a wee dram to start the day off."

'I thanked him for the offer but explained that I was about to go training. Dod then said to Dawes, "Sid, you've got to stick with me," and Sid had a wee dram, though gin and tonic was his tipple, not whisky.

'The weather in Fiji was red hot for the match. I was sweating buckets, what with the heat and the booze, and I was never so glad to hear the whistle go for half-time. Steve Fenwick, always a bit of a wag, was sitting on the touchline and he could see that I was suffering from meltdown in the heat. He calls out, "Hey, Bobby," and he holds up an ice lolly. That only made me feel worse.

'Losing to Fiji just about summed up the whole f*****g trip. A tour to forget. To cap it all, there was a baggage strike at Heathrow, which meant it took us nearly 50 hours to get back. We landed and took off from so many airports that it felt like the pilot was playing a game of hopscotch.

'We were all knackered, exhausted by the long journey. Because I hadn't shaved and because I was wearing a Fijian straw hat, Judi walked straight past me. I'd grown a moustache. I hadn't seen her for over three months so now it was coochie-coochie time. She said, "You're shaving first."

While the Lions licked their wounds, the New Zealand Rugby Union counted the cash. Crowds of almost 750,000 watched the 25 matches, generating enough revenue for the hosts to make a profit of more than

2 million New Zealand dollars, which made the public antagonism towards the tourists all the harder to bear. It also made some of the Lions wonder why they had bothered in the first place to go so far for so long and end up with so little – and even less in gratitude.

9

....

EXPENSES SCANDAL

The Great Schism of 1893, as the Rugby Football Union described the breakaway of 22 northern clubs over the issue of broken-time payment, provoked a class war which lasted for a century. The secession of clubs like Wigan, St Helens and Wakefield Trinity followed their unsuccessful campaign for the right to compensate their blue-collar players for missing work on a Saturday morning.

Union amateurs played the game as a hobby, strictly for recreational purposes, as decreed by the Establishment, which meant turning a Nelsonian eye to many of the brown envelopes changing hands in South Africa and France, as well as to the overtly commercial activities of certain well-known England players shortly before the sport acknowledged the reality.

Until the custodians of the 15-a-side code plucked up the courage to end the shamateurism, which they finally got round to doing over a summer's weekend in Paris in 1995, when the International Board declared the sport 'open', league professionals were treated as outcasts. The union rule book railed against any kind of fraternisation and warned of dire consequences for anyone failing to give those tainted by a wage packet anything other than the coldest of shoulders.

In what was supposed to be a free world, the International Rugby Board, a body consisting of two delegates from each of the eight foundation countries, imposed a draconian set of measures on a worldwide basis. A union player who had committed the cardinal sin of 'going north' was not to be allowed back on the premises of his former club, nor could he hold any position in any union club after his retirement.

Ludicrously, anyone rubbing shoulders socially with one of those dastardly people who had sold his soul for a pot of northern brass was deemed to have professionalised himself, although quite how that would have stood up in a court of law is a moot point. Many were shunned like lepers as the Unions operated a rigid enforcement of an apartheid which demanded that a league 'turncoat' be treated as a social outcast.

David Watkins, the Wales and Lions fly-half of the '60s, was a classic example. In October 1967, barely twelve months after playing in the last of all four Tests for the Lions against New Zealand, his transfer from Newport to Salford rugby league club broke all records. He received an £11,000 signing-on fee plus £1,000 a year for each of the five years of his contract, and that at a time when £5,000 bought a detached house with room to swing more than a cat.

Back in South Wales on a weekend break, Watkins experienced the prejudice against league players for himself one night in the Athletic Club at the Arms Park when Hubert Johnson, the Cardiff chairman, invited him into the members' bar. Watkins remembers all too well what happened next. In *Lions of Wales*, he recalled: 'While [Hubert] was ordering me a drink, another very well-known Cardiff official, Danny Davies, was on the opposite side of the bar. He said, "I see we are drinking with professionals tonight, Hubert, are we?"

'Hubert told him straight, "If you don't want to drink with us, Danny, I suggest you go and find somewhere else."'

Watkins subsequently found the Welsh Rugby Union unforgiving to the point where they as good as slammed the door to the national stadium in his face. 'I arranged to meet a photographer at the Arms Park for some pictures for my book,' Watkins said. 'They wouldn't let me in! I was refused permission to go inside the gates by Bill Clement. It wasn't his decision. It was the WRU's decision. All the photographs had to be taken outside the main entrance.'

At least they were consistent, if nothing else. Watkins was not the only Welsh stand-off to be denied admission when hired by the BBC, in his case to be part of the commentary team for a Cardiff–Llanelli game. 'I was sent my pass to the press-box but at eleven o'clock on the morning of the match BBC Wales phoned to say that I had been refused entry to the press-box,' Watkins said. 'The BBC were sorry but they said they could not overturn the decision and had to accept it, however reluctantly.'

A similar fate befell Jonathan Davies, in that he too rapidly found he had become *persona non grata*. His last match for Wales, a shocking home defeat against Romania in December 1988, led to a national inquest on a scale which only the Welsh could muster. The protracted debate over a variety of issues, not least Davies' captaincy, was still in full swing when 'Jiffy' took refuge on Merseyside and signed for Widnes in a move which would establish him beyond argument as one of the most complete rugby players on either side of the divide.

As part of their Welsh language coverage of the Wales–England match in March 1989, BBC Wales asked the WRU to issue a pass for Davies in his role as an expert summariser. Their refusal provoked a public outcry, not least in the House of Commons, where 24 members signed a motion condemning the WRU's action.

'Apparently the place from which I was going to be interviewed was under the stand in full view of the crowd,' Davies said in his autobiography. 'David East [WRU secretary] said the request was contrary to the International Board rules on amateurism. They make it clear that there can be no promoting or fostering of non-amateur rugby. If Jonathan Davies had been commentating, he would have been promoting himself and furthering professional rugby league.

'The press box was full of players who'd professionalised themselves. Why pick on me? If I wanted to set up a stall behind the goal, with a placard saying, "Sign Here for Rugby League" and a suitcase full of tenners, they might have had a point. But all I was going to do was talk in Welsh about rugby union. Rugby league wouldn't have been mentioned.'

The archaic rules were also enforced in respect of those who had never been paid a penny for playing the game, so that they too were ostracised from the sport they had served with distinction. Even the truest of true-blue amateurs found no immunity from the crass law which branded a clutch of famous internationals professionals for the heinous crime of writing a book about their careers and daring to keep the money.

After 11 years of yeoman service for queen and country, Fran Cotton found the door slammed on him at Twickenham on his first visit there after the publication of his autobiography in March 1982. As soon as England had beaten Wales, Cotton began threading his way from the middle of the West Stand down the stairway to the home dressing-room for some back-slapping bonhomie with his former Sale teammate, business associate and new England captain Steve Smith.

The Chin had seen off some very tough hombres and survived some fearsome moments in the line of national duty, but he had never been hit by the double whammy of Air Commodore Robert Weighill bolstered by the full weight of the International Rugby Board's regulations on amateurism.

'I was in a happy mood because England wins over Wales were pretty infrequent in those days,' Cotton says. 'So straight after the match, I walked towards the dressing-room to congratulate my old mate and I got three-quarters of the way there when I was stopped by R.H.G. Weighill. He said, "What are you doing here?"

'I said, "I'm going to see my mate Smithy."'

'You are most certainly not,' Weighill told him. 'You must leave at once.'

Rather than make a scene by standing his ground, Cotton turned on his heel and walked sadly away. The cold war between the codes outlived the Berlin Wall as well as large chunks of the Soviet empire, and Cotton could always console himself with the knowledge that he was in good company, a similar fate having befallen such contemporaries as Bill Beaumont, Gareth Edwards, Barry John, J.P.R. Williams, Phil Bennett, Mervyn Davies and many more.

One of the last victims, in January 1993, was a much lesser-known player, Steve Pilgrim, Wasps' England B full-back. Fed up trying to make ends meet on a building site ('more miserable work for miserable money'), Pilgrim approached the Leeds rugby league club. They arranged for him to play in a reserve match against Wakefield Trinity under the anonymity of a nom de plume which had not stretched the imagination of whoever made it up: A.N. Other.

Unfortunately for Pilgrim, pictorial evidence of his illicit activity appeared in the *Yorkshire Post* on Monday morning. Some busybody recognised him and forwarded the cutting to the Welsh Rugby Union, who sent it on to their counterparts at Twickenham. They took one look at it and banned the hapless Pilgrim for life, reducing it to twelve months on appeal.

As for expenses, woe betide anyone claiming a cent more than he was entitled to. Cliff Morgan travelled to his debut for Wales, against Ireland in 1951, by double-decker bus from his native Rhondda, and when asked for his expenses by the secretary of the Union, Eric Evans, submitted a claim for the return travel from Trebanog to Cardiff of five shillings, or twenty-five pence.

Evans, according to Morgan, looked up the bus fares, rebuked the new outside-half and gave him four shillings and eight pence (twenty-three pence). Nothing had changed in that respect when Wales were at the height of their Grand Slam activity a quarter of a century later.

The 1976 National Squad Players' Reimbursement Claim Form as issued by the Welsh Rugby Union contained a pre-emptive strike against anyone trying to pull a fast one on mileage. Travelling expenses by car had to be based on 'precise mileage' at 5p per mile and heaven help anyone whose claim was found to be 5p more than it should have been according to the Union.

Each claim form stated: 'Where mileage allowance is claimed, departure points, destination and return points must be clearly designated, so that distances can be checked with AA figures.'

It conjures up an image of a battery of clerks armed with slide rules poring over maps at the Welsh Rugby Union offices in central Cardiff to find out which players had claimed a mile or two too many. Another note on the claim form stated: 'Where more than one player travels in the same car, only one claim for mileage will be paid.'

The first-class standard required of the players in the national cause did not extend to first-class travel. Those travelling on international duty by train had to travel second class. If they wanted to go first, they paid the difference out of their own pocket. A rigid limit was also imposed on food – £1 for lunch, 35p for tea, £1.50 for dinner, with a directive that 'such claims must be supported by receipted vouchers'.

For hotel stays on Five Nations duty in Dublin, Edinburgh, London and Paris, players were left in no doubt that they would have to foot the bill for any incidental expenses: 'Please ensure that all personal charges (telephone calls, newspapers, drinks, food, other than breakfast in bedrooms) are cleared before departure from the hotel on Sunday morning.'

On the morning of Thursday, 18 November 1976, Bobby Windsor set off in tandem with the rest of the Pontypool front row to Oxford to play for Major Stanley's XV at Iffley Road against the university as part of the Dark Blues' preparations for the Varsity match at Twickenham the following month. When the mucky stuff hit the air-conditioner over the petrol money incurred in their debut for the Major's team, all three were dragged before a court martial held by the Welsh selectors.

Bobby Windsor remembers it well. 'Nigel Starmer-Smith, who used to play for Harlequins and England, invited us to play and after the match he asked us about our expenses. John Dawes, who had just finished playing then, was there and when the subject was brought up we asked him, "What can we claim?"

'Dawes asked where we had travelled from and we said we'd come up from Pontypool. He said we'd need to buy a meal on the way home from Oxford and it was agreed that £25 would cover that and the petrol money. We thought that was fair, so the three of us filled out a form claiming £25 each.

'We heard nothing more about it until a little while later, when we went squad training with Wales and got called in by the Big Five. Keith Rowlands was chairman and he looked very stern. He said we had let down Wales, we had let down rugby union and that the Barbarians would never pick another Welshman. We looked at each other and thought, what the hell's going on here?

'Clive Rowlands then explained. "What we're on about," he said, "is that you went to Oxford to play for Major Stanley's XV and you claimed money for playing a game, which makes you professionals."

'As much as they like to call front-row forwards donkeys, we weren't that stupid. I said, "No, we did not take any money for playing. We claimed £25 for travelling up there and back and for a meal on the way home. If you check the mileage, I think you'll find that's a fair claim."

'"Ah," said Keith Rowlands, "but how did you get up there?"

'I said, "I drove there and back from Newport."

'The other two were not daft and twigged straight away. Charlie said, "I drove up on my own because I was working." And Pricey said he drove up from Pontypool.

'"Well," said Clive Rowlands, "that's fair enough. You can't argue with that. We understand that, boys, so off you go and thanks very much."

'That was the end of it, or so we thought. Obviously, we had gone up in one car. Anyway, mud sticks, and, although we didn't have a clue at the time, some of it was sticking with the Barbarians. The word was out that they wanted to pick the Pontypool front row, and to play for the Baa-Baas was always a great honour, the next best thing to an international. It never happened.

'Nobody ever told us why, officially or unofficially. I'd played several times for the Barbarians before that, but none of us was ever picked after that Major Stanley's business. We were working-class lads and the Barbarians was not a working-class club.

'If it was felt that we'd done something terribly wrong with our expenses claim for the Stanley's game, why didn't someone say, "Look, boys, you can't do that"? If they'd said that, we wouldn't have done it, but nobody said a dicky bird. The only conclusion we all came to was the obvious one: that we had been blackballed by those jolly good chaps who run the Baa-Baas.

'They have a song which goes along the lines of, "It's the way we have in the Baa-Baas and a jolly good way, too." It seemed that if you had a few bob and wore a collar and a tie you couldn't go wrong with the Baa-Baas. If you went to work on a bike in a pair of wellies, you felt they looked down on you.

'I'd been on the Easter tour of South Wales with them the previous season and I didn't like the way some of them talked down to me. Herbert Waddell, the president, always called me by my surname, which might have been the way they behaved in the public schools, but I didn't like it one bit. It was Windsor this and Windsor that. I felt like saying, "F**k you, Waddell."

'He thought he could get away with that sort of thing because he talked posh and knew the Queen. Well, I've got the same surname as her majesty, not that he ever bothered to ask me if I was related. At one stage on that Easter tour, at the Royal Hotel in Cardiff, Waddell told me to leave the bar and go to bed because we were playing Newport the next day. I said, "I'm not going to bed. I'm on tour and it's only ten o'clock," but he persisted.

'I went up to my room, packed my belongings and carried my suitcase down to the bar. I told them I was going home to sleep in my own bed. They rang me at nine the next morning to say that the other hooker, Duncan Madsen, had cried off and they said, "Bob, you'll have to play now because we haven't got anyone else."

'I said, "Don't worry about it. I'll be there and we'll beat Newport easily." We lost 43–0 and the Baa-Baas had never been stuffed as badly as that in their history.

'When one of their officials was giving out the expenses afterwards, he said to each player in turn, "All the best and thanks for coming." When he came to me, he said, "Goodbye . . ." I had a laugh then and I still laugh every time I think about it.

'I never darkened the Baa-Baas' door again. The one thing I can say, hand on heart, that I didn't miss was the golf, which had always been a tradition of the Easter tour and still is, as far as I know. Herbert

Waddell was a very keen golfer and while he may well have viewed me as a cheating so-and-so, he had me in his golf team because some joker had told him that I played off a handicap of six.

'I had never played golf in my life, although I have since learnt that anyone who plays off a handicap as low as six is a more than useful player. So we get to the first tee at the Glamorganshire Golf Club in Penarth and it comes to my turn to hit the bloody thing. I took a big swipe at it and missed.

'Waddell thought I was acting the clown. "I say, Windsor, what do you think you're doing?" he said, or words to that effect. "Stop making a fool of yourself, Windsor, and get on with it."

'I said to him, "Mr Waddell, I have never played golf. This is the first time I've ever had a club in my hands, so give me a break."

'"Come off it, Windsor. You're a six-handicapper."

'He expected big things from me, like I was some sort of Gary Player, but after a couple of hacks he got even more short-tempered. By then it must have dawned on him that one of the other lads had pulled his leg. Mike Burton was the main suspect.'

Before Windsor and the Barbarians went their separate ways, they were embroiled in another row, which would have made headline news had it ever became public knowledge. The Baa-Baas chose the Lions Test pack en bloc for a celebration match against the All Blacks at Twickenham on 30 November 1974, and the players had been invited to a reception hosted by the Prime Minister, Harold Wilson, at No. 10 Downing Street.

'Only a few months before we were being slagged off by the same Labour government for going to South Africa,' Windsor says. 'It seemed strange to us that now we were being invited as special guests. When we needed a bit of support, they didn't want to know us. Our attitude was "Stuff it and stuff them".

'All the Lions in the Baa-Baas team were unanimous. We would boycott the reception. We made our views clear to the Barbarians and in the end they begged us to go in for the sake of the Baa-Baas. They told us, "If you don't come to No. 10 with the rest of us, you will destroy the fine reputation of the Barbarian Football Club." So we relented and went in, but we were not happy, not happy at all.'

Before that season was out, Windsor would miss far more than a few putts and lose something far more important than his association with the Barbarians. Along with just about every other member of the Wales team, he missed the flight home from Paris, having lost another Grand Slam the previous afternoon.

'Charlie Faulkner dropped out of that match because of an injured shoulder and Glyn Shaw of Neath came in on the loosehead. Keith Rowlands, as chairman of the Big Five, got us together for a pre-match pep talk in Paris: "Right, boys. We're over here now – one for all and all for one. We stick together through thick and thin and we do what we have to do. We are all together, a solid party. Everyone together."

'We didn't do that well against the Froggies up front and lost the game because we didn't deserve to win it. We went to the dinner and then on the Sunday morning to Charles de Gaulle airport for the plane back to Cardiff. Fourteen of us went into the bar about midday or so for a pint and a laugh and a joke to try and ease the pain of losing.

'After a while, this airline fella came up and said, "Are you the Welsh team?"

'Phil Bennett, who was the captain, said, "Yes, we are the Welsh team."

'"Well," says this fella, "your plane's gone."

'So we said, "What do you mean, the plane's gone?"

'"Taken off, for Cardiff."

'We said, "No, the committee wouldn't go without us."

'"The committee are all on the plane."

'He offered to try to fit us on later flights to Cardiff, if and when seats became available. At eleven that night, three of us were still in the bar: me, Benny and Cob. The wives were not at all happy, especially Benny's missus, Pat, who was waiting to take him home from Cardiff airport, which was empty by the time we got there. We all got the usual grief about so-and-so getting back early, so why couldn't we have done the same. I don't think Pat was impressed by her husband's argument that as captain it was his responsibility to be last off the ship.

'When we next joined up as a squad, nobody said a word about it. As players, we didn't want to risk our places by kicking up a fuss. What were we going to do? Complain to the committee that they left us behind? You'd think that the selectors, all members of the committee, would have said something. Instead, it was as if the whole thing had never happened, which was typical. But it still makes me chuckle now about that one-for-all, all-for-one bollocks.

'We'd go to Twickenham by bus, as we did that season, and there'd be another bus behind us full of the committee and their wives. They'd stop in the hotel overnight. Lovely. As players, we'd be two to a room in twin beds. Nobody ever thought that our wives might like to stay overnight or, if they did, they did nothing about it. How mean can you get?

'The dinner after England matches in London was the worst in the world. The players would be split up on all sorts of different tables, which always seemed to be full of alickadoos, like the secretary of Old Bollocks' Old Boys somewhere in Surrey and the chairman of some club in Yorkshire you'd never heard of.

'So you had f**k all to talk about. Worse still, when the speeches were over, the players would leave and make space for the committee, their wives and guests to have a bit of a shindig. It wasn't much better before home matches in the Angel Hotel in Cardiff, where they held the committee dinner on the Friday night.

'We players would be sitting round in the foyer having a quiet orange juice, trying to kill a bit of time, and some of these committee types would come rolling over, half sloshed, wishing us all the best and singing 'Hen Wlad Fy Nhadau'. They were a bloody nuisance, but it was a very small price to pay for playing the game I loved.

'To be fair, things did improve in terms of the wives being looked after, but the players went on being treated like second-class citizens. You put your bollocks on the line for your country, but then they kicked you in the nuts with their meanness off the pitch. The free bar put on at the dinners after home matches closed as soon as the dinner finished. After that it became a pay bar.

'At times, it seemed to be all take and no give, with the players doing the giving. We checked into our hotel in Dublin on one occasion and I wanted to phone home to let Judi know everything was all right, because she knew how I hated flying. I made the call thinking the Union would pay for it.

'On the Monday morning, I did a television interview. The WRU obviously saw it because they sent me a letter pointing out that I could not keep the fee and that I should pay it into one of their charities. I had no problem with that because I knew the score. But I had a big problem when another letter from the WRU arrived at my home a few days after that. This one contained the bill for my phone call home from Dublin and asked if I would please settle it by return post.

EXPENSES SCANDAL

'You did as they said because the Unions ruled with a rod of iron and nobody wanted to rock the boat. So they took advantage of us by giving us as little as possible. We got two tickets per home international per player, with the option to buy two more, when we should have been given ten each. The Unions were making hundreds of thousands of pounds out of international matches even then and they kept telling us it was a players' game. I'm still trying to work that one out . . .'

Discovering that the committee had abandoned them at Charles de Gaulle was not the only travel drama to engulf the Wales team and their hooker, whose phobia of flying reduced him to a state of high anxiety during even the smoothest flight. Some 14 months after finding themselves lost in France, many of the same players became the hapless victims of a row which threatened to cause the biggest diplomatic incident involving a British sports team in Australia since the Bodyline Test series of 1932–33.

It happened before the first of two internationals against the Wallabies in June 1978. Wales accused their hosts of breaking the tour agreement on referees by appointing the Queenslander Bob Burnett to take charge of the first Test on home soil in Brisbane without prior consultation with the tourists' management, headed by Clive Rowlands and Terry Cobner, the new captain following Phil Bennett's decision to retire from international rugby.

'We noticed a surprising amount of hostility towards the Welsh right from the start of that tour,' Windsor says. 'The row blew up when the Aussies, instead of allowing us to choose from a panel of three referees as had been laid down in the tour agreement, said, "You're having this chap [Burnett] whether you like it or not."

'Clive was a good manager, a players' man and he said, "No. You give us the names of three referees, as per the agreement, and we'll choose one."

'They said, "You're having who we are telling you to have."

'Clive called us all to a meeting, explained the position and said, "Boys, we're not having this, because it isn't fair. If we don't get our way on this, we're flying home – tomorrow." That was the day of the Test. We couldn't see the Aussies backing down, so we started to pack our bags. As far as we knew, it was a simple matter – either they changed the ref or we were going home. We were all ready to go to the airport when we got called to another meeting at nine o'clock on the Saturday morning.

'The feeling in the camp was that we were definitely sticking to our guns – who did the Aussies think they were, anyway? We knew all about Bob Burnett. When he refereed the Queensland game, he turned up wearing the maroon and white Queensland socks, so it was fair to think that impartiality was not his strongest point.

'That night, there were some urgent phone calls between Brisbane and Cardiff. Clive wanted formal permission to bring the team home. On the Saturday morning, he was very upset that the Union in Cardiff hadn't backed him. He said the WRU had let us down, that they had told him we had to play whatever happened.

'Looking back, I can see that we were onto a loser, because if the governing body of the game had allowed us to scrap the Test and come straight home, they'd have set a precedent for every other touring team with a bee in their bonnet to do the same. It was no way to prepare for a game, so it hardly came as a surprise that we lost.'

Rowlands, addressing the controversy in his autobiography, wrote:

> Surely it was unacceptable to assign the task of refereeing a touring match to a resident of a particular state on his own soil? Despite a somewhat stormy meeting, it seemed that the Australian authorities were unperturbed and we seriously considered cancelling the tour.
>
> However, despite major misgivings, we swallowed our pride. Unfortunately, our worst fears were realised in the most extraordinary and biased display of refereeing I have ever experienced. At one stage in the game, Mr Burnett barked at Brynmor Williams [Wales scrum-half], 'It's not your ball, Williams. It's ours!'

Terry Cobner, captaining his country following Bennett's international retirement, became so exasperated at what he saw as Burnett's biased refereeing that the skipper threatened to take his team off the pitch in protest, an action unprecedented in Test rugby. Relations between the countries went from bad to worse during the final week, culminating in the second match at Sydney, in which Wallaby prop Steve Finnane broke Graham Price's jaw with a single punch.

'Cob got a crack on the back of the head in the first game in Brisbane which left a nasty, gaping wound almost the size of someone's mouth. It was horrible, but I said to Cob, "Don't worry, it's not so bad. We'll get some Vaseline on it."

EXPENSES SCANDAL

'A lot of things went on in that game which Burnett let go for them but didn't let go for us. I can understand Cob's frustration, but we just had to put up with it. Taking the team off wouldn't have done any good. One year later, Jeff Squire took the Pontypool team off in San Francisco because the referee was a joke, but Jeff shouldn't have done it. It was a stupid thing to do and the club got banned from touring for three years as a result.

'Finnane's punching of Pricey came during the second Test. Graham had a habit of dropping the scrum and if you do that, you leave yourself open to some sort of retaliation. Finnane did say to him, "If you're going to keep doing this, I ain't going to have it." He was losing his rag, so he let Graham have it. You could have cut the atmosphere with a knife at the after-match reception and the word was already getting round that Finnane would not be allowed into New Zealand with the Aussie team a few weeks later.

'Finnane came up to me at the bar and explained why he did it. I said, "Steve, I'm glad you didn't hit me." Things happen on the pitch. The worst part of that game was that we lost it and they won it on a drop goal that never was. We could see at the time that it was miles wide and some of the Wallabies who played in that game have since admitted that it never went over. They changed the ref for that game and gave it to another Aussie, Dick Byres.

'Instead of squaring the series, we lost it because the officials made a massive balls-up over that drop goal. You'd think one of them would have seen what happened. A win would have been some achievement, because by then we were so badly hit by injuries that J.P.R. had to play in the pack because we'd run out of back-row forwards.

'Dr J.P.R. was an amazing player. On the field, it always seemed impossible to hurt his feelings because he didn't have any. He never seemed to feel any pain. He did have a compassionate side to him, not that we saw it very often. Because he never felt pain, he assumed nobody else did either, which was why I'd rather have been stitched up by a sewing machine than J.P.R.

'Ironically, that tour was a turning point for Australian rugby. Until then, they were never considered among the best in the world, but after beating us it was only a matter of time before they joined the big league. They did a Grand Slam tour of the home countries a few years later, in 1984, and have never looked back.

'It didn't occur to me when we flew home that I would never have the privilege of playing for Wales in the southern hemisphere again. My motivation as a player was never to get anything out of it other than pure enjoyment, so I never felt disappointed if I was occasionally out of pocket. Playing international rugby put you in the limelight, especially in Wales. There was always the chance you would get a better job because of your rugby success. But I never expected to be given something for nothing.

'In that respect, a strange thing happened to me the night before we left for Australia, and it began with a tap on the shoulder.

'The bloke asked, "You're Bobby Windsor, aren't you?"

'He told me he was a farmer and that he wanted to give me some land so I could build my own house on it. It sounded too good to be true, but he was at pains to point out that he wanted to show his gratitude to me for what I had done for Wales. He also said he thought it was a disgrace that I was the only member of the team living in a council house and he wanted me to have a slice of his land.

'People don't come up with propositions like that without some sort of catch somewhere. I was a bit suspicious, but before the conversation went any further Charlie came up, all ears, and joined in. This chap turned to Charlie and said, "I'm trying to give Bobby two acres of ground and I don't seem to be getting anywhere with him."

'Charlie said something along the lines of, "OK, I'll have it."

'I said to the farmer who owned the land, "There are four of us from Pontypool in the Welsh squad – me, Charlie, Cob and Pricey. We've come through a lot together so maybe the two acres could be divided up between us." At that point, Pricey came up and said, "What's happening?"

'We explained the offer the gentleman had made and left it like that because we were going off on tour the next day. When I came back and went to my local boozer, I was upset to be told that Charlie and Pricey had been up at the land in question, near Bettws High School, putting pegs in the ground. I lived 200 yards from there and thought it strange they hadn't called in.

'It didn't leave a very good taste. I went to the council and made some discreet enquiries about the land to find out whether planning permission was ever likely to be given for it to be developed. I was told straight: no chance. I didn't tell the others. There were a few incidents like that. I was very fortunate in life that people often seemed to take a liking to me, but I was unfortunate in that I always seemed to have a parrot or two on my shoulder.'

On the same ornithological topic, there was another bird which Windsor and every other player in Wales since 1953 had been unable to remove from their shoulders: the flightless Kiwi. A quarter of a century had come and gone since New Zealand lost an international match to Wales, and at Cardiff Arms Park on Armistice Day 1978, the All Blacks were in grave danger.

With New Zealand losing 12–10 going into the final minutes and Wales anxious to secure their own lineout ball, Andy Haden activated a pre-match stunt hatched with his second-row teammate Frank Oliver. As they lumbered into position, Haden whispered the fateful words to his partner in crime: 'I'm going to take a dive.'

Seconds later, Haden plunged headlong from the lineout as if he had been shot out of a catapult, a piece of amateurish theatrics designed to win the penalty which might just further obstruct the course of justice by robbing the Welsh. Roger Quittenton, the English referee, duly gave the penalty, explaining later that he had done so against Geoff Wheel for barging at the front of the lineout and denying that it had anything to do with Haden's almost comical charade. According to no less a witness than J.P.R. Williams, captaining Wales after Cobner's unexpected retirement weeks earlier, Haden should have been sent off for ungentlemanly conduct. In that event, the penalty would have been reversed and history would have taken a different course.

Substitute full-back Brian McKechnie kicked the goal, the All Blacks stole it 13–12 and the whole of Wales has never forgiven them for theft on a grand scale. What made the ploy all the more cynical was that Graham Mourie, one of the most revered of all New Zealand captains, had reminded Haden 'over a few beers' before the match of how Taranaki had won a penalty by pulling the same stunt during a match against Colin Meads' King Country.

'We were talking about it and I said to Andy, "You should remember that. You might need it some day,"' Mourie recalls in his autobiography. 'During the game he came up to me and said he was going to do it and I looked at him quizzically. Guilty by silence . . .'

Stu Wilson, the All Black right wing who scored the game's only try, confirmed that the plot had been discussed widely within the team. 'We had talked about it,' he said years later. 'We all knew it was going to happen. We beat Wales 13–12 and, to be honest, we had to cheat with guys diving out of the lineout.'

Time has not soothed the burning sense of Welsh resentment. Even more than 30 years after his outrageous impersonation of Greg Louganis, Haden is still public enemy No. 1 in Wales. There has never been an apology, and nor will there be, for the simple reason that he believes he has nothing to apologise for. His attitude remains implacably unforgiving, as articulated before New Zealand beat Wales, yet again, in November 2009.

'Whenever I left the dressing shed to play, my attitude was always the same – don't finish up asking, "What more could I have done to win the game?"' Haden said. 'I have no regrets and I don't think there are any amongst the rest of the team that day. There's certainly never been any regrets about the final score. Gamesmanship in sport is alive and well.

'I remember going back to the hotel near the ground afterwards and the telephone girl rushing up to say, "Mr Haden, I've got 20 international calls waiting and they are all for you."

'I could see the switchboard all lit up. I reached over and pulled out every plug. "Don't worry," I told the telephonist. "They're going to be asking the same questions in 50 years' time . . ."'

What made it worse for Windsor was that he would never have another crack at the All Blacks. The chance of a lifetime had gone for good, as it had for the rest of those slumped around him in the dressing-room.

'The World Cup hadn't been invented, so beating the All Blacks was the biggest thing we could achieve outside the Grand Slam. Then you'd done it all. Those two blokes, Haden and Oliver, admitted they cheated deliberately, and they are heroes in their own country, which makes what they did all the harder to stomach,' he says.

'We all cheat in our own way and rugby gives you plenty of scope in that respect, but it's instinctive, heat-of-the-moment stuff. I never knew of anyone planning to cheat and carrying it out. You draw the line at doing that. The whole thing was a farce, but they got clean away with it and the score is there in the record books for everyone to see: Wales 12, New Zealand 13.

'I threw the ball into that lineout. I told Quittenton straight away, "Ref, you've been conned." I threw the ball to Geoff Wheel at the front. Oliver, who was their front jumper, was cleverer than Haden in that he didn't jump. He moved over, Geoff was jumping for the ball and when Oliver tipped him off balance he put his hand down to steady himself.

'Then Oliver shouted out and went down, which was more convincing than Haden's antics,' Windsor says. 'Haden was standing in the middle and as he dived he let out this scream, which quite frightened Allan Martin who was lined up against him. Haden looked a complete fool because the ball was nowhere near him. The crowd went berserk.

'As we were walking off, I went over to Quittenton and told him again, "They've conned you, ref. You'll find out soon enough." He never said a word and even now, after all these years, that incident and that decision always come up whenever people talk about Wales and New Zealand.

'To plan it the way the All Blacks did and then almost boast about it afterwards was unforgivable. I never thought they would stoop to such behaviour. I've seen the great Colin Meads on television when this business was put to him and he just shrugged his shoulders and said, "We won the game." This is the same Colin Meads who, when the All Blacks put three men into a scrum against the Lions the previous year, got up from his seat and walked out in disgust.

'In all my 27 years as a player, I never felt as disgusted by anything I'd seen on the pitch as I felt that day at the old Arms Park. It shattered us to lose that match, more than any other in all my time with the Welsh squad. People were crying tears of anger in the dressing-room afterwards because they knew they'd been cheated and there was nothing they could do about it. Clive Rowlands, the coach, was in tears. So was Ray Gravell.

'We took them apart up front that day. If only Gareth Edwards and Phil Bennett had delayed their retirement by a few months. With their experience at half-back, we'd have turned them over and justice would have been done.

'The minute Quittenton gave the penalty, we all knew McKechnie would get it. Brian's a nice chap and I bumped into him when he returned to Cardiff some years later. I said, "It's you, you bastard." And then, despite all the hard feelings, I bought him a drink.

'"Ssshh," he said, "don't talk too loudly, otherwise I'll get filled in."'

In a classic example of the biblical parable about reaping what you sow, McKechnie did not have to wait long to appreciate how it feels to be the victim of daylight robbery. A real all-rounder, the All Blacks' full-back strode out to the wicket at the Melbourne Cricket Ground on 1 February 1981 with New Zealand needing to hit the last ball of the match for six to tie their series against Australia.

McKechnie never had a prayer. In an act which outraged the cricketing world, the Australian captain, Greg Chappell, ordered the bowler, his brother Trevor, to roll the final delivery along the ground, making it impossible for the batsman to lift it over the ropes. The most cynical of ploys, branded a disgrace by the commentator Richie Benaud, prompted a furious protest from New Zealand Prime Minister Robert Muldoon.

He called it 'the most disgusting incident in the history of cricket, an act of true cowardice and I consider it appropriate that the Australian team were wearing yellow'.

Not a peep was heard from Mr Muldoon over the jiggery-pokery used by two high-profile citizens of his country to swindle Wales less than eighteen months earlier. On a sliding scale of disgusting incidents in the name of sportsmanship, that had to be right up there. Neither Chappell brother has ever made a public apology for what he did, and nor has Haden.

The way he sees it, why say sorry when there is nothing to be sorry about?

10

TRAGEDY

After all their years of hardship, the Windsors of Newport had ample reason to join the New Year celebrations over the advent of 1979. They were no longer on skid row, which had dogged them since their teenage wedding 15 years earlier. This blessed state of affairs suggested that the lean years of using springbok skins to cover the holes in the carpet had gone for good.

A double Lion and double Grand Slammer, Windsor was at the zenith of his career. The uncertainty brought about by short time at the steelworks had gone. Instead he had a new, better-paid job, one which allowed him ample opportunity to meet the ever-increasing demands rugby made on his time. Having spent his entire adult life hitherto cycling to and from work, the provision of a company car doubled his wheels from two to four.

When times had been at their worst, with Windsor temporarily out of work, he refused to sign on at the nearest labour exchange and take the state handout to which he was perfectly entitled as a victim of the depression of the steel industry. A fierce sense of personal pride drove him to look for work rather than put his feet up and rely on the welfare state.

Judi had her own part-time job close to home. The little Windsors – Joanne (14), Ricky (13) and Mandy (8) – were not so little any more.

If it would be an exaggeration to say that everything in the garden was rosy, in many respects they had never had it so good. A second Welsh Grand Slam in three seasons had been followed by the trip of a lifetime to Australia for Judi and a family reunion with two of her brothers who had swapped Newport for Sydney, old South Wales for New South Wales.

The Windsors had no way of knowing that they would be devastated by tragedy in a matter of weeks, that on a Thursday afternoon in high summer the grieving family would follow the hearse carrying Judi Windsor's coffin on the heartbreaking final journey from the funeral home, past the Royal Gwent Hospital, right at the roundabout into Belle Vue Lane and up the hill to St Woolos cemetery.

As the sun blazed from a cloudless sky, pushing the mercury high up into the eighties, they laid her to rest amid the tall pines and monkey puzzle trees of one of the oldest burial grounds in Britain. The black marble headstone reads:

> In Loving memory of Judi.
> Beloved wife of Bobby Windsor.
> Devoted mother of Joanne, Ricky and Mandy.
> Died 22nd July, 1979. Aged 33.
> Oh, for the touch of a vanished hand
> and the sound of a voice that is still.

Under two months elapsed between Judi's diagnosis and her death. A non-smoker, she had developed a cough and the initial prognosis after X-ray examination was that it could be treated without anything as drastic as surgery.

'Early in the 1970s, two of Judi's brothers, Kevin and Bernard, emigrated to Australia,' Windsor says. 'Their mother, Nan McCarthy, mentioned to me how she'd love to be able to go out and see the boys in their new home in Sydney, and I suggested to Judi she and her mother should make the trip together.

'She said we couldn't afford it, it was out of the question. I said, "We can afford it." I had some souvenir rugby jerseys which would be worth something and I knew a gentleman who was in the market to buy them. I got in touch with him, asked if he was still interested and he said he was. He came to the house, I sold him the jerseys and the money paid for Judi and her mum to go to Australia.

'Another 12 months and it would have been too late. It's always easy to put things like that off until another day. Judi and her mum had a great time. None of us ever thought in our worst nightmare that she'd be taken from us; she looked so well. It wasn't until many months later when her cough got worse that I began to worry.

'Whenever she lay down, she coughed. It got so bad that she couldn't lie down and that was when we put a deckchair in the bedroom. That eased the cough a bit. But it was clear that the medication was not doing her any good, so I insisted we were going to get something done about it.

'We went to the Royal Gwent Hospital for some X-rays. They said Judi had an infection on the lining of the lung. I rang a doctor friend of mine who I knew through rugby, explained the condition to him and he said it could be treated with drugs but that it could take some time. We felt relieved that it wasn't anything more serious and that it could be cured. I thought that was marvellous news, but I continued to worry because she didn't seem to get any better.

'In May 1979, Pontypool were going to America for a couple of end-of-season matches. She was as mad as I was about my rugby and when I told her I was in two minds about going to America she was adamant that I had to go and that she'd be OK. She said, "When you come back, I'll meet you at the end of Bettws Lane." When I got back to Newport from the tour, I caught a bus to Bettws and met her, as arranged. I found it hard to get over how ill she looked. She looked bad.

'I kissed her and asked her how she was feeling. Next day, we went straight to the Royal Gwent for more X-rays. After a nervous wait, I was called into a consulting room. They had Judi's X-rays pinned up and, in my ignorance, I thought they all looked clean and white. Desperate for good news, I said, "Well, they look all right."

'The consultant said, "No, the X-rays should be black. The white is cancer."

'We were then referred to a specialist at Sully Hospital near Cardiff. I went straight down there and he told me, "I'm very sorry, Bob. There is nothing we can do for your wife. Nothing. Nothing at all. The only thing we can do is make it as easy as possible for the time she has left."

'The news hit me like a sledgehammer. Then I said, "Well, she ain't staying here. I'm taking her home."

'The specialist said, "She's going to need oxygen and 24-hour care."

'I said, "I'll give her 24-hour care at home. There's a chemist near where we live, Mr Davies. He's a rugby supporter and I'm sure he'll help me."

'The specialist took the trouble to speak to him there and then. Mr Davies agreed he would be available 24 hours a day and would keep a stock of oxygen for Judi, no problem.

'Before I left, they gave me the medicine to ease her pain. It was explained to me that given a mixture of certain medicines in an egg cup Judi would feel no more pain, that she would slip peacefully away. Euthanasia is a very controversial subject and whether the person concerned should have said that or not is for others to make up their mind about.

'All I said was, "Oh, right."

'Judi had not been told that the illness was terminal and I decided not to tell her because she was going to fight and I was going to fight it with her. I wasn't going to do or say anything to undermine that fight. I left Judi at the hospital and told her I would be back tomorrow to take her home. I drove to my mother's house alone and screamed my head off all the way. It was uncontrollable. At home, I brought the bed downstairs, I got a commode and carried two bottles of oxygen from the chemist. Then I collected Judi from the hospital. She lived for about six weeks. I didn't leave her side during that time. The worst part for her, and me, was that awful period around four or five o'clock in the morning when the pain would be at its worst.

'I didn't know what to do. I tormented myself about whether to tell her what they'd said at the hospital. I asked myself, do I tell her? Am I being cruel by not telling her that there was a way out, that all she had to do was take an egg cup of the right medicine?

'When a particularly severe bout of pain had passed one night, she said, "Bob, I know I'm dying." I said, "No, you're not, we're going to fight this and beat it. That's why we've brought you home."

'She repeated, "Bob, I know I am dying. We've got to accept that and make a few plans. When I go, the first thing you have to do is find a mother for the kids. You've got to promise me. You can't look after them on your own. Those kids need looking after. Now you promise me you will get a mother for the children."

'I said, "If that's what you want, I will."

'Judi said, "Good. Now I need to get something else sorted and that's to see this lady called Lillian who's a Jehovah's Witness." I arranged for her to call at the house and made a cup of tea while she was talking with Judi. When Lillian left, Judi looked a picture of health. It was an amazing transformation, considering how close she was to death.

'Now I did tell her about the egg cup of medicine which would cure her pain once and for all. She thought about it for a minute, then said, "No, for two reasons. I want to see the kids for as long as I can. And if

TRAGEDY

I take that stuff and go to sleep, I know you'll take it too."

'She was absolutely right. I would have done. And Judi said, "What about the kids? If we're both gone, who's going to look after them with no mum and no dad?" Again, she was absolutely right, but I was in such a bad state emotionally that I hadn't thought about the consequences of taking my own life and leaving the children to be brought up as orphans. Her bravery was unbelievable.

'She was the strong one, not me. I was watching the love of my life suffer so terribly from this horrible disease and I couldn't believe that anything so cruel could happen to someone so young. Knowing that there was nothing I could do to help made it worse, if that was possible.

'I stayed by her side in those six weeks, except when someone came to see her and I'd go into the kitchen for a cup of tea and roll up a cigarette. The only time I left her was the day our youngest, Mandy, was playing the recorder in the school orchestra. Judi told me, "You've got to go down and support her."

'I made sure there was someone to look after Judi and nipped down to the school. I sat in the audience looking at Mandy, who was then eight years old, and listening to her playing "Bright Eyes". I cried my eyes out. To think that little girl was going to lose her mother in a couple of weeks and there she was playing beautifully and looking gorgeous, the spitting image of her mum in every way. That was heartbreaking.

'We'd paid for Joanne, the eldest girl, to go on a school holiday that summer to Spain. We'd been saving and planning for it for a long time. Judi would say, "I don't care how ill I am or even if I'm not here, Joanne must not miss that trip. I really want her to go on it."

'She was thinking how excited Joanne would have been. As it turned out, Judi died three or four days before the Spanish trip. Joanne said to me, "I can't go now, Dad."

'I said, "Joanne, you have got to because it was your mother's dying wish that you go." She had seen her mother suffer for the previous 12 months and I explained to her that mam had gone but that her spirit would be with us for ever, and that she had set her heart on Joanne going on that trip. She went and I am very glad she did.

'Lung cancer is something you associate with smokers. Judi didn't smoke and they said that she died of secondary cancer but that they never found the source of the primary cancer. Was it because her father came home from his job as a coal-trimmer down in the docks covered in dust?

Nobody will ever know. Judi's brother Gerard died from emphysema, and yet her mother outlived almost all of them.

'My wife was a beautiful woman and in that last week or so she asked me to take some more photographs for the children, which I did, but she was terribly ill. She was very clear about the funeral, how she would like it to be done. She stuck it out as long as she could and passed away at half past five one morning. They talk about people taking their last breath and when it happened with a lot of blood, it frightened me.

'Judi's sister-in-law Jean, a trained nurse, was there at the end. At that terrible time, my niece Sally McCarthy came over and looked after the kids, did some washing and organising. She didn't have to do anything, but she volunteered out of the kindness of her heart, and she deserved a medal. I shall never forget the help Sally gave. There was something else I wouldn't forget either, and that was the malicious gossip which arose.

'Sally was 18. She had been courting, got pregnant and later gave birth to a baby girl, Shelley. The boy who she'd been going out with completely deserted her. Her mother, Jean, was also wonderful in the time she gave to help us out.

'The rumour reached me that Sally and I were cohabiting. That angered me no end. I said to Jean, "Sally can't stay any more because someone's putting it about that she and I are having an affair."

'I knew where I could find the boy who had abandoned her and his family. I found him in a pub and told him straight: "If I hear one word more about this nonsense, I'll put you in the Royal Gwent." And that was the last I ever heard of it.

'My duty to Judi was to make sure her wishes were carried out. She didn't want a religious service at the funeral, despite the fact that she came from a staunch Roman Catholic family. That put me at odds with them because they, naturally enough, wanted it done the Catholic way. They were on about getting the priest over straight away and I had to tell them Judi didn't want that. I had to say at one point, "You said that as long as Judi gets what she wants, you'd be happy. Well, all I'm doing is making sure Judi gets what she wants. She's asked me to do it this way and I'm doing it this way. I ain't going to change it. The service will be in the funeral home at the undertaker's opposite the Royal Gwent. Her friend Lillian will speak, then up to the cemetery at St Woolos."

'And what a fantastic turnout she had. So many people from the rugby brotherhood lined the route that they virtually closed off the main road. There were police all along the route on traffic duty. As we followed the hearse to the cemetery, the policemen saluted as it passed. That was a wonderful touch, one I shall never forget. It was extremely moving.

'After the funeral, it was down to my old rugby club at Newport Sarries, where they put on a lovely spread. I had the kids with me and Ricky, who was 13 at the time, dropped the jackpot on the one-arm bandit. Amazing. I left early with the children, went back home and sat in the kitchen. That's when it really hit me.

'Then Judi's family started saying the burial was a disgrace because it wasn't done on consecrated ground and they were going to get a priest up there the next day to bless the ground. I said, "You aren't doing that for Judi, you're doing that for yourselves. But if it's going to make you feel better, it's up to you."

'It was a bad day all round and a rough couple of weeks. We got on with life as best we could and the kids began to get used to fish fingers and mash. That was about the limit of my cooking skills. They had enough fish fingers in those weeks to last them a lifetime.

'Joanne came back from Spain and took over the reins from her mother. She was old enough at 14 to be able to run the house in a brilliant fashion, even if at teatime she did say occasionally, "For goodness' sake, Dad, can't you do something other than fish fingers, just for a change?"

'She pulled me through it.

'The rugby community, almost like a Freemasonry, came out in their droves to attend the funeral and offer support. Individual players were outstanding, two in particular. Terry Cobner came to stay in the house with us straight after Judi's passing and played with the kids. Nothing was too much trouble. He was the best ever. Peter Wheeler was also incredibly supportive. He wrote me a lovely letter and offered to arrange a holiday for myself and the children. It was a case of, if there is anything we can do, all you have to do is ask. And I knew they meant every word.'

Rugby had been a passion for Windsor since the perceptive Hedley Rowland began weaning him off soccer, but now the game was to play a critical part in helping him come to terms with his grief. When Wales opened their 99th season at home to Romania, patronising their opponents by refusing to grant the fixture Test status, Windsor was there, as good as ever, even if Wales needed a drop goal to sneak home 13–12.

THE IRON DUKE

There was no doubt that the selectors, blissfully unaware that their hooker was two years older than he had led them to believe, saw him as good enough at supposedly thirty-one for one more season. The chain of circumstances which would conspire to prevent him ever going into battle for Wales again in a full international had begun some months earlier, on 10 March 1979, against Cardiff at Pontypool Park.

Windsor's presence against Scotland, Ireland and France in the Five Nations took his tally of consecutive capped appearances to 28, in a reign stretching back to November 1973. He finished the match at the Parc des Princes – where Jean-François Gourdon belatedly got some of his own back by eluding J.P.R. Williams long enough to score both tries in a home win – with no reason to suspect that fate was about to play another trick on him.

While Wales were waltzing to a home victory over England which gave them the Five Nations title and the Triple Crown, Windsor was detained in the burns unit at the St Lawrence Hospital in Chepstow, to which he had been admitted the previous Sunday.

'Part of the pitch at Pontypool Park needed to be marked out for the Cardiff match and the groundsman was away ill so somebody else had to do the job,' Windsor says. 'Instead of getting the chalk stuff, he picked up the quicklime by mistake, but nobody had a clue about that until after the match.

'It was just my luck to slide over that particular part of the pitch with my jersey loose, which meant that the skin on my back got exposed to the quicklime. At the end of the game, my back felt as though it had been dragged over some rough sand. I came out of the showers and said to our first-aid man, Eddie Mogford, that I thought there was something wrong with my back.

'In the clubhouse that night, it was so sore that I must have drunk about 20 pints, not that the beer was going to cure it, but I thought it might ease the pain. I went home and had to sit up all night because I couldn't lie down. I drove to Port Talbot the next morning for training with the Welsh squad and my back was so painful that I had to lean forward to prevent it touching the back of the driver's seat.

'As soon as I got there, Ray Williams, then the coaching organiser of the Welsh Rugby Union, took some photographs of my back and had me sent straight to the St Lawrence Hospital. When I got there, one of the hospital staff took me into this room, stripped me off and put me on a bed. Then he said, "Grab hold of those bars on the bedstead, Mr Windsor, because this is going to hurt."

'He dabbed on a solution of vinegar, which neutralises the quicklime. It hurt like hell. On the Monday and the Tuesday, a couple of the Cardiff players involved in the same match came up to be treated for much lesser burns. I was there for ten days and beginning to feel sorry for myself until I saw the terrible burns suffered by kids at the hospital. Some had burned their hands by falling on electric fires and I heard them screaming with pain every time they flexed their hand muscles, which they had to do as part of the healing process.

'Somehow Bobby Windsor missing a match against England didn't seem that big a deal compared to the suffering of those little children.

'Shortly before that match against Cardiff, I'd given Newport Sarries a load of my international jerseys and blazers. They gave me a ring one day to say they'd sent them all to the cleaners and when they went to collect them there were two missing, including one Triple Crown blazer with a nice badge on the breast pocket. The club went to see a solicitor, who got in touch with the WRU to see if there was any legal action they could take.

'The Union's advice was that the blazer was worth about £45 and they couldn't sue for anything more than that so it wouldn't have been worth the bother. The other issue was over compensation for the burns. As an amateur, I couldn't make any claim for missing the England match, as the WRU was quick to point out, but in the end I got a sum of £1,000 from the council, who owned Pontypool Park.

'And that, strangely enough, paid for Judi's funeral and the headstone on her grave. So some good came from it after all.'

When Wales picked their squad for the 1980 Five Nations, Windsor was there alongside Alan Phillips of Cardiff, who had replaced him against England at the end of the previous season. By then, the Iron Duke, as the French president had called him some years earlier, was beginning to show signs of metal fatigue and a new crack had been put there by one of those routine occupational hazards, an accidental kick in the back.

'After a certain time, a lot of front-row forwards start getting trouble with their calf muscles,' Windsor says. 'Experience tells me that it all comes from the back and the effect of the bone-breaking pressures which you subject it to every time you put your head in a scrum. Before going off on the Lions tour two years before with Cob, Pricey and Charlie, who was on standby, I'd go running with them every day after work.

'On one particular evening, out at Llantarnam, a sharp pain stopped me in my tracks. I'd pulled a calf muscle. The first thing I did was tell John Dawes, the Lions coach. The tour was only about ten days away and I was worried the injury would force me to pull out. He was very reassuring, saying I would be fine. Well, I wasn't fine, because I had to have physio treatment on my calf everywhere we went in New Zealand.

'It gave me a lot of gyp and I'd be kidding myself if I denied that it affected my game. When I got home, I went to see Eddie Mogford, the trainer at Pontypool and one of the great men of club rugby. He manipulated my back and I could hear it click. Suddenly, I had no more trouble from calf muscles. Marvellous.

'I played at the start of the following season, which is when I got the accidental kick in my back. I had a lot of pain in my leg and then more trouble from my back after the Romanian game. I went to see a chiropractor and various other people before I was referred to Robert Weekes, a neurologist at the University Hospital of Wales in Cardiff.

'He took one look at me and said, "I want you down at the hospital tomorrow." They put me on a table and I could watch the dye they put in my neck going down the spinal column. Mr Weekes explained that some of my discs were broken and said, "We'll operate on you in 48 hours' time."

'The first thing I did after the op was to lift my right leg. For the first time in ages, I could do it without any pain. So they've done it, I thought. I will be able to play my beloved game again. Wonderful. I got up to go to the toilet, not realising that I shouldn't have gone anywhere unattended so soon after surgery. As I turned round after relieving myself, everything went black and I hit the deck, flat on my face. They must have heard the splattering sound all over the hospital.

'So one hour after my first operation, I was having another, this time for a broken nose. By a happy coincidence, Stan "The Pies" Thomas, now Sir Stanley, was in the same ward at the same time for the same kind of back surgery. There was a big fight on the television a few days later and he suggested we nip out and watch it in a club near the hospital in the same part of Cardiff.

'We put on our dressing gowns and walked along the concourse out to the front of the hospital, where Stan's chauffeur was waiting in the Rolls. He took us to the club and we sat having a few drinks watching the fight. We got back to the hospital at half past eleven at night to find that all hell had broken loose.

TRAGEDY

'They'd called the police because we'd gone missing. Uniformed officers were combing the grounds. The hospital didn't know whether we'd been drugged or kidnapped or whatever. The first person we bumped into back in the ward was the matron. I could tell by the look on her face that she was not pleased.

'So I said, "Hello, my lovely. How are you?" She ripped us to bits and the next morning we were told, "You are free to dress and leave when you like." We were kicked out.

'I didn't play for the rest of that season. Eleven months on, in September 1980, I was in the squad for the start of the WRU's centenary season, which told me that I was still in with a chance of getting my place back, even though I was 34. As far as the Union was concerned, I was only 32, otherwise they might not have picked me.

'That was a favour Mervyn Davies did me when I first got into the squad back in the early '70s. At my first training session with Wales, I was given a form requesting personal information, like height, weight, place of birth, date of birth and so on. I'd begun to fill it in when Swerve whispered in my ear, "Knock two years off your age and two stone off your weight."

'I said, "Why?"

'He said, "Do yourself a favour. If they think you're too old, they'll boot you out even though you may still be playing well enough. Buy yourself a bit of time."

'I was 16 st. 4 lb at the time so I put down 14 st. 10 lb. For my date of birth, I did as he told me and put down 31 January 1948. That date was used in every programme for every match I played. Who knows, if I'd put down my real date of birth, I might not have lasted as long as I did.

'After the operation, Mr Weekes explained that bits of my disc had been stuck to the sciatic nerve, causing it to jam when it moved. They took the discs away from the sciatic nerve, which had been bruised. Because of that, they said I would lose the feeling in my left leg and they proved it by sticking pins into it. I couldn't feel a thing.

'They said I'd done some damage to my vertebrae. I reckoned that was because I'd been advised to do sit-ups on the basis that my back couldn't get any worse, even though I'd virtually scream with pain every time. Anyway, Mr Weekes came straight to the point: "Bob, pack it up now. Take up something lighter. I know you're a sportsman, so do another sport. But my advice to you is to forget about rugby. I know that won't be easy, but it's for your own good."

'I couldn't bring myself to quit. When I reported for squad training a few months later, the WRU told me that Mr Weekes was unable to give them a clean bill of health for me to continue playing. That meant there was an insurance problem, which was fair enough, because I had to be given medical clearance to play. That was that, the end of my career with Wales but not with Pontypool.

'Packing up completely was the only sensible option, but common sense didn't come into it. I just could not face life without rugby. I didn't say anything to the club about my back and I played for another seven years, until I was forty-one. During that time, I experienced some of the hardest rugby of my life as captain of the second team, the Athletic, because I was a target for every young bull who fancied making a name for himself, which was fair enough. I would have done the same.

'I'd only been playing a few months after ignoring Mr Weekes' advice when I found myself back in hospital wishing I'd done as he'd said. Playing against Bedford in November 1980, I got caught in a double tackle. I came out of a ruck and got hit in opposite directions at the same time. I hit the deck and couldn't move, not a muscle.

'Peter Lewis, our full-back and a doctor by profession, came up and said, "All right, Bob?"

'I told him, "I can't move."

'I was lying there and they got the pins out and started putting them into my leg and hand. I wouldn't have known they were doing it if they hadn't told me, because I felt nothing. In my mind, I was thinking, I am paralysed for life. I was terrified. Eventually, they got me off the pitch on a stretcher and the ambulance never went above five miles an hour on the journey from the rugby ground to the hospital because of my paralysed condition.

'I still couldn't feel anything and now I was thinking I was going to be spending the rest of my life in a wheelchair. They did all kinds of tests and about three hours had gone by since it had happened and I was still paralysed. Then one of the top specialists at the hospital came in and asked me, "Have you got any feeling whatsoever?"

'I said, "The only feeling I've got is as if I've got a hundred needles stuck in my balls."

'And the specialist said, "Thank God for that. That probably means you have stunned a nerve, and that's what we've been hoping to find. We're going to check you every five minutes because if this is not what I think it is, we are going to have to do something else."

'After half an hour or so, I could move my fingers. Gradually, the feeling came back to the rest of my body. The hospital staff were great and I was so relieved that I wanted to jump about. They advised me not to do anything silly. Half an hour later, who should come in but the coach himself, Ray Prosser.

"How did we get on, Pross?"

"We won. How are you anyway?"

"Not so bad."

"All right, we'll see you at training next week."

'And that was that – from being scared out of my wits that I'd be paralysed for life to being reminded not to miss training. I did train the following Thursday and I did play in the next match. People will think I was crazy to go on pushing my luck when I'd had a couple of scares, but me without rugby would have been like a junkie without a fix. The worst part used to be in the summer, waiting for September to come round. I couldn't wait, so I'd get hold of some players from the Sarries and the steelworks. Then I'd round up a few more Pill Labour boys and others from Pill Harriers until we had enough players.

'Then we'd go to the nearest park and have a game. We usually managed to talk someone into being the ref and off we'd go. All those knock-about games in the summer were great crack, even though I was in the Welsh squad then and not far off winning my cap. Somebody else in my position may have thought twice, but I loved rugby so much that I'd have played seven games a week if only it had been possible.

'I was always going to play until I was physically unable to play any more, and to hell with the risks. Many people will think that irresponsible in view of the medical advice, and they would definitely have a point. I thank my lucky stars that I got out in one piece, but I'm also very glad that I went on until the very end.

'I missed the big stage, the buzz of the occasion, the build-up to the internationals and being in the "bubble". That was marvellous, something which you had to experience to appreciate how good it felt. At least I was still playing, although I knew that the more matches I played, the sooner the time would come when I'd lose my place in the first team.

'There can't be any room for sentiment at any club worth its salt, and Pontypool hadn't got to the top by being sentimental about anything other than winning rugby matches. Pross had to look to the future and consider what was best for the team, because at that time he had a good hooker who was pushing me all the way, Steve Jones, or "Junna", as everyone called him.

'Now, whether Pross had any inside information on my back or not, I don't know, but he said to me one day, "Bob, I think we'll play you and Junna on an alternate-match basis."

'I said, "No, you won't. I'll play for the seconds. I'd rather do that than sit on the bench.'"

The news of Windsor's retirement from first-class rugby appeared on Monday, 5 January 1981 in the *South Wales Argus*, where Ray Prosser, Pontypool's perennial coach, paid tribute to the player's generosity. 'This is a wonderful gesture and only a man like Windsor could do it,' Prosser told Robin Davey, the paper's rugby writer. 'I've been trying to persuade him to carry on but he wants to step off the first-team rota to give Steve his chance of a cap.

'It's always difficult comparing players but Bobby is head and shoulders above any other man in the position I have ever seen. Since he went out of the international team, the Welsh scrum drive has gone. He is the only tight forward I have seen who could alter the course of a game by a run to set up a try. You expect that of a class back-row man but never of a tight forward.'

For Windsor, it was far from the end, merely a drop to second-team level, and while he would continue to fill in for the first team whenever the situation demanded, often to prop the scrum on either side, he had left the way clear for Jones to stake his Wales claims without hindrance.

'I was sad and upset because I thought I could go on and on, but I also had to recognise that Junna was a good player and that his time had come,' Windsor says. 'I wanted to help him as best I could and the best way of doing that was to let him play and not have him kicking his heels on the bench once a fortnight watching me play.

'Stepping down into the Pontypool Athletic team, I knew I was making myself a target for every youngster from Treorchy to Cwmbran who fancied making a name for himself. Some of them would be thinking, there's an old British Lion out there, let's rough him up. I knew I'd get some stick, but that was all part of the crack.

'I captained the seconds for two years and we had some great fun with the young players. I got a lot of my kicks from being able to tell them that I'd been playing at the very same level 20 years before. I understood everything about their hopes and ambitions and their frustrations.

TRAGEDY

'You got your satisfaction then in a different way, from helping them become better players. I related to them and they related to me because they knew that I had once been where they were, a local kid in love with the game. I'd encourage them and advise them the best I could, even if that was to advise them to go to another club. We had a young lad who turned out for the Athletic and I'll tell you straight, he was f*****g useless. I knew that because I played alongside him.

'He came to Pontypool Athletic as a prop from Ynysybwl seconds. Nothing wrong with that, but after one scrum when he looked as though he couldn't hold his mother up, I switched him to hooker. I said, "You go into the middle, I'll prop and look after you."

'Fair play to him, he trained like a dog. He listened and he learned. Pross, who always had a nickname for everyone, called him "Roundhead" because he thought he had a head like a billiard ball. And that was Garin Jenkins, who went on to play for Wales in three World Cups and become the last coalminer to win a cap.

'Nigel Meek was another promising young hooker who came to the club from Ebbw Vale. Alan Davies [then Wales coach] came up one Saturday in the early '90s and asked me whether I thought Nigel was ready for a cap. "Not yet," I said. "Give him a bit more time and then you'll have a player who will be good enough for a few years."

'When you rush players in before they're ready, it can do them more harm than good. Anyway, Alan ignored me, put Nigel straight in and he was straight out again after three games. If only they'd waited.

'I was still getting my occasional games for the first team. Pross had asked me a few times to help him with the coaching, but I always wanted to play. The last tour I went on was with Pontypool to Canada in 1985, to celebrate winning another Welsh Championship, ahead of Cardiff, Neath and Swansea. The last match of the trip was in Toronto and the local paper reported that I had made history because I had just become a grandfather and a father on the same day. I'd remarried by then and my son Luke and my granddaughter Charlene had been born the day before – the 21st of May.

'When I read about it in the paper, I thought perhaps, at 39 years of age, it was time I stepped aside and did a bit of coaching . . .'

11

IN LOVE AGAIN

'Judi had made me promise that I would find another wife, and it was only 11 months after her death that I met Lynne. People might think that was a bit too soon. Perhaps it was. I'd got married at 18, I liked married life and I wanted a really close friend, which is what a wife or husband should be.

'I was looking for love, not for a one-night stand. Without wishing to sound big-headed, there was plenty of that available. I wanted to give love as well as find it, love of the kind I had known with Judi, which would be for life. In my case, I had to find a wife who was prepared to take on three children, which was never going to be easy unless I was extremely lucky.

'As my doctor told me, "Could be a problem, Bob. You ain't the best looking and you've got three kids. How are you going to find someone who will accept you and the kids? And then, you've got to consider awkward questions like whether the kids will accept the new woman."

'There were never any single girls at Pontypool Rugby Club, only wives or girlfriends of committee men and players, so going to the clubhouse was a waste of time in that respect. I always went there on a Sunday night, though, when they had an organist and a cracking sing-song. On this particular Sunday night, 10 June 1980, I saw a girl sitting there with an older lady and I did something I'd never done in my life before. I asked one of the older chaps at the club to introduce me.

'I asked him, "Who's that girl over there?"

'"Oh," he said, "that's Lynne and her stepmother."

'So I said, "I haven't seen her before. Is she married?"

'"No," he said.

'We got chatting and Lynne said she'd never heard of me because she was a football fanatic – she supported West Ham United. At the end of the evening, we arranged to meet again two days later. We went to a restaurant in Caerleon and had tournedos Rossini, which was showing off a bit on my part. We had three courses and all the trimmings. Lynne is quite petite, but she ate everything that was put in front of her and never stopped talking. I thought she was brilliant.

'When I first took her to meet the kids, they were very hostile, which was not that surprising because of what they had gone through. Joanne was the acting mother of the house so, naturally, she was not happy at the idea of someone else coming in to take Judi's place. She felt threatened, which was perfectly understandable.

'Lynne had a little boy, Mark, then three years old. They came to stay for a bit, but things were difficult and it got to the point where she decided to move out again. I said, "If you go, there's no turning back. You either stay and see it out or that's the end."

'She changed her mind and decided to stay, but not long after that she caught a severe dose of chickenpox and got it into her mind that the illness was the work of Judi's spirit, which she said she could sense in the house. The upshot was we sold the house to Joanne and the chap she had been seeing. After paying off the mortgage, I had £10,000 left to put down on the "dream house" we found in Garndiffaith on the outskirts of Pontypool. It had great views down the mountain. I was earning good money then, so we built some stables for a couple of horses and everything was hunky-dory.

'Lynne and I got married at Pontypool Registry Office on 11 June 1983, four years after Judi died. I had a stall in Pontypool market and did some sales repping, and after that I started up in business with a friend of mine, Steve O'Donoghue, a Cardiff boy who'd been a hooker for Pontypool and Newport. We did all right and after a couple of months I started my own company called Gwent Chemicals, specialising in cleaning materials.

'It was hard work. I was going round getting the orders, coming home and mixing all the stuff into containers, labelling it and delivering it the next day. The horses had gone by then, so I used the stables as a warehouse. I was also clearing drains. I'd often go out at one in the morning in the pissing rain, driving a Land Rover with a trailer carrying my small drain-clearing machine. With a bigger machine, I stood to pick up more business, so I discussed it with the bank manager, explaining I'd need twelve grand to buy one. He was one of the last of the old-style bank managers. He gave me the loan.

'Shortly after I bought the machine, I met a fella who had picked up a lot of work in London from Westminster Council cleaning graffiti off the subways. I hired another machine and we went to work in London. It meant working all night every night, because the faster you got the job done, the more money you made. We wiped out every bit of graffiti from every last subway, half-hoping that someone would come along behind us, put the graffiti back on again and keep us in business!

'The boys working for me used to joke about going round with an aerosol can spraying it on again. We got £36,000 for that job, which helped me no end in paying off the loan. The business built from there and we began diversifying into emptying tanks and going into waste management.

'I went to a company in Cirencester who had a combination unit tanker, which I bought for less than the first machine. My son Ricky could see the possibilities and he worked hard to get his heavy goods vehicle licence. He came on board driving the tanker, which carried water for jetting and a suction tank with a capacity of 1,500 gallons where you sucked up the rubbish.

'We kept the name Gwent Chemicals, but we were also trading as Aquadrain. I was very lucky in that 99 per cent of the time we had good workers, but I was always the one who went out knocking on doors, giving them a bit of the old bullshit or whatever it took to keep the orders rolling in. Life was good. For the first time since Judi passed away, I'd got to the stage where I didn't have anything to worry about.'

And then, in the summer of 1989, ten years after Judi's death, Windsor and his expanding family suffered a double tragedy of almost indescribable cruelty. Within a matter of weeks, Ricky, his eldest son, lost both his daughter, Nicole, and his 24-year-old wife, Dawn. The nightmare began with a horrible coincidence.

'As soon as we began to think that Dawn was seriously ill, I drove her to Velindre, the cancer hospital in Cardiff, to have her checked out,' Windsor says. 'The same doctor who'd told me the news about Judi ten years earlier then told me the same terrible news about Dawn. He said, "Bob, she is riddled with cancer. I'm dreadfully sorry about this, but I've got to tell you the same awful thing I told you about your wife."

'For the second time in my life, I was in the same dilemma. I didn't know what to do. I didn't tell Dawn, but I had to tell Ricky, and we all decided we'd fight it with everything we'd got. Just when we thought things couldn't get any more horrific, they did. Nicole, who was eighteen months old, died one week later from what was diagnosed as a condition known in the medical profession as a floppy windpipe.

'When she was in the cot lying on her back, her throat closed and that was it. Dawn's condition got progressively worse. She suffered horribly but never complained. She'd say, "I'm not worried. Nicole has gone ahead of me and she's waiting for her mother. Soon I'm going to be with Nicole again."

'It was a very, very sad time. Once she and Ricky decided to get married, Dawn asked me to make all the arrangements for the wedding at Bettws church in Newport and the reception at the Horseshoe, out in the country at a place called Mamhilad. Time was running out fast for Dawn. On the morning of the wedding, the people from the hospice got in touch to say they didn't think she was going to make it.

'We rang them back a couple of hours later and by then Dawn was asking them to help get her dressed. She walked down the aisle, although it took so much out of her that she had to sit by the altar for the ceremony. She was happy, it was a gorgeous occasion, but she had to go back to the hospice after an hour. She died about two weeks later.

'Dawn was a beautiful, beautiful girl, but two days before she passed away the cancer had reduced her to not much more than a skeleton. I cannot understand why anyone should suffer from such a horrific illness, especially one so young. Over a period of ten years, Ricky had lost his mother, his wife and his daughter.

'Every time I think that I've had a bad time, I think about Ricky and how much worse it was for him. Nobody deserves that and it says a lot about his character that he picked himself up from each of those devastating blows to make a success of his life. A lesser man would have been broken by the torment and grief.

'We always make a point of going to the cemetery on the anniversary of Nicole's death and putting flowers on her grave. By a very strange coincidence, my youngest son, Sean, was born on 10 June 1991, the second anniversary of my granddaughter passing away. They do say, don't they, that the Lord gives and the Lord takes away.

'I was doubly blessed to have three more children with Lynne – Mark, Luke and Sean. I was also lucky that all the children got on, that there was never any split. Sometimes in life you go through a period where every door seems to be slammed in your face, and I'd had my share of hard times, so it made a nice change to find things going my way. A lovely wife, a loving family and a business going from strength to strength. It felt like I didn't have a care in the world.'

And then, for the third time, cancer reared its ugly, terrifying head. Windsor, the hard man who had withstood the annual battery by France as though fortified by a piece of reinforced steel borrowed from the hot mills where he used to work, found himself crushed by another sledgehammer blow shortly before Christmas 2004.

'I found out completely by accident,' he says. 'The fella who'd done my life insurance for 15 years rang me up and said, "Bob, your policy has matured. You can have your money back and take out a smaller one if you so wish."

'That was fine by me and he said he'd have to arrange for someone to do a quick medical. I pointed out that there was nothing wrong with me and that I wasn't into wasting time or money. He insisted and they'd almost completed the medical when I was asked to pee on a straw.

'They took the sample away to have it tested. A few days later, they told me they'd found a touch of blood in my water. They asked me if I'd had any difficulty going to the toilet. I said, "No problems. Same as normal."

'They did further tests and then I saw a specialist. He said, "I'm not happy with this. I want you in the Royal Gwent as soon as possible."

'They took some stuff out of my prostate, did biopsies and called me back in at the beginning of March. The surgeon, Mr Carter, told me, "Bob, you've got cancer."

'I knew something was up because when I went in to see him they called the nurse in as well. Maybe they thought I was going to break down. The news stunned me. My first reaction was to ask, "Right, what do I have to do now?"

'He said, "There are things you can do with prostate cancer. There's radiotheraphy and there's a new treatment, which has not been tried and tested, which involves putting radioactive seeds in the prostate to try and kill off the cancer. But, in your case, there is no choice. We operate."

'There was worse to come. "You've got one of the most aggressive cancers you can have," Mr Carter said. "We're going to have to operate and we're going to have to get it seen to right away."

'I said, "Operate? Hang on, Wales are playing on Saturday and I've arranged to go."

'He said, "Do you want to see Wales play next year? And the year after that?"

'"Yes, of course I do."

'"Well," he said, "you'll have the op whenever I say so – tomorrow."'

The Duke did not dissolve into a flood of tears. Nor did he hold his head in his hands and wallow in self-pity. Windsor being Windsor, he did something which, very probably, only he would have done. He told a dirty joke about how the in-hospital treatment for patients with testicular ailments varies according to whether they are on the national health or members of a private health scheme.

'I went into hospital the next day, and before the operation Mr Carter said, "With this type of surgery, there can be side effects. If we damage the nerve, you might not be able to get an erection again. Drugs like Viagra can help."

'This rocked me, and later on, because of the domestic situation with my wife, I almost wished I'd never had it done, that I'd carried on and died. That would have happened had they not caught my cancer when they did. They said that had they not discovered it for another three or four months, there would have been very little they could have done. So I was very lucky in that respect.

'I was going to have to take my chances on the erection front, because I didn't have much choice, not when the alternative meant I'd be pushing up daisies in a matter of months. The operation knocked me for six, more than I'd imagined, and during the early stages of my convalescence I struggled to cope with the pressure of that and running the business. There was also the added problem preying on my mind as to the possible physical side effects. On top of all that, there was no guarantee that I was going to live that long anyway.

'Whether it was because of my illness I don't know, but, for whatever reason, my marriage wasn't right. It began to annoy me, and that in turn meant that I couldn't sleep at night. I kept tormenting myself with the same questions: how was I going to cope and what kind of a future did I have, if I had any future at all?

'I worried constantly about the children, whether the first three I had with Judi were still getting on with the three I had with Lynne. How was all this going to affect them? Thank God, it didn't. Thank God, they had the strength of character and the loyalty to stick together through it all, because it can't have been easy for any of them. As Luke said to me one day, "Have no fears on that score. It's not a case of them or us. They are all my brothers and sisters and they always will be."

'I went in for my operation afraid that once I'd been opened up the cancer would spread like wildfire. I thought I was a goner. Another company wanted to buy us out and I decided the best thing to do was to sell, to make sure everyone was looked after. The people who'd taken us over asked me to stay on. Everything was agreed before I went in for the operation in March 2005. I signed the papers to sell the company that April, after I came out of hospital.

'The arrangement was that I'd work for the new owner for a year. It was a good deal, but, sadly, we had to fight like hell over a period of three or four years to get our money. By then, we were into waste management, cleaning out underground tanks for big customers like Welsh Water. The health and safety issues became very stringent and that was another reason why I'd made the right decision. From my wife's point of view, it seemed like the worst decision I'd made. Everything in my private life went completely wrong.

'I was rough for a while. I'd never touched another woman from the day I met Lynne. I'd always been sexually active. Now I wasn't performing like I used to. I wasn't a stallion any more, but I could still get there with the help of medication. After a while, my mind went altogether. I went straight down into a big black hole.

'My second marriage disintegrated around this time. I suppose the news that your partner is seriously ill and could die soon could have such a frightening effect that you walk away. Theoretically, I could have consoled myself with the possibility of starting a relationship with someone else, but how do you cope if you meet a woman who really likes you and you can't do anything? Do you say, "I'm sorry, but we're not going to go to bed. How about a game of cards?"

'I did one thing badly and I will admit to it. Lynne booked a holiday in Spain with all the kids. I said, "You know how much I hate flying and you want me to get on a plane with all my children?" Every time I got on board a plane, I thought it was going to crash. I told her, "I can't do it."

'I know it was selfish because that fear of planes didn't stop me touring South Africa and New Zealand with the Lions. She went with the kids. They said it was great. In hindsight, I can see that I should have gone. I should have made the effort and put myself out for them. That is my biggest regret – my biggest mistake in my relationship with Lynne. I let them down. Too late now . . .

'As for my cancer, you never have the all-clear. As the specialist said to me, "Bob, you're a cancer survivor, that's what you are." You have it checked every three months. If your blood count is 0.001 – marvellous. It means you've got it in check.

'On the worst days, I tried to think of Broonie, my dear friend Gordon Brown, and how bravely he fought cancer before it killed him in his early 50s. Lying there thinking of him and what a wonderful chap he was lifted my spirits. I rang Gordon most weekends over the last months of his life, and every time, before I rang off, I told him I loved him. And that is something I had never told another bloke before or since.'

Brown described Windsor as the archetypal loveable rogue. 'In rugby, you get bankers and brickies, doctors and dockers, teachers and tearaways,' he told Robert Philip of the *Daily Telegraph*. 'Bobby was a hard-as-nails Welsh steelworker. When he came to your house, you put away all the cutlery. When he shook hands, you had to make sure you still had your watch and rings!'

The Scot loved his fellow Celt's reaction to McBride's famous introductory speech before the Lions left London in May 1974, when the tour was being battered by anti-apartheid campaigners. 'Willie John said, "If there is anyone here with any doubts, go home now,"' Brown recalled. '"If you don't leave within the next two minutes, you are here for the next four months. I have been in South Africa before and there's going to be a lot of physical intimidation, a lot of cheating. So if you're not up for a fight, there's the door." There was a brief silence after McBride finished speaking until Bobby, who loved fighting more than anything, jumped up and shouted, "I'm going to bloody well love this."'

Brown's bravery was impossible to overstate. They staged a dinner in his honour attended by the great and the good in London on 28 February 2001. When McBride, his old Lions captain, helped him gently to his seat that evening, there wasn't a dry eye in the house. The Scot knew time had all but run out. With his life expectancy reduced to a matter of days, Brown defied the ravages of his illness to climb out of his wheelchair and walk on his own two feet, albeit with a little assistance.

'This is the last supper, Willie John,' he told McBride by way of whispered thanks as 1,400 guests gave him a standing ovation. 'But I'll tell you this – it's going to be one hell of a night.'

It was, too, and how typical of the man that, right to the very end, nothing could dilute his sense of fun, no matter how severe his pain. He still found the courage to smile and give every impression that it was just another rugby dinner, to be enjoyed to the hilt.

Somehow, he found the strength to stand unaided and regale his last audience with a few of the old stories. He recounted how, as a budding sixteen-year-old goalkeeper in a Troon Juniors' Cup tie, one career ended and another took off when he rugby-tackled an opponent, provoking such uproar that he required a police escort before seeking refuge the following Saturday at the local rugby club.

His father had kept goal for Scotland, his mother was a hockey international and it was surely only a matter of time before Gordon joined his eldest brother, Peter, in the Scottish pack. Gordon was in and Peter out at the start, only for the roles to be rapidly reversed for the next match, Wales in Cardiff.

'I'm back in the team,' an ecstatic Peter told his brother.

'Great,' says Gordon. 'Who's been dropped?'

'You.'

Then there was the one from the '74 Lions tour about Johan de Bruyn and his glass eye and what happened after he had been hit by Mike Burton, the Englishman having followed McBride's orders to 'stoop to the lowest of the low'.

'His good eye closed up immediately and the glass one fell out,' Burton says. 'We're all looking for it and there was an awkward silence until Gordon piped up. "Johan," he says, "where exactly were you standing when Mickey hit you?"'

The 'last supper' at one of London's finest West End venues took so much out of Brown that, instead of flying to America the next morning in search of some miracle cure, he was taken straight to hospital in London. 'I remember holding his hand that morning,' McBride recalled. 'He was even smiling then, saying what a great night it had been. I found that evening very difficult because Gordon was dying, but he loved it. My greatest memory of Broonie will always be his wonderful zest for life, right to the end.'

Brown died less than three weeks after the London dinner, on 19 March 2001, at the age of fifty-three. Windsor, whose cancer nightmare descended a few years later, has since become an ambassador for the prostate cancer charity Progress, urging men of all ages to take pre-emptive action against a form of cancer which kills more than 10,000 in the UK every year.

'Most men think it could never happen to them and most young men don't even think about it at all,' Windsor says. 'Over the last 30 years, rates of prostate cancer have nearly trebled. There are something like 35,000 men diagnosed with it each year; more than three-quarters of them survive the disease for more than five years because more are waking up to the screening test.

'That's the message I keep hammering home whenever I have the chance to do a talk on behalf of Progress and help raise funds for better treatment facilities. There was one form of treatment which, at that time, was available only in England. We successfully campaigned for it to be extended to Wales.

'I always try to be as humorous as possible, but I'm deadly serious in getting the message across about this illness. It's all about raising awareness. My old mate Fergus Slattery tells me that he makes sure he has it checked out every few months.

'Whenever I speak to rugby clubs at their dinners, I always say at the end, "Boys, have a great night. I've really enjoyed your company, hope you've enjoyed mine. Just one thing. If you haven't had a blood test, go on Monday and get rid of the stupid idea that it could never happen to you."

'I thought that myself. If I hadn't found out by a complete accident, I'd have been a goner a long time ago.'

12

....

THE £20-MILLION CIRCUS

The first covert operation to launch a professional circus took place during the early months of 1983. More than two hundred players from the British Isles and the three southern hemisphere superpowers signed contracts promising six-figure sums and a series of matches kicking off with an ambitious double-header at Stamford Bridge in London on 14 January 1984 – England versus Wales followed by Australia versus New Zealand.

World Championship Rugby, a round-robin tournament involving England, Ireland, Scotland, Wales, France, the Wallabies, the All Blacks and South Africa, was going to change the game for ever, according to its creator, an imaginative Australian journalist called David Lord.

He conducted a series of clandestine meetings with the world's leading players and made the idea sound so plausible that they put pen to paper in their droves. In the end, Lord had everything he needed: eight international squads of twenty-eight players plus eight international coaches. Everything except the £20 million to make it work.

Before the prospective backers evaporated into thin air, Lord assured the players that his flight of fancy would get off the ground. At best, it may have reached an altitude of three feet, but while its would-be inventor found himself derided by the Establishment, there could be no denying that Lord would have done for professional rugby what the Wright brothers and their flying machine did for the aviation industry had he not been a man too far ahead of his time.

'Had there been pay TV then, the game would have turned professional with me,' he said, looking back later after the sport recognised the reality and declared itself open. 'The problem was that terrestrial television networks were worried that traditional advertisers would not advertise on a channel showing a professional rugby circus. There was so much bad feeling. No one has been more pilloried or ostracised than I was then. Lepers, communists and terrorists were all treated better. I found it staggering that people you had known all your life suddenly thought you were the arch-enemy.'

Twelve years after Lord's attempt bit the dust, another Australian struck a ten-year deal, worth £336 million, with the South African, Australian and New Zealand Unions to televise the Tri-Nations. Rupert Murdoch's move to secure the Unions invited every other big beast in the business jungle, notably Kerry Packer, to secure the most valuable asset of all, the players.

'The Rugby Unions were so busy patting themselves on the back, they didn't think to sign up their own players,' Lord said. 'Had the Unions lost control, they would only have had themselves to blame. They've had one hundred years to sell the game but they've spent all that time looking after themselves.'

A professional circus in 1983 would have been manna from heaven for those players nearing the end of their careers but whose reputation earned on the battlefields of Lions tours gave them an enduring commercial cachet. Bobby Windsor had another, more pressing reason for hitching himself to the Lord bandwagon, beyond the fact that the notion of signing up appealed to his rebellious nature.

What motivated Windsor then more than anything else was the grim discovery that no amount of success on the rugby field could pay the bills. 'I remember the day I was tapped up about the rebel tour,' he says. 'We met at the Angel Hotel in Cardiff and everything sounded perfect. We were going to be paid a lot of money to play all over the world. Everything would be taken care of, we'd still be playing the game we loved and get a big screw into the bargain.

'When they got the contracts out and asked us to sign, I don't think anyone turned it down. The contract was a declaration to say, "Yes, I am interested and if it comes off, I'm in."

'Lord explained to us that the contracts would be kept in the safe of a solicitor's office in Sydney. I thought, what if someone gets hold of those? We've had it. We'll all be banned for life.

'Lord assured us, "Have no fears – if nothing comes of this, the contracts will be destroyed. No one will ever know." We'd be like international footballers, travelling all over the place and getting paid for a job we'd all done for nothing. Brilliant.

'Since then, there's been a lot of talk about professional circuses, but this was the first one. They were very professional in the way they explained it all. I wanted it to happen, but the more I thought about it, the more doubtful I became. When news of it got out, the Welsh squad were told by the Union that if any of us were in discussion about a professional game, we would be booted out.

'It didn't matter whether you'd signed or not. You'd be banned for life just for talking about playing the game for money. Those sorts of threats didn't bother me, but some of the younger players would have been frightened to death. When I walked out of that meeting at the Angel Hotel, I thought it all seemed a bit too good to be true. And that was the last I ever heard of it.

'I could have done with something, because I'd been out of work month after month. The steel industry was so depressed, the job was hardly worth having. Times got so bad that there was hardly any money to be earned there and pretty soon I was out of a job.

'As luck would have it, I'd only been gone from there six months when they started offering redundancy packages. The trade union tried their best on my behalf, but without any luck.

'Steve Fenwick, Tommy David and Derek Quinnell were all doing really well as reps selling industrial chemicals and I was offered a job doing the same thing for a different company, selling gloves, boots and the like. Now I had more money and the petrol all paid for.

'Brian Clark, the former Cardiff City footballer, was with the same company and he showed me the ropes. He was a really top man, but, with industry generally having a rough time, it slowly dawned on me that it was the wrong job at the wrong time.

'That also spanned the time Judi died. Less than a year after that, I was in hospital having an operation on my back. All I got for my trouble was the sack – talk about kicking a man while he's down. So there I was with three kids and no job. When you're wondering how you're going to pay for the next meal, never mind the mortgage, a lot of thoughts flash through your mind.

'I was on my uppers, an ex-Welsh international, but there was never any way that the super-duper stars I'd played alongside were going to be in the same predicament. There was always something for them to do. Some of them were directors of this company and directors of that company to the extent that the only thing they didn't direct was the traffic. They had no qualifications for those jobs. They got them on the back of their rugby fame.

'Every day, I was racking my brains. What the f**k am I going to do? I never signed on for the dole because I was too embarrassed. I knew I was entitled to, but I couldn't do it. Then someone gave me the idea of taking a stall at Pontypool market. I made a few enquiries, found out that I could put a stall up there for £1 a week. John Perkins, my old Pontypool teammate, made me up a stall with doors which I could lock.

'As a club, Pontypool were going through a bad stage of not being that well liked by some of the teams they played against, and I was watching a film on television one night with Steve McQueen riding his mean machine. It gave me an idea, so the next day I went to this chap in Cardiff who was an embroiderer.

'I asked him to make me a print of a rugby team who looked like a bunch of maniacs with a few words printed underneath saying: "Pontypool RFC – the Mean Machine". I was onto a winner straight away. I sold thousands of them as T-shirts and sweatshirts. People were sending them to their relatives all over the world. That was a cracker, but it only had a short shelf life.'

Bristol's refusal to play ball with Pontypool any more after a match there in April 1984 would doubtless have been all grist to the Windsor mill as a timely public-relations boost. The mean machine appeared all the meaner in the light of Bristol's decision to cancel fixtures until further notice after they had been put to the sword by 46 points to 18 on the last Saturday of March.

'Bristol have been unhappy about the excessively physical nature of play by Pontypool players in recent years,' the Bristol chairman, the late Dave Tyler, said. 'We feel the game is played for enjoyment by young men who are amateurs and have to go to work the next day.'

In their letter formally notifying Pooler of their decision, Bristol secretary Tom Mahoney wrote: 'We brought over a weakened side who, we felt, gave a good account of themselves. But to be subjected to violence when you already had the game easily won is not only unpleasant but completely unnecessary.'

Pontypool rejected the allegation of violent conduct as 'absolute nonsense', not that the spat did any harm at all in ensuring that their old hooker's roaring trade roared on a little longer. 'It was brilliant while it lasted, but it wasn't going to last for the rest of my working life,'

Windsor says. 'Working in the market, it was all cash, so you always had a wad in your back pocket. You had to keep busy, especially in winter, otherwise you were liable to go down with hypothermia. There was no heating in the market, so in the winter it was freezing.

'J.J. phoned up one day to ask how it was going. He said he'd met people up in Solihull who were looking for a rep in South Wales. I said I wasn't keen to go through all that again because I'd had a bad experience with Derek Quinnell.

'He was working for a company called Gremer Chemicals. They were going to break away and form their own company called Triple Crown Chemicals. At the last minute, Derek pulled out, leaving Steve Fenwick and Tommy David on their own. Derek stayed with Gremer and then advertised for a rep in Gwent, which would have been brilliant for me.

'Derek was the sales director. I rang him up and said, "That job you've advertised would suit me down to the ground. That would be great."

'He said no, that because we'd been friends and mates in the same team, he wouldn't be able to talk to me the way he could talk to someone he wasn't friendly with, on a purely business footing. He said it wouldn't work. The fact that I was out of work didn't seem to come into it.

'In my mind, that job was going to be my salvation. It would have meant that much to me. That was one of the biggest kicks in the guts I've ever had. I have never ever spoken to Derek about it from that day to this. I hope he reads about it in this book, rings me up and says, "I remember that, Bob." Years later, when I was in business, I took Derek to certain companies so he could get some business.

'Anyway, J.J. said this repping job was with a company he recommended called Dimex, which specialised in cleaning materials. He arranged for them to call me, I went for the interview and got the job.

'After a while, they made me sales manager, which widened the area beyond Gwent. As the company prospered, I got a number of the Welsh players jobs – Phil Bennett, Gary Pearce, Ian "Ikey" Stephens, John Perkins, Steve Sutton, Bernard Thomas and a few more. I gave them the help which I hadn't got a couple of years before, other than from J.J., who's been a really good buttie over the years.'

Despite standing down to give Steve Jones a clear shot at the Wales position, which continued to elude him, Windsor was still in sufficient demand for one final appearance at his old stamping ground, Cardiff

THE £20-MILLION CIRCUS

Arms Park. Pontypool's first Welsh Cup final, on 30 April 1983, brought them an 18–6 win over Swansea, preventing the Whites from completing a cup and championship double.

Pontypool did what they did best during a season when the uncapped David Bishop announced himself as a scrum-half par excellence, his 33 tries leaving no doubt about his complete recovery from a broken neck earlier in his senior career. A dominant pack squeezed Swansea into conceding enough penalties for full-back Peter Lewis to kick the goals and left wing Bleddyn Taylor to score the only try. Far from being the result of a dazzling three-quarter move, it came from a Mike Goldsworthy drop kick; when the ball rebounded off a post, Taylor seized the ball and touched it down while Swansea were still dithering.

Windsor, recalled for the occasion to fill the propping role performed down the years by the retired Charlie Faulkner, damaged a hamstring ten minutes into the match and limped off to be replaced by Mike Crowley. The following season, with their old stager happy to spring out of the supporting cast every now and again, Pooler proved themselves the most consistent club in the British Isles.

They won forty-two of their forty-six matches, drew two and lost the other two, 10–9 at home to Cardiff on 19 October and 10–8 at Neath on 2 March. The following week, they avenged the Cardiff defeat by winning at the Arms Park 16–11, having seen Neath off at Pontypool Park the previous autumn to the tune of six tries to one.

All told, they scored almost 1,500 points and 219 tries, 36 from the still uncapped Bishop, a figure which would probably have topped 40 had it not been for an enforced six-week absence after he was sent off for stamping during a routine home win over Saracens. As well as the north London club, they beat every other English opponent they came across that season – Gloucester, Bath, Coventry, London Irish, Bedford, Bristol, Sale, Leicester and Waterloo.

There were tries galore, an average of almost five a game. Chris Huish weighed in with a season's haul of 24 from the back row, Goff Davies with 22 from one wing, Lee Jones with 19 from the centre, Eddie Butler with 13 from number 8 and Perkins managed to join them in double figures, no mean feat for a second-row forward. Graham Price helped himself to six, an unusually high return for a tighthead prop.

Butler's background – public school followed by Cambridge University, not quite the natural habitat for Pontypool forwards – could scarcely have been more different to Windsor's – Brynglas Secondary Modern and the University of Life. Rugby's egalitarian society united them in a common cause once the student had opted to leave Newport and join Pontypool, taking note of his father's sombre advice about Pooler's reputation for being 'very rough' but discounting it on the basis that he would rather play for them than against them.

Butler's first match for Pontypool, as a nineteen year old, was at Swansea in September 1976; his last came during the end-of-season shindig in Canada nine years later. By then, the embryonic captain of Wales had seen more than enough of Windsor at close quarters and from afar to know precisely where he stood amongst the finest internationals of his time.

'Bobby Windsor was the best player I ever played with,' Butler says. 'Simple as that. He was also vicious, the most cold-hearted brute you would never wish to see standing over you at a ruck. He was the undisputed leader of the Viet-Gwent, a ferocious figure who rode the crest of a gigantic wave after the '74 Lions tour. Our Bob was always a big lump, but on that tour he turned it into almost 17 stone of muscle. He was fighting fit, in every sense, and he kept that going.

'He was also sublimely skilful, a good footballer who was very quick, especially off the mark. The great Pontypool rolling maul crushed many an opponent, but without Bobby there was no such weapon. He controlled the whole thing by getting his grubby little mitts on the ball and driving it from the back.

'Some hookers are good at some parts of their trade and not so good at others. Bobby was the master of them all. He was a very good technician whose squat running style with its low centre of gravity made him unstoppable. He was the heart and soul of a particularly destructive scrummage and rolling maul.

'He was also tough. If you were going to punch Bobby, you had to make sure it was a good one or not bother. I remember a match against Tredegar in the mid-'80s, when he and I were both sliding out of the game. Bobby clipped Ian Lewis, the Tredegar scrum-half, early in the game and Ian, fair play to him, caught the Duke with a good one.

'Bobby spent what time was left trying to exact what would have been horrible retribution. Ian Lewis wisely kept out of his way and went scarpering off the field at the end with Bobby in hot pursuit, leaving the rest of us thinking, what's he going to do now?

'Windsor, the story goes, stormed on into the Tredegar dressing-room, put an arm round Lewis and said, "I know you're frightened, but the game's over. As soon as you get changed, we're going to have a couple of pints together."

'In his own peculiar way, Bobby was very conscious of the traditions of the game. He was of his time and he played according to the laws of that time. On the Lions tour of 1977 to New Zealand, he was overtaken by another wonderful hooker who shared many of the traits of cruelty, Peter Wheeler. But, for at least a couple of seasons, Bobby was a towering force in the game, as he would have been in any era.

'Had he been playing today as a professional, he would have served a bit of time and been fined heavily, but he would have adapted easily, not least because he always had an eye for the commercial opportunity. As a coach, he was excellent, with a broad vision of how the game should be played.

'What made him such a lovable character was that he had a natural sparkle and wit. I've seen him woo audiences full of blue-rinse ladies, not necessarily by modifying his language but by being very quick on his feet. He always had a sharp mind, which meant he could always leave them laughing. He's always been a gravel-voiced hoot who says what he thinks.'

That readiness to give everything straight from the shoulder made him a big hit as a television pundit for BBC Wales on their own version of *Rugby Special*, not that the mandarins at the Welsh Rugby Union necessarily found him that much of a hoot. Windsor was nothing if not candid, brutally so at times, and if that ruffled a few feathers within the Establishment, then so much the better as far as he was concerned.

Sadly, it proved to be his undoing. The Welsh Rugby Union, in their hypersensitivity, found him too straight for their liking and requested his removal. Butler, then embarking on a career in broadcasting and journalism which would take him to the pinnacle of his field, could not save his former colleague from being given something which Windsor usually made a point of giving the French – the order of the boot.

There were times, then, when the Union invited ridicule, most notably over the farce surrounding their participation or non-participation in the old South African Rugby Board's 100th birthday party celebrations in September 1989.

Former president Rhys (R.H.) Williams denied that he was attending, only to climb aboard an SAA 747 for Johannesburg at Heathrow airport the following day. Clive Rowlands, his successor as president, resigned in protest at the decision of ten Welsh players, among them his son-in-law Robert Jones, to accept invitations and disobey the presidential instruction to stay at home in preparation for the All Blacks match later in the autumn.

David East, the former chief constable of South Wales who had been appointed secretary of the WRU only months earlier, also resigned after learning that other Union members had gone behind his back in their dealings with the South African Board. Unlike Rowlands, he did not withdraw his resignation.

In a classic case of closing the stable door after the horse had bolted – or ten of them, in the case of the players – the WRU decided at an extraordinary general meeting to banish all contact with apartheid South Africa.

The following motion was carried by a vote of 306–62, with six abstentions:

> For so long as any rugby player living in the Republic of South Africa is the victim of racial discrimination under the laws of that country, neither the Welsh Rugby Union nor any of its member clubs will become involved in any matches organised under the authority of the South African Rugby Board. Nor will the Union, nor any of its members, permit teams under the jurisdiction of the South African Rugby Union to play in Wales.

The scandal left the Union no option but to set up an inquiry, headed by a Cardiff barrister who would rise to become the single most influential figure in the world game as chairman of the International Rugby Board during the momentous period before and after professionalism, until his tragically premature death in April 2003 at the age of 57. Vernon Pugh, QC, knew that players had been paid to go to South Africa but was unable to name names.

'There is evidence that two of the Welsh players were seeking to transfer monies to the UK from bank accounts held for them in Luxembourg,' he wrote when the inquiry published its findings in 1991. 'All the players denied receiving any money or promise of money or any payment in kind or otherwise.

'We concluded that responses to questions on this point had been discussed between the players beforehand. This was evident from the manner of the answers given. It was evidence which was clearly rehearsed. We are unable to advise the Union that the evidence makes us sure that the players received remuneration.

'All the players went to the inquiry but other witnesses who could have shed light on this matter refused.'

Pugh's damning verdict uncovered evidence of involvement by some senior Welsh Rugby Union members which he said gave rise to 'the gravest cause for concern for both the present and future for rugby football in Wales'.

His report stated: 'While individual lack of circumspection or even deceitful behaviour might be explicable, the vitally disturbing feature was that such behaviour seemed so widespread as to be almost endemic to the whole system and its operation. We were told untruths by at least three witnesses who currently held positions of responsibility and influence within the administration of the Union. Despite their appreciating that we recognised parts of their evidence as being untrue, and were likely to so record in our report, there was an evident lack of concern as to that fact.'

John Ryan, then Wales coach, told the inquiry that he expected only two or three players to travel to South Africa and that such a number would not harm the Welsh team's prospects for the early-season internationals. He did not know that ten would go or who they were, the report stated. He said that only two players (Phil John and David Pickering) troubled to speak to him as to the acceptability of their accepting invitations.

The other eight Welsh players involved were Paul Thorburn, who had been identified as the ringleader, Mike Hall, Phil Davies, Paul Turner, Robert Jones, Mark Ring, Anthony Clement and Robert Norster. Only one has since revealed how much he was paid to make the trip.

Ring came clean in his autobiography, admitting that he had agreed a payment of £35,000 – at a time when even to take a penny for playing was sufficient to incur a life ban for contravening the amateur regulations. Ring also admitted that he was one of those referred to in the inquiry report as using a bank account in Luxembourg and that he had lied to Pugh.

'I remember Vernon Pugh asking me point-blank in my interview whether I had received payment for going to South Africa,' Ring said. 'I just smiled and said no, but there was a look between us that made it clear we both knew I was lying . . . The tax on the fee was all paid and the loot . . . was paid into an account in Luxembourg. I was instructed that if I wanted any of it, I would have to make the demand two days earlier to allow time for the transaction to go through, then I would have to get a train to London to an address where I would meet a South African businessman and he would hand over any money in cash. For a fair while, I was nipping back and forth to London and getting my hands on wads of cash and living the life of Riley . . .'

And to think the Pontypool front row were frozen out by the Barbarians over a £25 expenses claim for petrol and fish and chips! Ring's bonanza illustrated the amount of money sloshing about in places like South Africa for what was still, at least in theory, an amateur game.

Money was also a major driving force behind the advent of the World Cup. The Australian and New Zealand Unions moved quickly under the leadership of Nick Shehadie, a Wallaby prop who became Lord Mayor of Sydney, to create the tournament as a pre-emptive strike against a Kerry Packer or a Rupert Murdoch beating them to it and effectively hijacking the sport at Test level. In 1986, when Shehadie's delegation asked the Scottish Rugby Union for their votes in favour of a World Cup, their honorary treasurer, Gordon Masson, protested, 'Over my dead body.'

Shehadie told him not to bother coming to the tournament and there is an apocryphal story about a subsequent meeting: when Shehadie took his seat in the royal box at Twickenham for the 1991 final, he looked around and, to his surprise, found the aforesaid Masson sitting in the same box, whereupon Shehadie grabbed him by the wrist. When Masson enquired as to what he was doing, Sir Nicholas supposedly said, 'Just checking your pulse to make sure you're alive.'

For reasons only they know, the International Board took another six years after the grubby South African centenary celebrations of 1989 to grasp the nettle of professionalism. They would probably have gone on navel-gazing had one of the most influential figures in the world game not come clean and confessed all during the Board's historic meeting in central Paris on the last weekend of August 1995.

Dr Louis Luyt, a one-time second-row forward in the Orange Free State who began his working life as a railway clerk with the South African equivalent of two brass farthings in his pocket, drove a convoy of Voortrekkers' wagons through the fanciful notion that nobody was paid for playing the game. The Board's then chairman, Vernon Pugh of Wales, who had been appointed to head an investigation into professionalism, called on the New Zealander Rob Fisher to kick the debate off. He promptly passed the ball to Luyt, who writes in his autobiography *Walking Proud*:

A heavy cloud hung over the room and everyone's eyes turned to me. Perhaps they were hoping that I would, as they did, tiptoe around the issue and save everyone embarrassment. Instead I decided to tackle the 'pro' word head-on. The time had come, I felt, to talk honestly and openly about professionalism instead of hiding behind euphemisms and obscurantisms.

'First of all, Mr Chairman, I am here today to declare SARFU [South African Rugby Football Union] and South African rugby as professionals to your organisation,' I said. 'But now, if I have the chairman's permission, I would like to go round the table and ask each and every one whether they have ever paid their players in one way or another. Let's start with England . . .'

You could hear a pin drop. Several board members shuffled in their chairs and rearranged the papers in front of them. The first answer. Yes, England did, in fact, pay its players but it was through a trust fund.

'Does it matter?' I asked. 'The end result is the same.'

Next, Scotland, in the affirmative. One after another, everyone admitted to some form of payment, except Argentina. In fact, I was surprised at the amounts paid by some of the nations. It had always been my impression, judging from the constant criticism heaped upon us, that South Africa led the field. But we did not.

When Syd Millar of Ireland took his turn, he remarked, 'Yes, Louis, we do pay, but only a few thousand pounds a year. Nothing like the big money that some others are throwing around.'

'Syd, with all due respect,' I responded, 'there is no such thing as being a little bit pregnant.'

The young lady who provided the simultaneous translation into French sniggered but Millar and the others were not amused. I had cleared the air but muddied the waters. No one likes to be shown up as a hypocrite and, in a single session, I had succeeded in sullying every single 'shamateur' who had managed to hide behind the door while taking cheap shots at SARFU and me.

THE IRON DUKE

Professionalism came too late for Windsor and his contemporaries, but they had been left with the sort of indelible memories which no amount of money could ever buy, of a time during the '70s when the Lions ruled the world, and Wales, more often than not, ruled Europe, a time when to have been an international rugby player guaranteed a lot more fun than it does today.

Windsor scored his last try in first-class rugby during a 15–7 home win over Munster on 19 September 1985. He went out in fitting style in his 42nd year: his last match for the first team was a 38–0 rout of Nuneaton at Pontypool Park on 18 April 1987. It marked the end of an adventure spanning a quarter of a century, from Whitehead's to Newport Saracens, Cross Keys to Pontypool via Cardiff, Wales to the Lions, Monmouthshire to the Irish President's XV, the Barbarians to Crawshay's.

It consisted of almost a thousand matches, the best part of fifty thousand scrums, the odd scrape, more broken noses than he could ever remember, a million laughs, heart-breaking tragedy and rarely a dull moment. As a player who reached his Everest with the Lions in 1974, he spent the rest of the decade roaming around in the upper reaches of the Himalayas before helping Pontypool set mountainous records of their own.

Along the way, he only once signed a contract, for an Aussie journo with a good idea but not the wherewithal to make it happen. Somewhere, 10,000 miles away in an office in Sydney, still more dust must be gathering on a document signed in the name of R.W. Windsor, Esq.

13

. . . .

BEYOND A JOKE

Ray Prosser has seen them all over a period of 60 years, from the up-close-and-personal exchanges when he propped for Wales and the Lions down the decades to retirement and a more detached view of the best in the professional business. He has witnessed a veritable battalion of front-row forwards come and go since the '50s, first as an international in his own right, then as the most successful one-club coach in the British Isles and, latterly, as an educated spectator.

Nobody is more qualified to pass an opinion on the most technical area of the game because nobody has a clearer insight into the darkest recesses of the scrum and a better grasp of the physical and mental strength required to survive. For a whole generation, from the late '60s to the late '80s, Prosser turned Pontypool into a byword for scrummaging power, built around his special creation of the all-Lions front row, the Viet-Gwent.

In assessing the crème de la crème, he has a distinguished list to choose from, including one of his earliest opponents, the legendary Alfred Roques. If Prosser thought the Welsh selectors kept him waiting unduly long, until shortly before he turned 30, he was a whippersnapper compared to the mighty Alfred, who had gone 33 when he made his Five Nations debut, against Prosser at Cardiff Arms Park in 1958.

Later that year, Roques terrified the Springboks into ultimate submission during the famous French series win there. At one point, when the fur was flying at its thickest, the France captain, Lucien Mias, turned to his fearsome prop and whispered, 'Alfred, now is the time to unleash the dogs of war.' Not for nothing did the South Africans call him 'The Wild One'.

A peasant farmer's son who had played soccer until his mid-20s, Roques was almost 38 when he bowed out of the Test arena, against

Scotland in January 1963. Years later, when a reporter enquired as to what rugby had given him, Roques replied, 'I drive a refuse lorry in Cahors and, thanks to rugby, they put me in a tuxedo and I shook hands with the Queen of England.'

Many of his successors maintained the tradition, players like the master of menace, Gérard Cholley; the great bear of the Pyrenees, Robert Paparemborde; and the tragic Armand Vaquerin, the Béziers prop who played one game of Russian roulette too many at his bar in the centre of the town.

The All Blacks were no slouches when it came to looking after themselves, even if the brooding Keith Murdoch took it a bit far, hence his last sighting being ushered off the premises at Heathrow prior to deportation for assaulting a security guard at the New Zealand team's hotel in Cardiff. They had props like Kevin Skinner, who doubled up as New Zealand amateur heavyweight champion; the inestimable Sir Wilson Whineray; and Steve McDowell and Olo Brown, to name but two more.

There were great Scots – Hugh McLeod, Sandy Carmichael, Ian 'Mighty Mouse' McLauchlan, David Sole and 'Whispering' Tom Smith. The Irish had, amongst others, Tom Clifford, Syd Millar, Ray McLoughlin, Sean Lynch and Gordon Wood.

There were many more, like Fran Cotton and Jason Leonard from England, the Springboks captain Hannes Marias, the Australian-converted Argentinian Enrico Rodríguez, Graham Price of Wales and the durable Argentinian Diego Cash. When it came to hookers, Prosser was spoilt for choice all the more with the likes of Bryn Meredith (Wales), Alain Paco, Raphaël Ibañez (both France), John Pullin, Peter Wheeler (both England), Tane Norton, Sean Fitzpatrick (both New Zealand), Colin Deans (Scotland), Phil Kearns (Australia), Keith Wood (Ireland), John Smit (South Africa) and a South American most deserving to be in the highest company, Mario Ledesma of Argentina.

'I played with some good hookers in my time and I've seen many more good ones down the years,' Prosser says. 'But, to be quite honest, Bobby Windsor was in a different league. As well as being the best hooker, he was also the best front-row forward I ever saw. He stood out above the rest, not by a little bit but head and shoulders. And I'll say that to my dying day.

'Bobby was lethal. He was strong, quick as a three-quarter and utterly ruthless. He was so accurate that he'd kick a gnat's eye out from six feet. A lovely, affable bloke off the field, but he could be a dirty, vicious bastard on it. He used to frighten me at times and it takes a lot to do that. As a geriatric prop myself, I'd have maybe thought twice about having a go at him.

'When I watched him play, I used to think, thank goodness I wasn't born in the same era. I'd have hated it. Bobby could carry the ball and make big holes in the other team just by dipping his shoulder and bouncing people out of the way. He was so well balanced and quick that it always took more than one tackle to put him down. More often than not, he just ran through them.

'As a scrummager, he was such a powerful man that he could park his arse close to the ground and from that low a position drive through the opposition. Mind you, he was lucky to have two good props either side of him in Charlie and Pricey. Alfred Roques would probably have been as near to Bobby as anyone in my day. Roques was a hard man and ruthless, too.

'They were all hard men back then. There seemed to be a bit of the ape in some of them because they'd do anything to get an advantage. As well as the usual punching and booting, they'd have taken the corner flag out and tried to stick it up your backside if they had half a chance so you needed to be a bit apish to look after yourself.

'You didn't have television cameras covering all the angles in my day, as they do now. You could get away with blue murder in the scrums because nobody had much of a clue as to what was going on. A lot of the roughness seems to have disappeared from the game. People will think this is just an old front-row forward talking, but the modern props seem to lack the edge which used to be taken for granted. If you didn't have it, you didn't survive, because punching and kicking were part and parcel of the game. I even got bitten in one match against France.

'Maybe the game then would have been too dirty for today's players, although they have to contend with three referees and a citing commissioner. It's very different, but good players would stand out in any era – players like Bryn Meredith. I was lucky enough to be on the 1959 Lions tour to New Zealand with Bryn, a very good player and probably next best to Windsor as a hooker.

'Bobby was better because he had more power. Windsor was as strong as a bull. If he had a weakness, it was his passing, but he could compensate for that by knocking people out of the way. For a coach, he was a dream because you could do anything with him. He'd train like a dog and then come back for more. Some chaps would be difficult to handle, but you could speak your mind with Bob, give him a gee-up and off he'd go.'

Cross Keys against Pontypool during the 1972–73 season was the game which changed Windsor's rugby life more than any other. Prosser, then in the course of taking Pooler to the first of several championship titles, had signed one front-row forward from Cross Keys, Charlie Faulkner, the previous summer. Windsor left such an impression that Prosser made it his business to relieve Keys of their captain:

'Straight after the match, I said to Charlie, "Do you know that black-haired bastard of a hooker?"

'Charlie said, "Do I know him? I work with him in the same steelworks. Known him since we were kids. Why?"

'"Jesus Christ, I'd like to have him at Pontypool."

'"Leave it with me, Pross. I can get him."

'And so Charlie persuaded Bobby to join us. He did tell me he was getting a few quid at Cross Keys, but I told him straight, "We're a dry bread club. You'll get sweet f**k all here, but you will get the honour of playing for Pontypool." Tony Symons was the match secretary then and we didn't believe in paying. The same applied to me and often I'd have to dip into my own pocket.

'Bobby was ready straight away for Wales and the Lions. His power and pace set him apart from the others. Not only was he a brilliant player, but he was the best of blokes.'

The ruthless streak which underpinned Windsor's warrior-like ferocity did not dilute his generosity of spirit. Acutely conscious of Roy 'Shunto' Thomas's predicament as his international understudy – Thomas sat on more benches than most High Court judges without ever getting onto the pitch – Windsor thought of a scheme to feign injury in the closing minutes and clear the way for Thomas to win his cap. He ran the idea past Prosser.

'I said, "Pross, if we're doing well late in the game against Ireland on Saturday, I'm thinking of coming off with an injury and making sure Shunto gets his cap." We were good friends and I thought it would be a decent thing to do, because I'd have been going nuts if I'd been in his position.

'Pross went ballistic. He said, "Don't you dare cheapen the Welsh cap. Get this into your thick skull – you are never given a cap. You earn it. If they think Roy Thomas is worth a cap, they'll pick him and you'll be out on your ear."'

Prosser admired Windsor the man as much as Windsor the front-row forward. 'Bobby had principles,' he says. 'In fact, he had more principle in his little finger than some had in their entire body. I couldn't fault him on or off the field, but if I thought very hard my one criticism of him would be that sometimes he'd say, "I'll see you at so-and-so's place tonight at such-and-such a time." You'd get there and he'd be nowhere to be seen. But that was nothing, really.'

During the final period of his long haul as Pontypool coach, Prosser guided the club to a hat-trick of Welsh Championship titles. In three seasons of unprecedented supremacy, from 1983 to 1986, they played 136 matches, won 120, drew 4 and lost 12. They rattled up almost 4,000 points and conceded fewer than 1,500.

When Prosser stood down, Windsor took over and proceeded to regain the title at the end of his first season as coach in tandem with the former prolific-scoring wing Goff Davies. During that 1987–88 campaign, the new coaches redefined Pontypool as more than a pack of forwards, using the inimitable talents offered by David Bishop at scrum-half and another Cardiffian, the multiskilled Mark Ring, whether at outside-half or centre.

In a season of staggering achievement, they won forty of their forty-two matches, losing at home to Bridgend in the first month of the season and to Neath at Cardiff Arms Park in the semi-final of the Welsh Cup six months later. They topped forty points on eight occasions, most notably at home to Llanelli in October, before completing the double at Stradey Park in February.

Had the European Cup been invented ten years earlier, in time to catch the end of Béziers' long reign as the most formidable club across the Channel, the first final would probably have guaranteed a duel reminiscent of Wales–France for most of the '70s.

Windsor followed the landslide success of that debut season as coach by resigning, a move which stretched the old adage about quitting while ahead to absurd lengths. His decision followed an internal dispute over the choice of captain. The Pontypool committee wanted Bishop, Windsor wanted Ring.

'Bish was a fantastic player, but I had two good reasons for wanting Ring,' Windsor says. 'First, I knew for certain that it was only a matter of time before Bishop went north to rugby league, because it was obvious that the Welsh selectors would go out of their way not to pick him.

Second, I knew he was too abrasive for the rest of the players and his style wouldn't have gone down at all well with some. Bish would have been the first name down on any team of mine, but we also had to think about protecting the good spirit we had in the dressing-room.

'The art of good captaincy is in being able to handle different players in different ways to make sure you get the best out of all of them all the time. You have to put an arm round some and give others a boot up the backside, but Bish would have handled them all the same way. He would not have been the right choice.

'One of the reasons we lost that semi-final to Neath was because he got involved in a physical confrontation with Phil Pugh, the Neath flanker. He was one of two blindsides in their back row that day, and because of that our plan was to get the ball out into the backs and expose their lack of pace. It worked a treat, with Sean Hanson scoring in the corner, but once Pugh had wound Bish up, all he wanted to do was take them on physically.

'David was one of the very best rugby players I have ever seen. How he only got the one cap is something I will never understand. His antics off the field obviously had something to do with it, because the chairman of selectors at the time, Rod Morgan, was a chief inspector in the South Wales Police. Some people thought of Bish as an extra Kray twin, but while he could be a handful on the odd occasion, he was a soft-hearted bloke who was usually as good as gold.

'That didn't influence my judgement on his ability to captain Pontypool. I told the match committee that I wanted Ring because I knew he was going to stay and because I thought he would get more out of the team. I thought they would back me, particularly in view of the success we'd had the previous season. When the vote went for Bish, I decided to finish there and then.

'Although I resigned as coach, I stayed on the committee. When it came to appointing a new coach, I voted for Charlie Faulkner, as did Goff Davies. I was again outvoted and the job went to John Perkins instead. Before the autumn was out, Bish had gone north, as I'd said he would – not that I took any pleasure in that, but I thought it proved I'd been right in wanting someone else as captain.

'I didn't take any pleasure either in seeing the team finish that season in the bottom half of the table, beneath the likes of Newbridge, Newport, Abertillery and Ebbw Vale. So from being the best in Wales, we went to being the fifth best in Gwent. Even then, when I was 43, I couldn't resist playing the odd match at a lower level. If anybody was hard enough up to give me a shout, I'd always give it a go.

'I turned out twice for Garndiffaith and then twice for Talywain. Wherever we played, you could tell what the young bulls were thinking: "There's old Bobby Windsor. Let's give him what for." I couldn't have got more of a booting if I'd taken the front doormat from the house and strapped it to the back of my jersey. I knew I'd get a lot of stick, and none of the opposing teams disappointed me in that respect.

'Every time I got caught at the bottom of a ruck, it didn't make any difference whether the ball was there or not, they kept booting me just the same. But as the rest of the boys said after one game, "The more attention they pay you, Bob, the easier it is for us."

'I suppose I'd have been disappointed had it been any other way, but there had to be a limit to how often I was prepared to take the abuse. I decided the time had come to take a back seat.'

The '80s brought Wales one Five Nations title, twice as many wooden spoons and recurring humiliation. On successive Saturdays in June 1988, New Zealand swept Wales aside on a torrent of 18 tries. When North Auckland delivered four of their own to win 27–9 at Whangerei, a bugler in the crowd applied the last rites by sounding the Last Post.

When Romania rounded the year off by following their home win in Bucharest with another at the Arms Park, the Wales captain, Jonathan Davies, considered Welsh rugby such a hopeless case that he finally succumbed to Dougie Laughton's persuasive persistence by signing for Widnes rugby league club. Davies was not amused at Windsor sending him on his way with a flea in his ear.

'The *Sun* newspaper contacted me just after I signed, offering me £5,000 if I would "slag off" the Welsh Rugby Union,' Davies writes in his autobiography. 'I turned them down and paid the penalty because they immediately signed up the ready mouth of former Welsh and Pontypool hooker Bobby Windsor to write an article headed, "Good Riddance to Selfish Davies". It appeared *The Sun* didn't mind who was slagging whom off, as long as someone did, and Bobby must have needed the money.'

Windsor stands by what he said. 'I never got a penny for that article, unlike those who went north for money and came back home for money,' he says, referring to Davies' subsequent transfer from Warrington to

Cardiff. 'I said "good riddance" because at times Jonathan gave me the impression that he was running backwards faster than the other side were going forwards. There were some matches when I thought he wouldn't have been able to tackle his granny. Widnes had the sense to put him on the wing and, fair play, he had a great career in league.'

Just when Welsh rugby thought it had seen the back of the worst decade in living memory, along came the '90s. In terms of dragging the sport to hitherto unplumbed levels of shame, they outstripped the '80s by turning Wales into a periodic laughing stock. The most shameful episode took place on 21 July 1991 in Brisbane, when a team captained by Paul Thorburn conceded 12 tries to Australia without reply, losing 63–6, or 75–6 under current scoring values.

It would have been bad enough had it stopped there. By the end of that night, certain Welsh players did their best to ensure that the disgrace off the field matched that on it by fighting amongst themselves around the dance floor of the banqueting suite at Ballymore Stadium, where the post-match dinner was being held. The Australian players, their wives and girlfriends looked on aghast at witnessing the sort of fight which had been sorely lacking during eighty one-sided minutes earlier in the day.

To round off the weekend, the Welsh party flew home the following morning without a word of regret for the boorish behaviour of some of their party, although an official apology was subsequently sent to the Australian Rugby Union. The following season's *Rugby Annual for Wales* appeared etched in black on the front cover with a terse sentence of explanation in the editorial: 'Welsh Rugby at senior international level is dead.'

There must have been a resurrection of sorts, because Wales staggered on through a decade which brought the surprise of a Five Nations title in 1993–94, the year after Ieuan Evans' opportunist try famously caught the English napping at the Arms Park. That Wales finished rock bottom the season before they finished top and rock-bottom again the season after made such fleeting success appear almost miraculous.

The beatings went on: 34–9 by Samoa in Apia in 1994, an aggregate hammering of 98–28 in successive Tests in Australia in 1996, 51–0 by France at Wembley in April 1998 and, worst of all, 96–13 by South Africa in Pretoria two months later. The only thing that could be said for Wales that day at Loftus Versfeld was that they avoided the century, or rather the Springboks avoided it for them by bungling more than one late try.

By then, they had scored 15, but at least there were some mitigating circumstances, whereas there had been none to excuse the calamitous events in Brisbane seven years earlier. Wales had been forced to go to South Africa without 18 front-line players, the vast majority of whom had just returned from a winning series in Argentina, leaving them no alternative but to cobble together a team of sorts.

Worse was to follow. More injuries caused further disruption, to such an extent that three captains presided over the sorry mess at varying stages of the mismatch in Pretoria – the Ebbw Vale flanker Kingsley Jones, Pontypridd scrum-half Paul John and Swansea hooker Garin Jenkins, who had started on the bench.

The WRU's response, as articulated by its then chairman, Glanmor Griffiths, was to search the world for the best available coach. Instead of confirming the planned appointment of Mike Ruddock, the Union left him high and dry, hiring Graham Henry on a five-year deal at £250,000 a year which made the New Zealander comfortably the best-paid coach of all at a time when Clive Woodward was building an English empire to conquer the world for considerably less.

Henry wasted no time playing fast and loose with the International Board's regulations on international qualification and the governing body's wretched failure to police it by making even a half-hearted request for documentary proof. Their attitude can be seen in retrospect as naive in the extreme: 'We take our Unions at their word.' Henry picked so many Kiwis, Australians and South Africans that it was hardly surprising that the Board eventually tumbled to the fact that they had broken the rules in some cases.

They did so only after newspapers dug out the birth certificate of Brett Sinkinson, a New Zealander who played in the back row for Neath. Wales justified his selection on the false premise that his grandfather came from the country before emigrating. Sinkinson, on the day of his selection, was not sure whether his grandfather came from Carmarthen or Caernarfon. No wonder. The following year, in March 2000, the birth certificate revealed that he was born in Oldham.

A two-day inquiry resulted in Sinkinson and another Kiwi, Sale full-back Shane Howarth, being declared ineligible. Wales were also found guilty of breaking the rules by picking Swansea's South African lock Tyrone Maullin for their A team on the assumption that he met the three-year residency criteria, which he did not. That, however, did not prevent

Henry putting him on the bench against the United States of America in August 1999, his employers having failed in their responsibility to tell him he had no right to do so.

Three others claimed by Wales from the colonies, Matt Cardey, a New Zealander, Jason Jones-Hughes, an Australian, and Peter Rogers, a South African, were cleared. It would have been worse had another South African, the Neath back-row forward Shawn van Rensburg, not been exposed as ineligible shortly before he was due to play in a Welsh international trial alongside an Englishman, James Storey, who subsequently withdrew.

Jones-Hughes had been rushed into the Wales squad for the 1999 World Cup despite a legal wrangle between the Welsh and Australian Unions. The Australians, with some justification, claimed him as one of theirs, on the basis that he had been capped at Under-21 level, had played for their second team, the Australian Barbarians, and been a member of their full Test squad.

In the end, the International Board ruled in favour of Wales because Jones-Hughes had Welsh parents. He proved to be another of those here today, gone tomorrow expensive signings, recurring knee and ankle problems limiting him to two starts, against Japan in the World Cup and France in the following year's Six Nations. At least Jones-Hughes sounded Welsh, but Windsor, for one, will never forgive Henry's readiness to throw Welsh caps at non-Welsh players.

'Henry didn't put any trophies in the showcase during his time with Wales,' Windsor says, 'but he sure put a lot of money in the bank. He embarrassed my country by bringing in players who had no right to play for Wales because they weren't Welsh. Worse than that, he made us a laughing stock.

'Whatever Henry wanted, he got. He wanted Iestyn Harris and it cost the Union over £1.5 million in wages and a transfer fee to the Leeds Rhinos, all that for a player who had never played union before. In the end, they had to cut their losses, just as they had to do over Jones-Hughes. If he played half a dozen matches for Newport, that was the absolute limit.

'What sort of a message did those two deals, and many more, send out to the young players in Wales?

'At one stage, he had a plan to sign up a group of young players from South Africa and give them all contracts so that after three years they would be eligible to play for Wales. How cynical was that? If he'd got away with it, the second language for the Welsh team would have been Afrikaans, not Welsh. Luckily, the word got out and some of the wiser heads on the general committee of the Union told him to get stuffed.

'To be dragged up in front of the beak charged with picking ineligible players was a disgrace. It was unbelievable that the WRU and Henry were let off scot-free. No fine, no suspensions, just a severe reprimand, which was a fancy term for a tap on the wrist. Maybe the only reason they got away with it was that the International Board didn't want to open a can of worms in respect of New Zealand picking endless players from Samoa, Fiji and Tonga.

'Graham Henry had never coached an international side when Glanmor Griffiths and Terry Cobner, in his role as the WRU's director of rugby, chucked all that money at him to come over from Auckland and run ours. What did Henry know about the tribal nature of Welsh rugby? He didn't have a clue about the difference between West Wales and East Wales and how the two areas hate each other.

'And to think they called him "The Great Redeemer". What a joke. The Union made another awful blunder when they allowed Henry to take charge of the Lions in Australia in 2001. His appointment was an insult to every other British and Irish coach. They would have given their right arms for the privilege.

'A lot of good judges reckoned that was the strongest Lions squad since we went to South Africa in 1974. The Test team was built around the great English team which went on to win the World Cup two years later. Let's be fair, they were a great team – Martin Johnson, Danny Grewcock, Richard Hill, Lawrence Dallaglio, Jason Leonard, Matt Dawson, Jonny Wilkinson, Jason Robinson and so on.

'Then you had people like Brian O'Driscoll, Rob Howley, Scott Quinnell and Tom Smith, the Scottish prop. How could you go wrong with that lot? Henry did, because they allowed a not-very-good Australian team to scramble off the ropes and win the series. That was bad enough, but there was a knock-on effect for Wales, because the tour ruined Henry's relationships with some of the senior Welsh players. I always knew it was going to end in tears for Wales, with Henry laughing all the way to the bank.'

The end came ahead of schedule, Henry responding to calls for his head by resigning a few days after watching Wales take their worst beating at Lansdowne Road, 54–10 against Ireland on 3 February 2002. When a group of Welsh fans spotted the players filing through Dublin airport the next morning, they began singing, 'We've got the worst team in the world.'

In his farewell statement, Henry complained of 'burn-out': 'In the light of recent results, I have had to take a good look at myself in the mirror and ask myself some hard questions. I still think I am a good coach, but I don't think I'm coaching as well as I can. The intensity of the rugby that Wales and the Lions have played since I arrived, as well as the all-consuming nature of the job I came into, I believe has led to a burn-out factor in my coaching.'

Henry had gone with some 20 months left on his contract, which was supposed to have taken him through to the end of the World Cup in November 2003. Despite resigning, he negotiated a severance payment from the WRU understood to have been in the region of £80,000. One senior member of the Union revealed that a large amount of Henry's salary had been paid in advance and that he was owed less than a year's pay when he quit.

After another New Zealander, Steve Hansen, had done his stint, the WRU decided it was high time they put the top job back in Welsh hands. In March 2005, Mike Ruddock succeeded where every Welsh coach had failed since John Dawes in 1978, landing the Grand Slam. Less than 12 months later, he too had walked away, amid Machiavellian theories that he had been ousted by a dressing-room rebellion, the hapless victim of player power.

'I knew Mike back in his early days with Blaina and Cross Keys,' Windsor says. 'A good man, Mike, but how can you win the Grand Slam one season and quit the next? Wales had made themselves a joke. If Mike had trouble with certain players, he should have been man enough to have got rid of them. Instead, it seemed to me that he behaved like a wimp.

'Player power? Don't make me laugh. Tough coaches never had any trouble with player power. I grew up under a coach, Ray Prosser, who never thought twice about getting rid of any player he felt had the wrong attitude. Paul Turner was one, the same Paul Turner who went on to play for Wales and become a successful coach.

'As a young lad at Pontypool, Paul had a head the size of a bucket. You get a good idea of what people are like on tour, and Paul came with us to America, way before anyone had heard of him. Pross didn't like anyone if he felt his attitude left something to be desired, no matter how good a player he might have been. So, with Paul, it was a case of, "Good night . . .'"

14

. . . .

SUICIDAL

As Sunday, 18 June 2006 dawns, a ridge of high pressure promises another warm summer's day over the southern half of the United Kingdom with Fahrenheit temperatures climbing towards 80 degrees. Delia Smith wakes up to her 65th birthday, Sir Paul McCartney, exactly 12 months younger, no doubt celebrates with a rendition of 'When I'm 64' – made particularly poignant by the announcement, a few weeks earlier, that he and his second wife, Heather Mills, are to separate after four years of marriage. On a sweeter musical note, ground staff are clearing up at Twickenham after Headquarters rocked to the sound of the Eagles and the all-girl Texan country band who had the courage to speak out against President Bush over Iraq, the Dixie Chicks.

Warren Buffett, the world's second-richest human being, is preparing to reveal that he is giving most of his £30-billion fortune to the only man who is worth a few bucks more, Bill Gates. A report commissioned by the National Health Service in Scotland warns that people in the 40–60 age bracket are drinking more than previous generations and that an increasing number are suffering from cirrhosis of the liver.

At the Olympic Stadium in Munich, Brazil are beating Australia 2–0 in the football World Cup while thousands of exiled Aussies take over Shepherd's Bush to watch the Socceroos from afar. In Italy, newspapers from back to front are spitting blood over the Azzurri's embarrassing failure to overcome a USA team reduced to nine men.

In England, some are far from impressed with the national team's performances, despite two wins out of two. 'It's true we are not playing so well, but we are winning,' Sir Bobby Robson tells the *Sportsweek* programme. 'There's a lesson to be learnt here from the World Cup in 1990. After we drew our first game against the Republic of Ireland, the media were calling for us to be sent home. Yet we went on to reach the semi-finals.'

Back home, the *News of the World* reveals that Liverpool have offered Blackburn Rovers £6 million for the Wales striker Craig Bellamy. In America, the final round of the US Open starts at Winged Foot Golf Club in upstate New York, with one of three players, Jim Furyk, Colin Montgomerie and Phil Mickelson, expected to win the second major of the golfing year. It ends with all three clearing the way for the Australian Geoff Ogilvy to find himself the surprising new champion, despite the unusually high aggregate total of five over par.

All over the British Isles, rugby enthusiasts are digesting reports of defeats for all four home countries in the Southern Hemisphere. Scotland lose 29–15 to South Africa in Port Elizabeth, Ireland 27–17 to New Zealand in Auckland, Wales 45–27 to Argentina in Buenos Aires and England 43–18 to Australia in Melbourne, where Wallaby scrum-half George Gregan plays his 120th international, eclipsing the world record set by Jason Leonard of Harlequins.

Historically, 18 June marks the anniversary of events of global significance, like the Battle of Waterloo, in 1815, which led to Napoleon Bonaparte's second, and final, abdication from the French throne. On the same day in 1940, Winston Churchill addressed the House of Commons on the stark reality of Britain standing alone against Nazi Germany after they had overrun northern Europe, the Prime Minister finishing his speech with the famous sentence, 'Let us therefore brace ourselves to our duties and so bear ourselves that if the British Empire and its Commonwealth last for a thousand years, men will still say, "This was their finest hour."'

The day brings other anniversaries, including the 120th of the birth of George Mallory, the English mountaineer whose attempt to make the first conquest of Everest has been shrouded in mystery since he disappeared close to the summit in 1924. The date marks the anniversary of the Staines air disaster of 1972, in which all 118 on board were killed, and of the first official recognition of the Aids epidemic at a medical conference in San Francisco in 1981. The old rockers who were there will always remember the date as the night Jimi Hendrix burnt his electric guitar on stage at the Monterey Pop Festival in 1967.

In Newport, a famous rugby player in a depressed state is oblivious to all that and the fact that it is Father's Day. Bobby Windsor has decided that Sunday, 18 June 2006 will be his last day on earth, that before the sun goes down he will have taken his own life. He would have had no way of knowing that all major-league baseball in America that day was being played in aid of a disease which kills one man in every six, prostate cancer. There was a terrible irony about that, because one of the two factors behind Windsor's suicidal state was the fear that the same cancer would kill him, too.

To those who remember him as the laughing cavalier who willingly shed his own blood for the cause while also ensuring that others shed theirs, he would seem just about the least likely player in the game to contemplate suicide. His passion for life, roguish sense of humour and an expanding family would seem to eliminate any such possibility. The reality was that he spent months agonising over the most effective means of carrying it through. It seemed the only way out. With the rugby community at large unaware of the demons driving him to the edge of oblivion, he wrote a suicide note, left it on the kitchen table and made what he intended to be his final journey, a one-way drive some eighty miles westward from Newport to the Pembrokeshire seaside resort of Tenby and the caravan site where he and his family had spent many a summer holiday. Windsor had all the raw materials he needed: one hundred paracetamol tablets and a bottle of water. He did not intend to be coming back . . .

'I lost all hope and could see only one way out,' he says. 'There were so many things whizzing through my mind at the same time that I just couldn't cope. It would be easy now to pretend that I never thought about taking my own life – it's not something I'm proud of. But, ever since I can remember, I've tried to be honest with myself and the people around me. Looking back, I can see how selfish I was. Nobody in his right mind would deliberately leave six children without a father.

'The whole point about what very nearly happened that Sunday was that my mind was not right. What would have happened to the kids once I'd killed myself? A normal person, thinking properly, would have asked himself that question and shuddered at the stupidity of it and pulled himself together. I was so far gone I could see no other escape.

'I'd been in a suicidal state for months. I'd wake up at half past three in the morning and not be able to get back to sleep. I phoned the Samaritans and they were very understanding, suggesting that I put all my thoughts down on paper and read them back the next day. I wrote and wrote, about what I thought should be going on between me and my wife, and what wasn't. I asked myself all sorts of questions. How was I going to cope if it went on like this? What future did I have beyond that?

'The Samaritans were as good as gold and they told me I could ring them back at any hour, day or night. It helped up to a point, but at the back of my mind the thought was always there.

'I spoke to Ray Gravell. I didn't want to burden him by telling him what I had in my mind, but I'd read somewhere that his father had shot himself and that Ray had found him. I didn't want to go and hang myself and have the children find me. I spoke to another person, whose son had hanged himself, and she told me how she came back and found him. Then I thought, can I get hold of a gun and shoot myself?

'In the end, I decided that the easiest way was to take an overdose. Once I'd made my mind up on that, it was only a matter of when. After days of thinking about it, I decided the time had come. I sat down and wrote a letter, hoping the children would understand. I wrote: "I am sorry that it has come to this but I cannot take any more. So sorry. Try to think of me in the good times and always stick together and look after each other. I love you all."

'I put it in an envelope and placed it on the kitchen table, knowing that one of my sons, Luke, would be home from work shortly. I went and bought paracetamol tablets and a big bottle of water, then drove down to Tenby, where I had a caravan.

'Inside the caravan, I took all the tablets out of their packets and put them in a plastic bag. Then I walked out towards the headland, a really beautiful spot overlooking the sea. I felt calm. I didn't feel upset. I felt happy because, before long, I would go to sleep. It would all be over. No more pain, no more anguish. I wasn't worried. It was just a question of popping the tablets and getting the water down my neck. I was looking forward to the relief of not having to go on living in such a bad mental state.

'I was already as good as gone. Sometimes I went to bed at night praying I wouldn't wake up the next morning. I just could not go on living the way I was. The humiliation was the worst part. Every time I looked anyone in the eye, I felt as though they were thinking, "Bob, your wife is with somebody else." I convinced myself that everybody knew and it was driving me mad.

'Unbeknown to me, Luke had come home early from work and found the letter. He ran to tell two of my other children. They thought I might have gone to Tenby. They contacted some friends, Sue and Ron Webber. If it hadn't been for quick thinking and smart detective work, they would never have got to me in time. I still feel bad that I caused them so much bother.

'Sue knew Linda, the woman who owned the caravan next to mine. Sue rang her up and said, "We're worried about Bob. Have you seen him?"

'Linda, God love her, said, "Yes, I saw him walking up to the cliffs a few minutes ago." Her son, Chris, was with her, so they sent him after me, afraid that I was going to throw myself off the cliff. I didn't have enough guts for that. Linda was worried that Chris, a lovely lad who was then no more than 14, might fall off the cliff in his attempts to stop me, so they phoned the police. I was sitting there when I heard Chris shouting out my name.

'"You all right, Bob?" he asked.

'"Yeah, fine, Chris," I said. That was pretty daft, considering that I was about to take my own life. Chris had just got to me when I saw two coppers running up to where we were sitting.

'They took me back down to the caravan where they'd found the empty paracetamol packets. They asked me, "Where are the tablets?"

'I said, "I've chucked them away."

'They said, "If you don't tell us where they are, you're going straight down to the hospital to have your stomach pumped. We have to find one hundred tablets and we have to find them now."

'With that, I pulled the plastic bag out of my pocket and handed it over. The policemen counted every one of them. Then they contacted my wife to tell her that I was in a pretty bad state and could she come down, but, for whatever reason, that wasn't possible.

'The copper put the phone down and said, "Look, Bob, from what Linda here has been telling me, you're going through a bad time. This is no business of mine, but, from what I've heard, my advice to you would be to get on with your life. Don't worry about the children. We've told them and they're on their way."

'The police were really good. I apologised for all the trouble I'd caused – they were about to call the helicopter out when they found me. I was crying and thinking what a fool I'd made of myself.

SUICIDAL

'Shortly after, Ricky and Joanne got to the caravan. They said, "Dad, what are you doing? We love you and we don't want to lose you. We know you're having a bad time, but we'll all pull you through it."

'Then I began to think, what am I doing? My first wife fought every inch of the way before dying from cancer and I was doing this. Then I realised how stupid I'd been. I was broken-hearted, which might sound silly for a tough, macho man to say, but that's what I was: broken-hearted.

'Every time I think of all those sick people in the world fighting for their lives, especially the little children, I feel terribly guilty about what I intended to do. For that reason, I am disgusted with myself, even though I had hit rock bottom. I'm a very lucky chap. I'm still here and I've still got my children. They said, "Just because one person has hurt you, Dad, that's no reason for you to hurt all of us."

'The strange thing is that it never occurred to me that they would miss me. I thought they'd get on with their lives. It didn't strike me that I'd be hurting them. I realised then how selfish I had been. I thought to myself, you daft bugger, you've got six children here who think the world of you and all the grandchildren think the world of you, too. You don't know how lucky you are.

'Slowly but surely, I started to come up out of my black hole, thanks to my family and friends like Sue and Ron Webber and Gary and Karen Haigh. And I couldn't have wished for a better friend than Jennifer Rawlinson, landlady of the Crown Hotel in Varteg, near Pontypool. They were all brilliant. They were the people who got me back on the straight and narrow and made sure I stayed there. You find out who your real friends are when you are down and out.

'I was on antidepressants and sleeping tablets. The doctor would only give me half a dozen at a time. He told me, "You've got to watch it with these sleeping tablets because they're addictive." There was me worrying about getting addicted when I was planning to bump myself off. How's that for a piece of black humour?

'I can laugh about it now, but it was no laughing matter then. To say I fought my way back up is not completely true. The reality was that the kids dragged me back. I'd given myself an almighty shock. If young Chris had been a few minutes later finding me in Tenby that day, I'd have been a goner. Surviving an experience like that taught me about putting everything into perspective and realising how precious life is.

'I was hurt more by my wife walking out than by any rugby injury. I'd had my nose broken, been kicked in the face and bitten on the ears, but when Lynne walked out, my world fell apart. I'm not perfect, but I still ask myself what I did wrong and I still don't know the answer.

'Gradually, I started to look forward to life again. I got off the antidepressants and the sleeping tablets and went to prostate cancer classes organised by Progress. There were fellas there who had no hope – three of them died within a fortnight – but they were fighting to stay alive. They put me to shame, because I'd been ready to do away with myself.

'In the weeks and months after pulling me back from the brink, the kids were in constant touch, taking me out and making sure that I was occupied so that I didn't have a lot of time to think about what I'd tried to do. They were afraid I'd try again and that this time they wouldn't find me until it was too late. I can honestly say I haven't looked back from that day at Tenby to this. A lot of things have crossed my mind during that time but never the idea of committing suicide.

'One of the first things I did after selling the business was to start up my own consultancy in the waste management trade. That was a major turning point on the road back. It gave me something to get stuck into and occupy my mind, which was exactly what I needed. I'm not too sure, though, how I would have managed without the love and support of my family.

'Lynne walked out of my life in January 2006 and she walked back into it almost exactly two years later. She moved back into the house, but the relationship didn't work out. Christmas went badly. When it came to my 60th birthday the following month, I didn't think she wanted to celebrate it with me, so I went to the pub with a few friends instead. I guess that was the last straw for Lynne, because she didn't attend my mother's funeral soon after and I got the impression she wanted nothing more to do with me. The next morning, my son Luke came and took me down to Ricky's house in Newport. He gave me my own place, which I could have free of charge for as long as I wanted.

'I got myself back on an even keel fairly quickly. The invitations to speak at rugby clubs kept coming in and, instead of turning them down, I started to accept them and rebuild my life. I'd get a few bob here and there, which enabled me to help the odd friend of mine who needed a bit of help through the recession.'

SUICIDAL

Dave 'Dapper' Power, honorary secretary of the Welsh Charitables RFC and an old pal, was one such beneficiary of Windsor's spontaneous generosity. 'Bobby was the first to get in touch after I'd lost my job in the steelworks just before Christmas 2008,' Power says. 'He invited me to a couple of dinners and each time he put something in my top pocket. I didn't know what it was until I went home and pulled it out. He'd only gone and given me half his speaking fee, and he did that twice. That's typical of the man.'

Windsor was beginning to think there had to be an alternative to the ravages of the Welsh winter. 'I just needed a push in the right direction, and a good friend of mine, Peter Phillips, provided it,' he says. 'Peter told me I needed a good holiday. There were too many bad memories for me to stay. When he arranged the flights, I decided to take off to Majorca for a fortnight. Friends of mine had been out there for some 20 years and they fixed me up with a rented apartment.

'Buying a place in the posher parts of Palma would be easy enough provided you won the lottery three times in a row. I was advised to rent an apartment and have a good look round, which was what I did. I swim in the Mediterranean most mornings and do a lot of exploring.

'I only had to go back and experience the cold of winter in South Wales to realise I had made the right move. I was spending a few weeks back in Newport during the early part of 2010, attending to some family matters and going through the legalities of my divorce, when my mobile bleeped with a text message, just a few days before I was due to catch the plane back to Palma. It was from Lynne, asking how I was and how things were going.

'I have no doubt that some of the kids had been working behind the scenes to mend a few fences and see if we couldn't get together again. The break-up caused me the biggest problem of all, because I loved Lynne from the day I first saw her. Even though harsh things had been said by both parties, I was pleased that the opportunity had come along to try and repair the damage.

'So, being a romantic at heart, I arranged to meet her again at the restaurant in Caerleon where we had gone for that first meal nearly 30 years before. I even made sure we sat at the same table, although I had no way of knowing whether it would turn out to be the last supper.

'We had a chat, and there was a lot to chat about because of all the water that had gone under the bridge since we'd last spoken. I said, "I can't tell you any more than that I still love you but I'm flying back to Majorca in three days' time. Remember how we used to talk about retiring to a warm place at some stage far into the future? Well, the future is now the present. You will have to decide what you're going to do."

'She said, "I'm going to pack my job in and come over."

'Lynne arrived ten days later with our youngest son, Sean, and we decided to start afresh. The alternative was to get increasingly bitter and twisted about what had happened, and that's not a healthy way to live. Some bits are hard to get out of your mind, but we decided after that first heart-to-heart not to look back, to accept that what's gone is gone, to look forward not back.

'You have to be positive. Nobody needs to tell me how precious life is, that nobody should ever take anyone or anything for granted. I have learnt to make the most of every day. The pace of life in Majorca is a lot gentler, which suits me down to the ground. I love walking, which is just as well because it's about the only form of exercise I can do without knackering my back.

'I walk for miles and it's great because there is so much to see beyond the expensive boats of the multimillionaire set. Some areas are so posh that they pay £80,000 a year just for the mooring rights for their yachts. It's not a lifestyle I have a hankering for because most of it is done for show. That's never been my scene and never will be, even if I did have a few million.

'I've got involved in the rugby community in the area, and I like nothing better than sitting in the sun watching local teams like El Toro. That gives me as much enjoyment as watching any of the big matches on television because it's 30 blokes having a bit of fun and that takes me back over half a century to when I first played the game at school for exactly the same reason.

'I've got six children and twelve grandchildren. They all take it in turns to come out to Majorca and spend time with me. I'm also into golf, whenever my back allows. I used to be a member of Pontypool Golf Club – which is a story in itself, because they blackballed me for six years.

'Every year, my membership would be proposed and seconded. Every year, I'd get a letter saying they were sorry but it was the unanimous decision of the committee that my application to join could not be accepted. They never gave me an explanation, which is ridiculous but typical of the way golf clubs operate.

SUICIDAL

'Apparently, it only takes one member to object and that's you knackered. My friends got so cheesed off with this happening every year that they forced the club to hold an extraordinary general meeting. They argued that it was a slight on those members proposing and seconding people for admission to the club when all they got for their trouble was to have the application thrown back in their face. As a result of the pressure they created, the rule was changed and, the following year, I was accepted.

'After six years of being blackballed, that must be some sort of record. The first time I walked in as a member, the committee were all there to welcome me. "Lovely to see you, Bob," they said. "Great to have you as part of the club."

'And I thought, you two-faced so-and-sos.

'I was never given a reason for all the blackballing. There were rumours that a run-in I'd had with a local bank manager and a subsequent case which I'd won might have had something to do with it. I'll never know. I used to play every week in the summer but hardly ever in the winter, when you would be in danger of dying from hypothermia. Still, I managed to get my handicap down to 18, which was not bad considering that I was limited to a half-swing because 20 years of playing rugby had done a fair bit of damage to my back.

'It would be impossible for me to get a lower handicap than 18 because of the swing restriction. I'd love to see how much farther I could hit it with a full swing, but I'll have to die wondering. If I tried a full swing, they'd have to cart me off to hospital, my back would probably take months to recover and they'd tell me never to swing another club.

'Golf has allowed me to recreate a bit of the old rugby spirit which has all but gone from the game since it went professional. I play what I call social golf, 18 holes and a laugh and a joke in the clubhouse afterwards. Since going to live out in Majorca, I've encountered a new handicap: the extortionate cost of green fees. They charge a green fee of 100 euros and another 40 euros for the hire of a buggy.

'All the clubs charge the same, like a cartel. It's not good for the tourism business, because people keen on coming over from the UK for a few days' golf look at the cost and give it a miss. One hundred and forty euro is virtually one hundred and forty quid. At Pontypool, you can play for £12, or you could when I last played there.

'So, what with the cost and my back, I wouldn't go so far as to say I'm ready just yet for the Masters at Augusta, but when I string a few good shots together, sometimes I think to myself, "If only Herbert Waddell of the Baa-Baas could see me now."

'Then I have a laugh and realise what a wonderful world it still is and how lucky I am to be alive, especially after my stupidity a few years back. Lucky, also, to be back with the woman I love. As Lynne says, "We want to spend the rest of our lives together." I never thought I'd live to hear her say that.

'Ironically, we got back together shortly after the divorce had gone through and that's something we will have to reconsider at some stage in the future. Perhaps it feels better because we're living in sin! All that matters is that we're together again.

'The tunnel I went through was so long and so dark I thought I would never get out of it. Depression is a terrible thing and experiencing it has made me much more understanding of those who suffer from it. The mistake I made was to give up hope. The blows I took on the rugby field were nothing compared with those I suffered in my private life, but no matter what happens in the future, I will never lose sight of the fact that there is always someone worse off. I think of Judi and Dawn and how cruelly short their lives were, and of little Nicole, who had the shortest life of all.

'Over the years, I've tried my best to look after my kids financially and they appreciate that, to the point where they now say, "Dad, you looked after us when we needed it. Enjoy yourself and don't worry about us."

'Now I'm happier than I've been for a long, long time and at peace with the world, which will be shocking news for some of the tough hombres I fought with all those years ago.

'Love put me down and love has pulled me back up.'

15

THE GAME'S GONE SOFT

Legend has it that Gérard Cholley, the frightening front man in the frightening France pack of the mid-to-late '70s, once laid out four Scotland forwards in the same match, at the Parc des Princes on Saturday, 5 March 1977. One of the punches was such a peach that it moved the top man in France, Albert Ferrasse, to break with the tradition of sweeping it under the carpet along with everything else.

Instead, after a game in which the referee, Meirion Joseph of Wales, was roundly criticised for allowing Cholley to see out the full eighty minutes, Ferrasse, the great dictator of the French Rugby Federation, made a presidential point of apologising for one incident, not the other three, presumably on the basis that they were too ordinary to mention. Cholley complains that 'there is no fear in rugby any more'; that may be a direct result of his retirement.

They do not make them like that any more. A paratrooper and amateur heavyweight boxer, Cholley was at the heart of the Grand Slam team good enough to deny Wales a hat-trick of such titles. Behind him in the second row were the formidable Michel Palmie and Alain Estève, who would make the selection of locks for any Dirtiest Dozen XV a no-brainer.

Palmie won a clutch of French club championships with Béziers despite having been banned from the game at 26 after an incident involving Armand Clerc which left the hooker for Racing Club of Paris partially blinded in one eye. Palmie has long since returned to action of a different kind, forging a new career with the French Rugby Federation as one of its leading members.

When the balloon went up over the infamous brawl at the Bar Toulzac in Brive following Pontypridd's Heineken Cup match there in the autumn of 1998, who should the European Rugby Cup appoint to head the investigation into the fight? Michel Palmie. One of two French delegates on the board of ERC Ltd, he has done his share of sitting on disciplinary committees, the ultimate poacher turned gamekeeper.

Bobby Windsor tangled with them all in locations where angels feared to tread, up close and personal in the scrum, where he would often view them through a gory red mist caused by a cut above the eye and/or a broken nose. The same went for the French, more often than not.

'Drawing up a list of the hardest, meanest, dirtiest lot I ever played against, Palmie would have to be numero uno,' Windsor says. 'He'd boot anyone, anytime. Once the ball went out of the scrum, nearly everyone else, especially the referee, would be watching the ball. That's when Palmie and his henchmen did their dirty best. He'd see you trapped at the bottom of the pile, he'd give a quick look round to make sure the ref wasn't looking and then, bang . . .

'When I'd taken more than enough punishment from the French, I wouldn't bother binding on my tighthead prop. I'd put my left arm round Charlie Faulkner on the loosehead, leave my right arm free so I could hold it close to my face ready to give a bit back to them. After a busted nose and the makings of two black eyes, I'd have been stupid not to have done something to protect myself. The referees were never going to make a stand on your behalf, at least not in Paris.

'If any of them had penalised me for not binding on my tighthead, I'd have told them why I was having to do it. None of them ever did, which only hardened my view that you had to take the law into your own hands.

'Estève would be right up there with Palmie, but it would be wrong to create the impression that it was just the French and nobody else. Ian Robinson, the Cardiff lock who got a couple of caps for Wales in 1974, could put it about with the best. I can vouch for the fact that he could punch his weight because I felt it once during a Pontypool–Cardiff match.

'We were jogging back for a drop-out on the 25 when he hit me straight in the solar plexus. I was down on one knee struggling to breathe when the referee, Ken Rowlands from Ynysybwl, came up and asked, "What's the matter?"

'I couldn't tell him. I was still gasping for breath. Later, over a beer, Robinson said, "I'm awfully sorry about that, Bob. I couldn't help it." That sort of strengthened Robbie's reputation as a hit man, and after that I always made a point to watch what I was doing against Cardiff if he was playing and, more to the point, watch what he was doing. Another Cardiff player, John Hickey, gave me the impression during my brief time with the club that if I didn't put the boot into the opposition, he'd put it into me.

'Some of the Irish forwards would give you some stick. At times, they'd be so ferocious that it was as if they believed in their battle cry: "Kick ahead, any f*****g head." With the Irish, there was never any malice, or at least none that I could detect. Alastair McHarg of Scotland wasn't afraid to dish out his own sort of justice, and after he'd smacked Phil Bennett in one international, Benny said to me, "Make sure you get him."

'The Springboks thought they were hard men, and that Moaner van Heerden was the hardest of the lot. He'd go round the field belting any opposing player who came near him, but I didn't see him around at the end of the third Lions Test in 1974. We'd given him a dose of his own medicine and he hadn't been able to take it.

'They also claimed to have a front-row forward who was said to be the strongest man in the world. They went through so many props in that series that I don't remember this fella's name, but, whoever he was, they carted him off on a stretcher. I didn't give him anything worse than a tap with the boot, and we were wearing rubber studs, not the long metal ones.

'Over my career, I probably got as good as I gave. But for the grace of God and various other things, my Lions tour could have been all over after a couple of matches by the time Hannes Marias finished with me. The Springboks skipper was playing for Eastern Province at Port Elizabeth when he stamped on my ankle. I went to hospital and the X-rays showed that I had chipped a bone, or rather Hannes had chipped it for me.

'On that trip, if you picked up an injury that put you out for any longer than a fortnight, you were on the plane home. As coach, Syd Millar got me down early every morning, took me over the road to the beach and got me walking, knee-deep, in the sea. He'd been told they did it with horses and that the waves would have a massaging effect on my ankle and that it was my best hope of a rapid recovery.

'As Syd said, "If it's good enough for racehorses, it's good enough for a Welsh donkey." It worked a treat and I was ready to go for the next match.

'There's a big difference between being hard and being dirty. Against England, it was always hard but never dirty, certainly not in my time. You knew from your Lions experiences how good the English forwards were. They were a really top-notch pack, with strong self-discipline, and not as wild as the Celts. The same went for the All Blacks. They'd trample you on the floor, but that was nothing more than the order of the day.

'Once, against New Zealand, Graham Price went down on the ball and the All Black pack drove over him, eight men as one. Nothing new in that, but they liked it so much that they then did something which certainly was new: they turned round and went back over him again as if they'd decided they needed a bit of practice. It doubled the number of cuts on Pricey's head.

'Glyn Shaw, of Neath and Wales before he went to rugby league with Widnes, was a good example of a hard player, not a dirty one. He was tough and brave and he'd run all day, qualities which allowed him to make a name for himself when he went north.

'The Aussies used to have a crazy, long-haired wing forward called Ray Price. We ran into him on the 1978 tour and thought he was a headcase. He'd go round belting people to the point where we reckoned he was crackers. If there was never any danger of neutral referees stopping him, then the Aussie refs we had on that trip certainly weren't going to pull him up. They just let him get on with it.

'Nobody has ever accused me of being politically correct and I'm not about to break the habit of a lifetime on the issue of how the game has changed. The game of rugby union they play today is not the sport I used to play. When they stopped the booting, the punching and the trampling, they spoilt the game. That's not as shocking as it sounds.

'The lawmakers on the International Board have a lot to answer for, because they have taken the blood and thunder out of it. As a consequence, they have gone a long way to ruining the old saying about rugby union being a game for all shapes and sizes – fast boys on the wing, strong boys in the centre, clever boys at outside-half, nippy boys at scrum-half, fat boys in the front row, tall boys in the second row, hard boys in the back row. Now you can forget about making a living out of the game unless you are at least 6 ft 4 in. tall and more than 16 stone.

'In their obsessive quest for a faster game, the so-called experts in charge of the laws have diluted the scrum to the point where the titanic battles of days gone by seem to have gone for good. The lineout is no longer the fierce contest it used to be, where the specialist jumpers, one at the front, the other in the middle, pitted their athletic wits against their opposite numbers. Nowadays you don't have to worry about jumping because you've got two blokes to lift you.

'Why, oh why, are they trying to make it like rugby league only not as good? They have a better kicking game in league and a better chasing game. When you have so many rugby league coaches involved in rugby union, is it any wonder that it ends up looking like rugby league?

'As Ray Prosser always used to say at Pontypool, "If they want to make rugby union a more open game, copy rugby league and make more room on the pitch by dropping two back-row forwards."

'The danger for rugby union is that in taking the heart out of the game they run the risk that supporters will get cheesed off to the point where they will go to watch rugby league because they will be watching roughly the same game, except that they play it better in league. Look at the scrum. It makes my blood boil when I see some of the things I see now, like back-row forwards looking up before the ball is out.

'If I was playing today and any of the back row in my pack did that, I'd kick their arses until they stopped it. The back row has an important job to do in keeping the scrum straight and stopping it being twisted. A wing forward's job in the set piece, as Ray Williams used to drum into us when he was in charge of coaching for the Welsh Rugby Union, was to scrum, scrum and then scrum again – not to be leaning on the side of the scrum with one arm thinking what he was going to do next.

'If they're not going to restore rugby union's old-fashioned identity and values, like putting the ball in the tunnel between the front rows instead of straight into the second row, then I'd get rid of the two flankers and play Super League, because it's virtually the same game.

'Rugby is a naturally violent game, always has been, especially in the '50s when the Lions used to get a systematic booting all over the park. But nowadays it's gone from one extreme to the other. Everyone is over-protected. When you're on the floor now, you can be the bravest man in the world because nobody is allowed to touch you.

'It used to be that the tough men won the lineout. Now, all of a sudden, the two lines are kept so far apart that you could drive a tractor between them. Once your hobby becomes a job, everything changes and suddenly you have one player taking another to court over some alleged skulduggery. That's another example of how much it has changed: from a time when it was almost impossible to be sent off to the present, when players like me would find it almost impossible not to be sent off.

'The game's gone soft. What are they doing to it? Where are the skills? In the old days, we had seven first-class teams in Monmouthshire, every one within five or ten miles of another. You'd be watching Georgie Gladwin against Eric Phillips go at it hammer and tongs one week, then it would be another pair having a battle royal the next week and so it would go on, month after month. The crowd loved it in much the same way the crowd at the Coliseum in ancient Rome loved watching the Christians and the Lions.

'Welsh people always console themselves with the thought that if there had been a World Cup during the '70s, we would have won it. I have news for them. Wales would not have won it because we could never beat New Zealand. Even on the rare occasions when we had the beating of them, we still lost and the results are all there in the record book for everyone to see.

'When it comes to the All Blacks, Wales always seem to find a way of losing, and when they didn't, the Kiwis had a con trick up their sleeves, which they pulled at the Arms Park in 1978. On the other hand, they can't be all that good, because they haven't won the World Cup for nearly a quarter of a century.

'Buck Shelford and that lot were so far ahead of the rest that their victory at the first World Cup in 1987 was one of the biggest certainties in the history of the game. The Australian Grand Slam team of 1984 were pretty good, too, but when I think of great teams, I think of the Lions of 1974 and France of 1976–78. To stand any chance of beating them, you had to beat them to the draw on the violence and put it about before they did. The only problem with that was that you had to come blasting out of your blocks like a 100-metre runner to have any hope of beating them to it.

'The England team which won the World Cup in 2003 was a very good one. They had an outside-half in Jonny Wilkinson who played like an extra back-row forward, and a man after my own heart as captain in Martin Johnson. England packs have always been worth their salt, like unbending oak trees, even if they did pick one or two cissies along the way.

'Wales have had nobody to lead them the way Johnson led England

and the Lions. Johnson always reminded me of Willie John McBride, a hard, no-nonsense player who never yielded an inch, a true professional from top to bottom. They were men you would follow because you respected them and believed in everything they said or did.

'England have been through the mill and there were times during the 2010 Six Nations when you wondered what they were doing besides driving the fans away, but they are not far off being a good side. I can see England, because of their big resources, winning the World Cup again. Sadly, I can never see Wales winning it.

'I hope I'm wrong, but anyone thinking otherwise is deluding himself or herself. As well as the lack of commanding figures and the shortage of strength in depth, Wales have the added historical problem of being the worst tourists. Whenever a Welsh team goes overseas, too many are missing mummy and daddy. It sounds nonsense, but it's true. I know because I've been there and seen it.

'I cannot for the life of me understand why Wales has such a dearth of leaders. Where is the strong man to rally the troops when the going gets tough? Where's the Welsh McBride or the Welsh Johnson? Alun-Wyn Jones is a really fine player who could grow into the position with experience. In leadership terms, he is the one glimmer of hope.

'Ireland have been the most consistent team in Europe in recent years and I'd fancy their chances at the World Cup if they had a half-decent tighthead prop. John Hayes has won over 100 caps, and I'm sure he's a lovely bloke, a great team man and all that, but I've seen him get murdered in nine scrums out of ten and concede a whole stack of penalties. No team can expect to beat the world with a liability like that.

'Elsewhere, there aren't that many good Test props around. There's been a lot of fancy talk about Andrew Sheridan, but I don't rate him. He seems to miss a lot of games and I've got a theory that 6 ft 5 in. is too tall for a prop, even if Carl Hayman has been busy making a fortune out of it on 350 grand a season at Newcastle. At that height, with your back longer than your legs, you are bound to foul up the scrum.

'I never rated Jason Leonard that highly, but England do have some good hookers. Steve Thompson is one who has always impressed me, a big man who gets the job done and has the mobility to get round the field. Dylan Hartley is another. As for Wales, well, no disrespect to anyone in the national set-up, but who in the name of hell is teaching them to scrummage?

'They go on about Gethin Jenkins being the best loosehead in the world. I watch him when he scrummages and too often out comes his backside, which causes a crabbing effect. As soon as that happens, you lose the power from one of your second rows. Thank goodness for Adam Jones on the other side of the scrum. Long may he continue to be the saviour of the Welsh team.'

THE IRON DUKE'S BEST BRITISH AND IRISH XV

(WITH A FRENCHMAN THROWN IN BECAUSE IT WOULD SAVE THE AGGRO OF HAVING TO PLAY AGAINST HIM)

FULL-BACK: J.P.R. WILLIAMS (WALES)

Nobody else comes close. Before he arrived on the scene, all a full-back had to do was sit back, take the up-and-unders and kick the ball 60 yards. J.P.R. changed all that, and in doing so he changed the nature of the game. He couldn't kick the ball that well, so he ran it, and that suited Wales down to the ground. When he played his first Welsh trial, the other full-back was the best kicker of them all, Robin Williams. Unfortunately, he was too slow and never got a cap.

RIGHT WING: DAVID DUCKHAM (ENGLAND)

A close call and maybe people will be surprised that I've left Gerald Davies out. You've got to be more than half useful to keep him out, which says everything about Duckham. He had a five-yard side-step, pace and skill. Let him loose and nobody knew for sure where he was going, partly, I suspect, because at times he didn't know where he was going either. Terrific rugby player and human being.

OUTSIDE-CENTRE: MIKE GIBSON (IRELAND)

Two Scots, Ian McGeechan and Jim Renwick, pushed themselves forward for consideration, but Gibson was brilliant. It didn't make any difference whether he played at outside-half, inside- or outside-centre or on the wing. No wonder they called him pound-for-pound the best back produced in the British Isles of the amateur era.

INSIDE-CENTRE: DICK MILLIKEN (IRELAND)

The best in his position, although Ray Gravell ran him close. The Irishman's ball-carrying quality and all-round power made him the perfect foil for the likes of Gibson and McGeechan. Sadly, Dick proved a good example of the old saying that the next game can always be your last. After the Lions tour, he had only one more season with Ireland before he broke an ankle training with his club, Bangor. It was bad enough to finish him as an international at the age of 25.

LEFT WING: J.J. WILLIAMS (WALES)

A real winner from top to toe, with an attitude which could not be faulted. He trained like a dog to make sure he made the most of his natural ability, and his achievements are there in the history books for all to see, like his four tries in the four-Test series for the Lions in South Africa in 1974. A top player and a top bloke.

OUTSIDE-HALF: PHIL BENNETT (WALES)

Cliff Morgan was brilliant. So too was Barry John, but he'd finished by the time I first got into the Welsh squad. I could never understand why Barry retired too young, at only 27, when he had so much more to give. There's no doubt he would have gone on the '74 tour to South Africa. Instead, Benny stepped in to make a name for himself and finish up as one of the all-time greats.

SCRUM-HALF: GARETH EDWARDS (WALES)

Who else? Well, David Bishop, that's who. Wales were all the poorer for deciding that he was worth just the one cap, because he was the best I've seen since Gareth, and there were times when he was just as good as the mighty man himself. As well as the complete master of his art, Edwards was also a fantastic athlete who represented Great Britain as a gymnast.

LOOSEHEAD PROP: GÉRARD CHOLLEY (FRANCE)

You have to go a bit to be voted the most feared man in French rugby, but he managed it without breaking too much sweat. A fearsome bloke with a neck the size of an Aberdeen Angus bull, Cholley was a heavyweight boxer who was fond of stopping opponents well inside the distance. He played in the best pack I ever came up against. Definitely the sort of player you'd rather have on your side, if only because you'd save yourself a lot of aggro.

HOOKER: COLIN DEANS (SCOTLAND)

It wouldn't be the done thing for me to pick myself. Colin had only played one game for Scotland when he came up against us during the Grand Slam season of 1978. We pushed their pack into reverse gear and afterwards their coach told me he was going to make some changes. I said, 'Whatever you do, don't change the hooker. That boy Deans is the best I've played against – lightning fast. He struck every ball and it wasn't his fault that we shoved their forwards off it.'

TIGHTHEAD PROP: FRAN COTTON (ENGLAND)

A bit of a no-contest, because the only man to give him a run for his money wasn't British or Irish but French: Robert Paparemborde, the Bear of the Pyrenees, who was an amazing player. When you go to war, as the Lions did in South Africa in 1974, you form a special bond with the men around you. Frannie was massive on that tour, like a great English oak.

FRONT JUMPER: BILL BEAUMONT (ENGLAND)

Willie John McBride was a good man, but I wouldn't say he was the best lineout forward in the world. Beaumont joined the Lions in New Zealand as a sub and immediately made a great impact. Three years after that, he skippered England to the Grand Slam for the first time in yonks. Outstanding.

MIDDLE JUMPER: GORDON BROWN (SCOTLAND)

What a player, what a man. His record speaks for itself and there wasn't a weakness to his game – top-class lineout forward, top-class scrummager, top-class footballer. And if you were ever in any trouble which called for an old-fashioned bit of law and order, 'Broon o' Troon' was the No. 1 man. I can never praise him highly enough.

BLINDSIDE FLANKER: JEFF SQUIRE (WALES)

The rain made nearly every pitch in New Zealand in 1977 look like it had come straight out of a film about the Battle of the Somme. Squire revelled in the conditions. Before I helped persuade Jeff to leave Newport, the best forward I ever played with at Pontypool was Brian Gregory, a man who never played for Wales, probably because his face didn't fit.

OPENSIDE FLANKER: FERGUS SLATTERY (IRELAND)

In South Africa in 1974, Fergus was as fast as any of our backs, and that's saying something. He did his sprint training with people like J.J. Williams, who had been an international sprinter. Unlike some loose forwards who lived off the sweat of their front five, 'Slats' gave everything he had to the cause every time he played.

NUMBER 8: MERVYN DAVIES (WALES)

The Lions would have won the series in New Zealand in 1977 if only Swerve had been there at the helm, as he would have been but for the brain haemorrhage which nearly killed him the year before. And had he been there, the tour would not have disintegrated from the management down. A real forwards' number 8 who worked like a dog, he had another quality which stood out above the rest: in times of trouble, he kept his head when others were losing theirs.

BOBBY WINDSOR: CAREER STATISTICS

Born Newport, 31 January 1946

HONOURS FOR WALES

GRAND SLAMS (2)

1976, 1978

FIVE NATIONS TITLES (4)

1975, 1976, 1978, 1979

TRIPLE CROWNS (4)

1976, 1977, 1978, 1979

BRITISH AND IRISH LIONS TOURS (2)

South Africa 1974
New Zealand 1977

TEST MATCHES

FOR THE BRITISH & IRISH LIONS – 5

8.6.74	South Africa, Newlands, Cape Town	won 12–3
22.6.74	South Africa, Loftus Versfeld, Pretoria	won 28–9
13.7.74	South Africa, Boet Erasmus, Port Elizabeth	won 26–0
27.7.74	South Africa, Ellis Park, Johannesburg	drawn 13–13
18.6.77	New Zealand, Athletic Park, Wellington	lost 12–16

THE IRON DUKE

FOR WALES – 28 (2 TRIES)

30.11.73	Australia, Cardiff Arms Park	won 24–0
19.1.74	Scotland, Cardiff Arms Park	won 6–0
2.2.74	Ireland, Lansdowne Road	drawn 9–9
16.2.74	France, Cardiff Arms Park	drawn 16–16
16.3.74	England, Twickenham	lost 12–16
18.1.75	France, Parc des Princes	won 25–10
15.2.75	England, Cardiff Arms Park	won 20–4
1.3.75	Scotland, Murrayfield	lost 10–12
15.3.75	Ireland, Cardiff Arms Park	won 32–4
20.12.75	Australia, Cardiff Arms Park	won 28–3
17.1.76	England, Twickenham	won 21–9
7.2.76	Scotland, Cardiff Arms Park	won 28–6
21.2.76	Ireland, Lansdowne Road	won 34–9
6.3.76	France, Cardiff Arms Park	won 19–13
15.1.77	Ireland, Cardiff Arms Park	won 25–9
5.2.77	France, Parc des Princes	lost 9–16
5.3.77	England, Cardiff Arms Park	won 14-9
19.3.77	Scotland, Murrayfield	won 18–9
4.2.78	England, Twickenham	won 9–6
18.2.78	Scotland, Cardiff Arms Park	won 22–14
4.3.78	Ireland, Lansdowne Road	won 20–16
18.3.78	France, Cardiff Arms Park	won 16–7
11.6.78	Australia, Ballymore, Brisbane	lost 8–18
18.6.78	Australia, Sydney Cricket Ground	lost 17–19
11.11.78	New Zealand, Cardiff Arms Park	lost 12–13
20.1.79	Scotland, Murrayfield	won 19–13
3.2.79	Ireland, Cardiff Arms Park	won 24–21
17.2.79	France, Parc des Princes	lost 13–14

UNCAPPED MATCHES FOR WALES – 6 (1 TRY)

6.10.73	Japan, Cardiff Arms Park	won 62–14
27.11.74	New Zealand, Cardiff Arms Park	lost 3–12
21.9.75	Japan, Osaka	won 56–12
24.9.75	Japan, Tokyo	won 82–6
16.10.76	Argentina, Cardiff Arms Park	won 20–19
6.10.79	Romania, Cardiff Arms Park	won 13–12

BOBBY WINDSOR: CAREER STATISTICS

NON-TEST MATCHES FOR THE LIONS – 21 (1 TRY)

15.5.74	Western Transvaal, Potchefstroom	won 59–13
27.5.74	Boland, Wellington	won 33–6
25.5.74	Eastern Province, Port Elizabeth	won 28–14
1.6.74	Western Province, Cape Town	won 17–8
15.6.74	Transvaal, Johannesburg	won 23–15
29.6.74	Orange Free State, Bloemfontein	won 11–9
6.7.74	Northern Transvaal, Pretoria	won 16–12
20.7.74	Natal, Durban	won 34–6
21.5.77	Hawke's Bay, Napier	won 13–11
25.5.77	Poverty Bay, East Coast, Gisborne	won 25–6
4.6.77	Manawatu-Horowhenua, Palmerston North	won 18–12
11.6.77	Southland, Invercargill	won 20–12
25.6.77	Canterbury, Christchurch	won 14–13
29.6.77	West Coast–Buller, Westport	won 45–0
5.7.77	Marlborough–Nelson Bays, Blenheim	won 40–23
13.7.77	New Zealand Maori, Auckland	won 22–19
16.7.77	Waikato, Hamilton	won 18–13
20.7.77	Junior All Blacks, Wellington	won 19–9
3.8.77	Thames Valley–Counties, Pukekohe	won 35–10
9.8.77	Bay of Plenty, Rotorua	won 23–16
16.8.77	Fiji, Suva	lost 21–25

OTHER MATCHES FOR WALES – 6 (1 TRY)

30.5.73	Alberta, Edmonton	won 76–6
5.6.73	Ontario, Ottawa	won 79–0
15.9.75	Waseda–Railway XV	won 32–3
24.5.78	Victoria, Melbourne	won 52–3
30.5.78	New South Wales Country, Cobar	won 33–0
3.6.78	New South Wales, Sydney	won 18–0

BARBARIANS – 6

27.12.73	Leicester, Welford Road	won 16–7
27.3.74	Moseley, The Reddings	lost 22–25
13.4.74	Cardiff, the Arms Park	lost 9–11
15.4.74	Newport, Rodney Parade	lost 0–16
30.11.74	New Zealand, Twickenham	drawn 13–13
20.4.76	Newport, Rodney Parade	lost 0–43

OTHER REPRESENTATIVE MATCHES – 7

7.9.74	Irish President's XV v Ireland, Lansdowne Road drawn 16–16
30.9.74	Carwyn James' XV v Welsh Valleys, Penygraig won 45–13
29.10.74	Carwyn James' XV v Newport, Rodney Parade won 44–28
19.4.75	England–Wales v Scotland–Ireland, Lansdowne Road lost 10–17
21.1.76	Gwent v Australians, Pontypool Park lost 15–26
29.9.76	East Wales v Argentinians, Rodney Parade lost 22–25
29.11.78	Monmouthshire v New Zealanders, Rodney Parade lost 9–26

CRAWSHAY'S WELSH RFC – 4

OTHER MATCHES FOR MONMOUTHSHIRE – 9

FIRST-CLASS CLUB HISTORY

CROSS KEYS (1970–73)

122 matches, 24 tries

CARDIFF (1970)

9 matches, 2 tries

PONTYPOOL (1973–87)

325 matches, 87 tries

NON-FIRST-CLASS CLUB HISTORY

WHITEHEAD'S RFC (1962–68)

Not known

NEWPORT SARACENS (1968–70)

50 matches, 19 tries

BOBBY WINDSOR: CAREER STATISTICS

PONTYPOOL ATHLETIC (1983–87)
Not available

WALES B – 2
21.10.72	France, Cardiff Arms Park	won 35–6
20.11.73	France, Toulouse	lost 12–24

WELSH INTERNATIONAL TRIALS – 6
1971–77

TOTAL CAREER IN SENIOR RUGBY
Matches: 556

Tries: 118

Sent off: once – for Cross Keys against Swansea, September 1972

BIBLIOGRAPHY

Bennett, Phil, with Williams, Martyn, *Everywhere for Wales*, Stanley Paul, 1981

Billot, John, *History of Welsh International Rugby*, Roman Way Books, 1999

Cotton, Fran, *An Autobiography*, Queen Anne Press, London, 1981

Davies, Jonathan, with Corrigan, Peter, *An Autobiography*, Mainstream, Edinburgh, 1989

Davies, Mervyn and Roach, David, *In Strength and Shadow*, Mainstream, Edinburgh, 2004

Jackson, Peter, *Lions of Wales*, Mainstream, Edinburgh, 1998

Jackson, Peter, *Lions of England*, Mainstream, Edinburgh, 2005

Luyt, Louis, *Walking Proud*, Don Nelson Publishers, Cape Town, 2003

McBride, Willie John, and Bills, Peter, *Willie John: The Story of My Life*, Portrait Books, London, 2004

McLean, T.P., *Kings of Rugby*, A.H. & A.W. Reed, Wellington, 1959

McLean, T.P., *The All Blacks*, Sidgwick & Jackson, London, 1991

Morgan, Cliff, with Nicholson, Geoffrey, *Cliff Morgan: The Autobiography*, Hodder & Stoughton, London, 1996

Mourie, Graham, with Palenski, Ron, *Captain: An Autobiography*, Moa Publications, Auckland, 1982

Parry-Jones, David, *The Dawes Decades*, Seren Books, Bridgend, 2005

Reason, John, *The Mighty Lions*, Whitecombe & Tombs Ltd, Christchurch, 1971

Ring, Mark, with Parfitt, Delme, *Ringmaster*, Mainstream, Edinburgh, 2006

Rowlands, Clive, and Evans, John, *Top Cat*, Mainstream, Edinburgh, 2002

Thomas, Clem, and Thomas, Greg, *History of the British and Irish Lions*, Mainstream, Edinburgh, 2005

Thomas, J.B.G., *Trial of Strength: The 1977 Lions*, Pelham, London, 1977

INDEX

INDEX

INDEX

INDEX